THE HUMAN RIGHT TO EDUCATION

To Ann and Chuck (my parents, friends and educators)

Programme on International Rights of the Child
Series Editor: Geraldine Van Bueren

Titles in the Series:

Children's Rights and Traditional Values
Edited by Gillian Douglas and Leslie Sebba

Cultural Pluralism and the Rights of the Child
Michael Freeman

Of Innocence and Autonomy
Children, Sex and Human Rights
Eric Heinze

The Human Right to Education
Douglas Hodgson

Legal Secrets, Cultural and Scientific Truths
Katherine O'Donovan

Childhood Abused
Protecting Children against Torture, Cruel, Inhuman and
Degrading Treatment and Punishment
Edited by Geraldine Van Bueren

The Human Right to Education

DOUGLAS HODGSON
Faculty of Law
The University of Western Australia

Ashgate

DARTMOUTH

Aldershot • Brookfield USA • Singapore • Sydney

Published by
Dartmouth Publishing Company Limited
Ashgate Publishing Limited
Gower House
Croft Road
Aldershot
Hants GU11 3HR
England

Ashgate Publishing Company
Old Post Road
Brookfield
Vermont 05036
USA

British Library Cataloguing in Publication Data
Hodgson, Douglas
  The human right to education. - (Programme on international rights of the child)
  1. Right to education
  I. Title
  344'.079

Library of Congress Cataloging-in-Publication Data
Hodgson, Douglas.
  The human right to education / Douglas Hodgson.
    p.   cm. -- (Programme on the International Rights of the Child series)
  Includes bibliographical references.
  ISBN 1-85521-909-3 (hb)
  1. Right to education. 2. Human rights--Study and teaching.
  3. Handicapped--Education--Law and legislation.   I. Title.
  II. Series.
  K3740.H63   1998
  344'.079--dc21   98-3167
                                      CIP

ISBN 1 85521 909 3

Printed in Great Britain by Galliard (Printers) Ltd, Great Yarmouth

Contents

Series Preface

The concept of international children's rights has come of age, and the Programme on International Rights of the Child Series is the first series of volumes dedicated to exploring specific aspects of international children's rights. The series comprises both sole authored and edited volumes, and single disciplinary and multi-disciplinary monographs, all considering issues which are at the rapidly expanding boundaries of international children's rights.

Geraldine Van Bueren
Series Editor
Programme on International Rights of the Child
Queen Mary and Westfield College
University of London

Acknowledgements

I wish to express my gratitude to my research assistant, Heather Goodwin, for her diligent efforts in accumulating materials and information to support this undertaking. I am also grateful to Jasmine Burkett for her assistance with correcting the manuscript.

I am also indebted to Geraldine Van Bueren, Director, Programme on International Rights of the Child, University of London, Queen Mary and Westfield College, for providing me with this research and writing opportunity, and for her encouragement and assistance.

Douglas Hodgson
Perth

PART I

DEVELOPMENTS AT THE NATIONAL LEVEL

1 Introduction

> [T]he child's right to education . . . is . . . a requirement of human dignity. It is unacceptable that in this world of ours, possessing a store of scientific and technical knowledge unprecedented in history, there should be, side by side with privileged people commanding access to the resources of knowledge, hundreds of millions, not only of boys and girls, but also of men and women, who are denied the possibility of simply learning to read and to write.[1]

In 1954 the United States Supreme Court stressed the fundamental importance of education for all in the celebrated case of *Brown v. Board of Education* [2] and asserted that "[i]n these days, it is doubtful that any child may reasonably be expected to succeed in life if he [or she] is denied the opportunity of an education".[3]

The concept of education can, of course, be variously defined. Education occurs in its widest sense in the interaction of the individual with the social and natural environment to which he or she belongs. This process transcends the school setting and includes informal sources of education such as the printed and electronic mass media. Education begins within the home where the child learns its first language and is socialised into the parental and sibling relationships. Individual attitudes and behaviour develop subsequently as a result of the child's interaction with family members and the wider social and natural environment.[4]

Education can be defined in the broad sense to encompass "all activities by which a human group transmits to its descendants a body of knowledge and skills and a moral code which enable that group to subsist".[5] In this sense, then, education is primarily concerned with the transmission to the younger generation of the skills necessary to effectively undertake the tasks of daily living and with the inculcation of the social, cultural, religious and philosophical values held by the particular community. The General Conference of the United Nations Educational, Scientific and Cultural Organization (hereinafter referred to as "U.N.E.S.C.O.") has itself defined the term 'education' to imply "the entire process of social life by means of which individuals and social groups learn to develop consciously within, and for the benefit of, the national and international communities, the whole of their personal capacities, attitudes, aptitudes and knowledge".[6]

3

Education can, in turn, be more narrowly confined to refer to formal or professional "instruction imparted within a national, provincial or local education system, whether public or private".[7] It is generally the case that the term 'education' is used in international instruments to refer to formal institutional instruction.   For example, the General Conference of U.N.E.S.C.O. has defined the term 'education' for the purpose of its *Convention against Discrimination in Education* of 1960 to mean "all types and levels of [formal] education, and includes access to education, the standard and quality of education, and the conditions under which it is given".[8]   The European Court of Human Rights has distinguished education in its wide sense from education in its narrow sense in the following terms:

> [education in the wider sense refers to] the whole process whereby, in any society, adults endeavour to transmit their beliefs, culture and other values to the young, whereas teaching or instruction refers in particular to the transmission of knowledge and to intellectual development.[9]

For the purposes of this monograph, 'education' will refer merely to formal teaching or instruction comprising the pre-primary, primary (elementary), intermediate (secondary), higher and adult levels of instruction.

It is generally accepted that formal education is an important function of the State.   The French Revolution and the American Revolution established the concept of education as an essential task of the State as a means of enlightening the citizenry and pursuing democratic ideals.[10]   In his famous treatise *On Liberty* John Stuart Mill asked "Is it not almost a self-evident axiom that the State should require and compel the education, up to a certain standard, of every human being who is born its citizen?".[11]   Indeed, the pre-eminent role of the State in the provision of education has received both constitutional and conventional recognition.   Article 119 of the *Constitution of Nicaragua* of 1986 forthrightly proclaims that "[e]ducation is an unrenounceable responsibility of the state" while Article 1 of the *Central American Convention on the Unification of the Fundamental Norms of Education* of 1962 acknowledges education to be "a primary function of the State, which shall offer maximum opportunities for education".[12]   The human right to education is essentially a welfare or "second generation" right which is to be provided to individuals primarily by governmental agencies. The state is generally the chief provider of education which involves the commitment of substantial budgetary resources to the education system as well as its regulation in the interests of efficiency and fairness.[13]

Nevertheless, there appears to be a recent trend towards recognising the utility of increasing the involvement of the non-governmental sectors in the provision of educational services. In this regard, Article 7 of the *World Declaration on Education for All* adopted by the World Conference on Education for All held in Thailand in 1990 acknowledges that although national, regional and local educational authorities have a unique obligation to provide basic education for all, they cannot be expected to supply every requirement for this task. Article 7, therefore, goes on to urge the formation of partnerships between government and non-governmental organisations, the private sector, local communities, religious groups and families to achieve a fuller and more comprehensive delivery of educational services.

Although children are the main beneficiaries, the right to education belongs to all individuals.[14] In proclaiming that "[e]veryone has the right to education", Article 26(1) of the *Universal Declaration of Human Rights* adopted by the United Nations General Assembly in 1948 implicitly recognises that education is a life-long and continuous process. Indeed, the Council of Europe has promoted the concept of "permanent education".[15]

This monograph will endeavour to provide a general overview of the content and development of the right to education at the international and regional levels as well as an examination of various associated topical issues. Part I will trace the historical development of the right to education at the national level. Part II will consider the recognition of the right to education at the international and regional levels and the emerging and controversial topics of minority and indigenous education. Part III will examine the obligation of States to provide human rights education while Part IV will canvass various forms of specialised education and topical issues such as the education of the disabled and parental involvement in decisions concerning the education of their children. Specific problems impeding the fuller realisation of the right to education will also be considered in the context of recent major setbacks in basic education in many of the least developed countries and significant cutbacks in governmental expenditure on education in certain industrialised countries.

Notes

1   Amadou-Mahtar M'Bow (former Director-General of UNESCO) "Introduction" in G. Mialaret (ed.) *The Child's Right to Education* (1979) 9, 14-15.

2   347 U.S. 483 (1954).

3   Id. 493.

4   A. Phillips *Education Rights and Minorities* (Minority Rights Group, 1994) 5.

5   M'Bow, op. cit., 11.

6   Article 1(a) of the Recommendation Concerning Education for International Understanding, Co-operation and Peace and Education Relating to Human Rights and Fundamental Freedoms 1974.

7   M'Bow, op. cit., 11.

8   Article 1(2).

9   *Campbell and Cosans v. United Kingdom*, Judgement of 25 February 1982, Series A, no. 48 (1982) 4 EHRR 433 at para. 33.

10   F. Volio "The child's right to education: a survey" in G. Mialaret (ed.) *The Child's Right to Education* (1979) 19, 22.

11   J. S. Mill *On Liberty* (London, 1859); the edition of G. Himmelfarb (Pelican Classics, 1974) 175.

12   Article 9 of *The Cairo Declaration on Human Rights in Islam* of 1990 recognises the provision of education as "a duty for society and the State" and imposes an obligation on States to "ensure the availability of ways and means to acquire education". Principle 4 of the *Official Statement of Principles* adopted by the Conference on the Legal Protection of the Rights of the Child held in Warsaw in 1979 states: "The duty to provide the means of education . . . falls in the first place on the State". Principle 7 of the European Parliament Resolution of 14 March 1984 concerning *Freedom of Education in the European Community* states in part that "it is the duty of the State to provide the necessary facilities for state . . . schools".

13   D. J. Harris, M. O'Boyle and C. Warbrick *Law of the European Convention on Human Rights* (1995) 540.

14   As will be pointed out in Chapter 4, however, although the right to education extends to both adults and children, the principle of compulsory education only applies to children.

15   The topic of "Adult Education" will be discussed in Chapter 11.

2   The Historical Development and Nature of the Right to Education

> I think by far the most important bill in our whole code is that for the diffusion of knowledge among the people. No other sure foundation can be devised for the preservation of freedom and happiness . . . Preach, my dear sir, a crusade against ignorance; establish and improve the law for educating the common people.[1]

Introduction

Despite its importance in the hierarchy of human rights, the right to education, as we shall see in Chapter 4, was not fully proclaimed at the international level until after World War II. The purpose of this chapter will be to provide a brief historical overview of the right to education and its contemporary constitutional recognition in the laws of selected States. The latter portion of the chapter will consider the nature of the right to education.

History of the Right to Education

Prior to the age of Enlightenment in Europe, education was primarily undertaken by parents and the Church. Education was considered a matter of public concern and State responsibility only with the emergence of the modern secular State.[2]   Beginning in the sixteenth and seventeenth centuries, certain eminent philosophers adumbrated in their writings the modern conception of the individual right to education. The imparting of knowledge and culture began to be conceived not only as a necessary moral and social obligation but also as a noble aim to which the individual might aspire.[3]   John Locke and Jean-Jacques Rousseau in the *Second Treatise of Government* and *Emile* respectively referred to the parental obligation to educate children until they became able to make full and proper use of their freedom and faculties. Education was perceived as being of such vital importance for human life that it was conceived as a pre-existing or natural right[4] superior to the positive law.[5]   The English jurist Sir William Blackstone described the source of general parental duties to their children in these terms:

> The duty of parents to provide for the maintenance of their children, is a principle of natural law; an obligation . . . laid on them not only by nature itself, but by their own proper act, in bringing them into the world . . . By begetting them . . . they have entered into a voluntary obligation to endeavour, as far as in them lies, that the life which they have bestowed shall be supported and preserved. And thus the children will have a perfect right of maintenance from their parents.[6]

The 'democratisation' of education received a fillip in the wake of the French and American Revolutions which established the promotion of education (for the benefit of the majority of citizens at least) as a State or public function. Public education was perceived as a means of realising the egalitarian ideals upon which these revolutions were based, and education was no longer the exclusive preserve of a particular social class or the select few, as had been the case in Ancient Greece and Rome.[7]   The unique value of education and the State's important role in promoting it were postulated by eminent men of their time including Thomas Jefferson who regarded education as necessary to protect a free people against tyranny.[8]

The common law of England gradually evolved to recognise parental obligations to nurture and protect their children and to provide them with a basic education sufficient to prepare them for adult life. Blackstone described the parental duty to children in this regard in terms of:

> . . . giving [children] an education suitable to their station in life: a duty pointed out by reason, and of far the greatest importance of any. For it is not easy to imagine or allow, that a parent has conferred any considerable benefit upon his child, by bringing him into the world; if he afterwards entirely neglects his culture and education, and suffers him to grow up like a mere beast, to lead a life useless to others, and shameful to himself.[9]

The right to education emerged rather belatedly in the history of civil liberties despite its importance.   The classical civil liberties instruments such as the English *Bill of Rights* of 1689, the *Virginia Declaration of Rights* of 1776, the American *Declaration of Independence* of 1776 and the French *Declaration of the Rights of Man* of 1789 did not contain any rights specifically related to the right to education. These instruments focussed instead upon basic political and civil rights such as freedom from arbitrary arrest, freedom of expression, opinion and religious belief, the right to life and security of the person, freedom and equality, and the protection of private property. Most of the rights contained in these instruments were freedoms concerning areas of individual conduct beyond the scope of State intervention. In the spirit of the *laissez-faire* doctrine, individual autonomy and liberty were emphasised; the State and the Government were perceived as a potential threat to such liberty and should seek not to interfere in human affairs to the greatest extent possible.

Two developments of the nineteenth century - the emergence of socialism and liberalism - placed education more firmly in the catalogue of human rights. The writings of Marx and Engels perceived the State as a paternal and beneficial institution whose main purpose was to secure the economic and social well-being of the entire community through positive governmental intervention and regulation. The demand for more rights during the course of the nineteenth century increasingly became a claim upon the State for basic welfare services and entitlements. *Laissez-faire* was gradually superseded by the perception of the State as a benevolent provider. Nineteenth century liberal and anti-clerical thought also influenced the definition of secular educational rights in continental Europe. These educational rights were formulated to defend and advance the ideas of freedom of science, research and teaching against interference by the Church and State.[10] Although wary of the dangers of too much State involvement in educational matters, liberalism advocated State intervention for the purpose of reducing the dominance of the Church and protecting the rights of children against their parents.[11]

During the latter half of the nineteenth century, explicit recognition of educational rights and State responsibility for promoting them occurred in national constitutions and legislation. The Constitution of the German Empire of 1849[12] contained a section entitled "Basic Rights of the German People" which devoted seven provisions (Articles 152 to 158) to educational rights. These rights aimed at striking a fair balance between the interests of children, parents, the Church, the State and operators of educational institutions. Education was affirmed as a function of the State, independent of the Church, and the right of the poor to free education was proclaimed. The rights of German citizens to establish and operate schools, to give home instruction and to choose and train for a vocation as well as the freedoms of science and teaching were guaranteed.[13] Similarly, the German Weimar Constitution of 1919 devoted an entire section of its bill of rights to "Education and Schooling" (Articles 142-150) which, *inter alia*, explicitly recognised the duty of the State to guarantee education by means of free and compulsory school attendance.

The emerging solicitude manifested towards children prompted the enactment of child welfare legislation. Compulsory education laws were introduced to make the State responsible for providing public education and for supervising private education, and to provide children with a basic general education and vocational training. These laws provided new educational opportunities for children and withdrew many of them from the labour force.[14] Child labour laws were also enacted to restrict the exploitation of child labour and to ensure that children were able to take advantage of these new educational opportunities. These laws regulated the working conditions of children and attempted to restrict the number of hours per day during which minors could be employed. The English *Factories Act* of 1833, providing for salaried inspectors to enforce labour regulations, dates from this period of social concern for the exploitation of children.[15]

The first instance of international recognition of the right to education occurred with the conclusion of various minorities treaties in the immediate aftermath of World War I as an adjunct to peace treaties signed by the Allied and Associated Powers with the defeated nations. These treaties sought to protect the religious and linguistic identity and educational rights of certain minorities which had been displaced through a redrawing of national boundaries in Europe. The *Treaty Between The Principal Allied and Associated Powers and Poland* signed on 28 June 1919,[16] the first of the series, sought to provide detailed guarantees of minority educational rights. Article 8 thereof stated:

> Polish nationals who belong to racial, religious or linguistic minorities shall enjoy the same treatment and security in law and in fact as the other Polish nationals. In particular they shall have an equal right to establish, manage and control at their own expense charitable, religious and social institutions, schools and other educational establishments, with the right to use their own language and to exercise their religion freely therein.

The second instance of the international recognition of the right to education under the auspices of the League of Nations took place with the proclamation in 1924 of the *Declaration of Geneva*.[17] The *Declaration* was adopted by the Fifth Assembly of the League of Nations on 26 September 1924, with President Motta proclaiming: "The Assembly, by approving the Declaration of Geneva, has made it the Charter of Child Welfare of the League of Nations".[18] While not directly recognising the child's right to education, three of its five operative principles implicitly adverted to such a right. Principle I states: "The child must be given the means requisite for its normal development . . ."; Principle II states: ". . . the child that is backward must be helped . . ."; Principle IV states: "The child must be put in a position to earn a livelihood . . .". The *Declaration of Geneva* represented the first step towards the development of international norms concerning the global protection of children, as earlier international agreements had merely focussed on particular problems affecting children such as working conditions and slavery. Its five basic principles for child welfare and protection formed the foundation of the *Declaration of the Rights of the Child* of 1959[19] which went on to formulate more precise standards. The *Declaration of Geneva* did not entail the assumption of legal obligations by States; it merely purported to be a declaration and acceptance by "men and women of all nations" of a set of moral duties. It was essentially an aspirational document, the Fifth Assembly of the League of Nations having invited "the States Members of the League [of Nations] to be guided by its principles in the work of child welfare". Thus, it was left to each League Member State to take appropriate action within its needs and resources.

An explicit human right to receive education with a corresponding State duty to provide it was prescribed for the first time by Article 121 of the Constitution of the Union of Soviet Socialist Republics of 1936. Pursuant to this provision, the right of citizens of the U.S.S.R. to receive education was guaranteed by free and compulsory education at all levels including higher education, a system of State scholarships and a system of vocational training in State enterprises.[20] The right to education was recognised thereafter as a prominent human right in the constitutions of socialist states.

The Contemporary Constitutional Recognition of the Right to Education

Aspects of the human right to education have been enshrined in national constitutions and bills of rights or recognised in non-constitutional or ordinary pieces of domestic legislation. The next three sections of this chapter will provide illustrative examples of such recognition as well as an examination of the judicial development of educational entitlements under the United States Constitution.

The Recognition of the Right to Education under National Constitutions

As of 1988, the right to education had been explicitly mentioned in the constitutions of some fifty-two countries.[21]   Many of these constitutions also specifically mention equality of opportunity in the exercise of this right. The subject of education may also be mentioned within the operative provisions of national constitutions of federal States in the context of a demarcation of legislative competence between the federal or central government on the one hand and the state, provincial or cantonal governments on the other. In Canada, for example, the regulation of the public education sector is a matter which falls within the exclusive authority of the legislature of each province.[22]

Examples of the national constitutional recognition of the right to education include the following:

- Article 121 of the Constitution of Nicaragua (1986) proclaims that all Nicaraguans shall have free and equal access to education, with basic education being free and compulsory.

- Article 45 of the Constitution of the Union of Soviet Socialist Republics (1977) declared that all citizens of the U.S.S.R. have the right to education which shall be free at all levels and universal and compulsory at the primary and secondary levels.

- Article 20 of the Constitution of Cyprus (1960) provides that every person has the right to receive instruction or education, with primary education being free and compulsory.

- Article 27 of the Spanish Constitution states that everyone has the right to education, with basic education being obligatory and free.

- The Constitution of Viet Nam (1992) assigns responsibility for the education of children to the family and the State.

- Article 42 of the Constitution of Ireland obliges the State to provide for free primary education, acknowledges the family as the primary and natural educator of the child and guarantees respect for the inalienable right and duty of parents to provide for the religious and moral, intellectual, physical and social education of their children.

- The Egyptian Constitution (1971) provides for full and compulsory education on the basis of equality of educational opportunity for all citizens.

- Article 26 of the Japanese Constitution states that education is a right of the people and that all have a right to receive equal education according to ability.

- Article 89 of the Paraguayan Constitution (1967) obliges the State to maintain public schools to ensure to all residents, free of charge, the opportunity to learn, and to ensure equality of opportunity for students.

- Article 72 of the Polish Constitution guarantees equal educational rights to all.

- Article 76 of the Danish Constitution states that all children of compulsory school age have the right to free education in primary school.

- Article 80 of the Finnish Constitution prescribes that education in primary schools shall be free for all and compulsory.

The Recognition of the Right to Education in Non-constitutional Legislation

References to educational entitlements and duties also appear in pieces of ordinary or unentrenched legislation both in countries with written constitutions and bills of rights and those with no such instruments. In terms of the latter category, for example, the principle of universal compulsory legislation is recognised in the English *Education Acts* by the imposition of legal duties on parents and local education authorities. The parental duty to educate is contained in Section 36 of the *Education Act 1944* which provides that "[i]t shall be the duty of the parent of every child of compulsory school age to cause him to receive efficient full-time education, suitable to his age, ability and aptitude, either by regular attendance at school or otherwise". Similarly, the Peruvian *General Law of Education 1983* requires all Peruvians to pursue primary instruction, guarantees free public education and prohibits discrimination on the basis of sex, race, language spoken, political affiliation or socio-economic status.

Among those countries which recognise the right to education both in their national constitutions and in their ordinary legislation, the following examples are illustrative and representative:

- Article 81 of the *Education Law 1949* of South Korea guarantees equal opportunity in education regardless of faith, sex or socio-economic position.

- the *National Charter of Education 1980* of Morocco guarantees to all its citizens the right to education and equality of access to it regardless of race or sex.

- the Japanese *Fundamental Law of Education 1947* guarantees equal opportunity in education regardless of race, sex or economic position.

The Judicial Development of Educational Entitlements under the United States Constitution

The United States of America represents an interesting case-study in so far as judges have relied on the federal and state constitutions in identifying and defining the parameters of particular educational entitlements. Education has been viewed traditionally as exclusively a state and local matter, subject to review by the courts, particularly the U. S. Supreme Court, to ensure that educational policies and practices developed and implemented at the state and local level conform with federal constitutional standards.[23]

Neither education nor the right to education is mentioned in the United States Constitution. The legal reform of the U. S. educational system by judges over the past four decades has tended to focus on non-discrimination and equal educational opportunity issues.[24] The concept of equality of educational opportunity derives, therefore, not from specific constitutional language about education or schooling, but rather from the more general constitutional provisions concerning equal protection or treatment under the law. Specifically, U. S. courts have applied the equal protection clause of the Fourteenth Amendment to the schools, with the first cases involving racial discrimination. Prior to 1954, the "separate but equal" doctrine sanctioning a system of segrated schools for black and white children had prevailed for over a century. In the famous 1954 desegregation decision in *Brown v Board of Education*,[25] the U.S.

Supreme Court construed the Fourteenth Amendment as prohibiting the deliberate separation of the races in public schools. In the course of its judgment, the Court also affirmed that the public interest is broadly served by education, a precept which has been generally endorsed by federal and state courts in education cases decided since 1954.[26] In the Court's view:

> Today, education is perhaps the most important function of state and local governments. Compulsory school attendance laws and the great expenditures for education both demonstrate our recognition of the importance of education to our democratic society.[27]

To secure compliance with the *Brown* decision, U.S. courts have exercised broad control over the organisation, administration and programmes of the public schools including the power to order state taxation for support of schools, the power to order the assignment of pupils and teachers to specific schools to achieve a racial balance and the power to order bussing to achieve such balance.[28] Ten years after the *Brown* decision, the effort to desegregate public education received a further stimulus when the U.S. Congress passed the *Civil Rights Act 1964* which prohibits racial discrimination in public education. As a result, both statute law and case-law now prohibit the denial of equality of opportunity in public education on the ground of race.

Although there is no constitutional right to education as such, if it is provided by the state, it must be delivered to all on an equal basis as required by the constitutional right to equal protection of the laws. The U.S. courts have also sought to dismantle other barriers to equality of educational opportunity including those based on sex. It has been held that discrimination in admission requirements based on sex violates the equal protection clause of the Fourteenth Amendment. In *Berkelman v San Francisco United School District* [29] the court struck down, on equal protection grounds, the school district's policy requiring a higher academic standard for girls than for boys for admission to a college preparatory public high school.

The low-water mark in U. S. constitutional jurisprudence on the issue of the extent to which the right to education is constitutionally protected occurred in *San Antonio Independent School District v Rodriguez.*[30] In its 1973 decision, the U. S. Supreme Court held that the right to be educated was not a fundamental constitutional right and that wealth discrimination did not amount to unlawful discrimination. In a five-to-four judgement, the Supreme Court upheld a Texas school financing scheme which resulted in significantly disproportionate per pupil expenditures on an interdistrict comparison. The financing scheme required the greatest proportion of each school district's funds to be raised through property taxes levied on property within the district. The validity of the scheme was challenged on the basis that education was a fundamental interest and that to the extent that substantial interdistrict disparity in per pupil expenditure reflected the quality of educational opportunity provided to the children in each district, the effect of the scheme denied poorer children the chance to receive an education of similar quality to that offered in wealthier districts, and thus constituted a violation of equal protection principles.

The majority of the Supreme Court in *Rodriguez* rejected the submission that education was a fundamental interest. After citing its opinion in *Brown v Board of Education* which characterised education as "a principal instrument in awakening the child to cultural values, . . . preparing him for later professional training, and . . . helping him to adjust normally to his environment",[31] Justice Powell, for the majority, stated that "the importance of a service performed by the state does not determine whether it must be regarded as fundamental for purposes of examination under the Equal Protection Clause".[32] The majority of the Court considered that it could not legitimately appropriate jurisdiction to itself to characterise important state or public services as fundamental interests when the subject matter of such services had not been accorded either explicit or implicit recognition in the Constitution.

The effect of the *Rodriguez* decision has been that children from poorer families disproportionately attend schools that struggle to meet minimal educational standards.[33] In response to *Rodriguez*, litigants asserting a right to equality of educational opportunity have turned to state constitutions and their interpretation by state courts.[34] Every state constitution in the Union contains provisions concerning education.[35] Article 9(1) of the Idaho Constitution, for example, imposes a duty on the legislature of Idaho to "establish and maintain a general, uniform and thorough system of public, free common schools". Article 10(1) of the Illinois Constitution declares that:

> [a] fundamental goal of the People of the State is the educational development of all persons to the limits of their capacities. The state shall provide for an efficient system of high quality educational institutions and services.

The state constitutional educational provisions are implemented, in turn, by state compulsory education statutes which generally require public school attendance for children aged seven to sixteen.[36]   Although constitutional litigation in the educational field at the state level has not always met with success, the right to education has been recognised as a fundamental legal obligation by numerous state supreme courts.[37]

Since its 1973 decision in *Rodriguez*, the U. S. Supreme Court has stressed the critical importance of education to all individuals, perhaps in the stongest terms ever in its history, in its decision in *Plyler v Doe*.[38]   In reaching its conclusion that a state's denial of public education to undocumented aliens constitutes unlawful discrimination under the equal protection clause of the Fourteenth Amendment, the Court observed:

> Public education is not a 'right' granted to individuals by the Constitution. But neither is it merely some governmental 'benefit' indistinguishable from other forms of social welfare legislation. Both the importance of education in maintaining our basic institutions, and the lasting impact of its deprivation on the life of the child, mark the distinction . . . The American people have always regarded education and [t]he acquisition of knowledge as matters of supreme importance. We have recognized the public schools as a most vital civic institution for the preservation of a democratic system of government, and as the primary vehicle for transmitting the values on which our society rests . . . In addition, education provides the basic tools by which individuals might lead productive lives to the benefit of us all. In sum, education has a fundamental role in maintaining the fabric of our society. We cannot ignore the significant social costs borne by our Nation when select groups are denied the means to absorb the values and skills upon which our social order rests.[39]

Over the last four decades, then, U. S. courts at both the federal and state levels have developed certain educational entitlements, particularly that relating to equality of educational opportunity, by relying not on direct constitutional language but through the application of more general constitutional guarantees. The U. S. experience marks a notable example of the influence of judge-made law on the development of constitutional principles in the educational field and their significant impact upon society.

The Nature of the Right to Education

It has been said that " . . . education is so intimately connected with what is of vital importance for human life that it is essential that it be granted to all 'as of right'".[40]   Several rationales can be invoked to support the argument that the right to education is deserving of recognition and protection as a fundamental human and constitutional right. Although these rationales are offered in the alternative, it is conceded that there may be some overlap between them.

Education: The Social Utilitarian or Public Interest Perspective

Certain arguments of social utility may provide a logical basis for the right to education. The critical functions performed by the delivery of educational services in contemporary society have been acknowledged, as we have seen, by the United States Supreme Court in *Brown v Board of Education* [41] and *Plyler v Doe.* [42] Public education is the primary means through which a community preserves its culture and values and transmits them to the younger generation. As Justice Brennan observed in *Plyler v Doe*, "[w]e have recognized the public schools as . . . the primary vehicle for transmitting the values on which our society rests". [43]

It is arguable that a proper education is a prerequisite to a more reasoned exercise of political and civil liberties. Article 21(1) of the *Universal Declaration of Human Rights* proclaims that "[e]veryone has the right to take part in the government of his country, directly or through freely chosen representatives". The attainment of a minimum level of competence is regarded as a necessary condition for the effective discharge of the right to vote and engage in political activity. [44] Indeed, the inability to participate effectively in the political life of one's community constitutes a significant civil disability. [45] A well-educated population may also be a prerequisite to maintaining democratic structures and ideals. As the U. S. Supreme Court stated in *Plyler v Doe*, ". . . some degree of education is necessary to prepare citizens to participate effectively and intelligently in our open political system if we are to preserve freedom and independence". [46]

A right to education can also be based on the need to train the younger generation as useful members of society and the world community. Various international human rights instruments recognise the right to education as a principal means to secure world peace through the training of its future citizens. Principle 7 of the *Declaration of the Rights of the Child* adopted by the United Nations General Assembly in 1959 states in part that the child " . . . shall be given an education which will . . . enable him . . . to become a useful member of society". Article 26(2) of the *Universal Declaration of Human Rights* provides that "[e]ducation shall be directed to the full development of the human personality . . . [and] . . . shall promote understanding, tolerance and friendship among all nations, racial or religious groups, and shall further the activities of the United Nations for the maintenance of peace".[47]

Education as a Prerequisite to Individual Dignity

The dignity of each human being comprises an important guiding and underlying principle of constitutional bills of rights and international human rights instruments. The first preambular paragraph of the *Universal Declaration of Human Rights* refers to "the inherent dignity . . . of all members of the human family [as]the foundation of freedom, justice and peace in the world". Some commentators maintain that an education that imparts knowledge of essential skills and trains the individual in logical thought and reasoned analysis forms the basis of individual dignity and self-respect.[48]   In those societies which esteem learning and achievement, there can be no dignity for those individuals deprived of an opportunity to benefit from such an education.[49]

Education as a Prerequisite to Individual Development

A third rationale for recognising the right to education is that without it human beings are unable to realise their potential and become   fully functioning members of society. The role performed by the educational system in the personal development of the individual has been acknowledged by several international human rights instruments. Principle 7 of the *Declaration of the Rights of the Child*, for example, states in part that the child shall be given an education which will enable the child to develop his or her abilities, individual judgement and sense of moral and social responsibility.[50]

Education: The Individual Welfare Perspective

Yet another foundation for the right to education is said to lie in its consideration as a welfare right. A "welfare right" has been defined as a right to have certain necessities provided by the community at large in circumstances of compelling need if one is unable to provide them for oneself.[51]   Well-established welfare rights include protection from starvation and the provision of basic medical care and shelter. To this list it has been sought to add education. It is argued that individuals cannot provide adequately for their own education and that they will suffer a significant and enduring disability if such is not provided to them. When conceived of as a welfare right, the function of education is to assist individuals to achieve at least a basic standard of literacy and numeracy so as to enable them to function adequately in the various spheres of life in their respective communities.[52]   A modicum of education will provide the individual with knowledge of the ways and values of the community as well as the ability to communicate and exist more independently.

Education may be regarded as a commodity to which an individual is entitled both as an end in itself but also as a means to other welfare rights.[53] In the latter sense, education may be conceived of as a secondary or derivative right whereby the provision of education to the required level will make it easier for the individual to secure employment and thereby to satisfy such needs as accommodation, health care and nutritional requirements.

Notes

1   Letter written by Thomas Jefferson to George Wythe in Paris on 13 August 1786 as quoted in F. Volio "The child's right to education: a survey" in G. Mialaret (ed.) *The Child's Right to Education* 19, 22.

2   M. Nowak "The Right to Education" in A. Eide, C. Krause and A. Rosas (eds) *Economic, Social and Cultural Rights* (1995) 189,191.

3   Volio, op. cit., 20.

4   "Natural rights" are those rights which can be deduced from the physical, mental, moral, social and religious characteristics of human beings which must be recognised for human beings to attain dignity and personal fulfilment.

5   Those provisions of the Constitution of Ireland dealing with family and educational issues are based on natural law concepts: see B. Walsh "Existence and Meaning of Fundamental Rights in the Field of Education in Ireland" (1981) 2 *Human Rights Law Journal* 319, 320. See also Article 120 of the German Weimar Constitution of 1919 which provided for the "natural right" and duty of parents to educate their children under the supervision of the State.

6   Sir William Blackstone *Commentaries on the Laws of England* Vol. 1 (1829) 435.

7   Volio, op. cit., 21.

8   17 *Writings of Thomas Jefferson* 417.

9   Blackstone, op. cit., 438-9.

10   Nowak, op. cit., 197.

11   Id. 191.

12   *Paulskirchenverfassung* of March, 1849 which, although never formally in force, had a strong influence on the development of constitutionalism in continental Europe. See Nowak, op. Cit., 191.

13   Nowak, op. cit., 191.

14   In many countries the age of 14 has been set to mark the end of the period of compulsory education for children.

15   D. Kelly Weisberg "Evolution of the Concept of the Rights of the Child in the Western World" (1978) 21 *The Review* (International Commission of Jurists) 43, 46.

16   112 *Great Britain Treaty Series* 232.

17   For more detail on the *Declaration of Geneva* see D. Hodgson "The Historical Development and 'Internationalisation' of the Children's Rights Movement" (1992) 6 *Australian Journal of Family Law* 252, 260-1.

18   E. Sharp *The African Child: An Account of the International Conference on African Children* (1931) Longmans, Green and Co., London, 97.

19   This instrument will be discussed in greater detail in Chapter 4.

20   Nowak, op. cit., 192.

21   George T. Kurian (ed.) *World Education Encyclopedia* (1988).

22   See Section 93 of the *Constitution Act, 1867* (formerly *The British North America Act, 1867* 30 & 31 Victoria, c. 3 (U.K.)).

23   Samuel M. Davis and Mortimer D. Schwartz *Children's Rights and the Law* (1987) 133.

24   Mark G. Yudof "Articles 13 and 14 - Right to Education" in Hurst Hannum and Dana D. Fischer (eds) *U. S. Ratification of the International Covenants on Human Rights* (1993) 235, 242.

25   347 U.S. 483 (1954).

26   Davis and Schwartz, op. cit., 132.

27   347 U.S. 483 (1954) at 493.

28   These cases are discussed in J. Hogan *The Schools, The Courts, and The Public Interest* (1985) 24-31.

29   501 F.2d 1264 (9th Cir. 1974).

30   411 U.S. 1 (1973).

31   347 U.S. 483 (1954) at 493.

32   *San Antonio Independent School District v Rodriguez* 411 U.S. 1 (1973) at 30.

33   C. de la Vega "The Right to Equal Education: Merely a Guiding Principle or Customary International Legal Right?" (1994) 11 *Harvard BlackLetter Journal* 37.

34   This new strategy has yielded inconsistent results. See William E. Thro "To Render Them Safe: The Analysis of State Constitutional Provisions in Public School Finance Reform Litigation" (1989) 75 *Virginia Law Review* 1639, 1641-42.

35   C. de la Vega, op. cit., 50.

36   Yudof, op. cit., 239-40.

37   S. Knight "Proposition 187 and International Human Rights Law: Illegal Discrimination in the Right to Education" (1995) 19 *Hastings International and Comparative Law Review* 183, 193 and n. 66.

38   457 U.S. 202 (1982).

39   Id. at 221 (citations and some internal quotation marks omitted).

40   Ivan A. Snook and Colin Lankshear *Education and Rights* (1979) 34.

41   347 U.S. 483 (1954).

42   457 U.S. 202 (1982).

43   Id. 221.

44   Snook and Lankshear, op. cit., 32.

45   C. A. Wringe *Children's rights: A philosophical study* (1981) 146.

46   457 U.S. 202, 221 (1982).

47   See also Article 13(1) of the *International Covenant on Economic, Social and Cultural Rights* to a similar effect.

48   William F. Foster and Gayle Pinheiro "Constitutional Protection of the Right to an Education" (1987-88) 11 *Dalhousie Law Journal* 755, 771.

49   Id. 772.

50   See also Article 26(2) of the *Universal Declaration of Human Rights* and Article 13(1) of the *International Covenant on Economic, Social and Cultural Rights.*

51   Colin Wringe "The Ideology of Liberal Individualism, Welfare Rights and the Right to Education" in M. Freeman and P. Veerman (eds) *The Ideologies of Children's Rights* (1992) 191, 192.

52   Snook and Lankshear, op. cit., 32.

53   C. A. Wringe *Children's rights: A philosophical study* (1981) 146.

PART II

DEVELOPMENTS AT THE INTERNATIONAL LEVEL

3 United Nations Instrumentalities Active in the Educational Field

Introduction

Although numerous United Nations agencies address educational issues as part of their mandate, the two most outstanding examples are the United Nations Educational, Scientific and Cultural Organization (hereinafter referred to as "U.N.E.S.C.O.") and the International Labour Organisation (hereinafter referred to as the "I.L.O."). The educational functions and activities of these two specialised agencies of the United Nations will be examined in this chapter.

U.N.E.S.C.O.

The French Government recommended at the San Francisco Conference in June, 1945 that the United Nations should set up an international organisation on cultural co-operation. The Conference for the Establishment of an Educational, Scientific and Cultural Organization was convened by the Governments of the United Kingdom and France and met in London in November, 1945. The Conference drafted the Constitution of U.N.E.S.C.O. and resolved that its headquarters be located in Paris. U.N.E.S.C.O. officially came into being on 4 November 1946.

Since 1946 the United Nations and U.N.E.S.C.O. have liaised closely in educational matters, including the elimination of illiteracy, the human rights education of youth and the eradication of discrimination in education. As its name suggests, U.N.E.S.C.O.'s primary fields of competence are education, science, culture and communication as well as the promotion of human rights. Recognition of the global responsibility for education as a basic human right was acknowledged in the Constitution of U.N.E.S.C.O. signed at London on 16 November 1945.[1] Article I(1) of the Constitution states that the purpose of U.N.E.S.C.O. is "to contribute to peace and security by promoting collaboration among the nations through education, science and culture in order to further universal respect for justice, for the rule of law and for the human rights and fundamental freedoms which are affirmed for the peoples of the world, without distinction of race, sex or religion, by the Charter of the United Nations".

To realise this purpose, Article I(2) states that UNESCO shall:

(a)   collaborate in the work of advancing the mutual knowledge and understanding of peoples, through all means of mass communication and to that end recommend such international agreements as may be necessary to promote the free flow of ideas by word and image;

(b) give fresh impulse to popular education and to the spread of culture;

by collaborating with Members, at their request, in the development of educational activities;

by instituting collaboration among the nations to advance the ideal of equality of educational opportunity without regard to race, sex or any distinction, economic or social;

by suggesting educational methods best suited to prepare the children of the world for the responsibilities of freedom;

(c) maintain, increase and diffuse knowledge;

by assuring the conservation and protection of the world's inheritance of books, works of art and monuments of history and science, and recommending to the nations concerned the necessary international conventions;

by encouraging co-operation among the nations in all branches of intellectual activity, including the international exchange of persons active in the fields of education, science and culture and the exchange of publications, objects of artistic and scientific interest and other materials of information;

by initiating methods of international co-operation calculated to give the people of all countries access to the printed and published materials produced by any of them.

The main organs of U.N.E.S.C.O. are the General Conference comprising all Member States, the Executive Board which is elected by the General Conference, and the Secretariat which is headed by the Director-General. To achieve its aims, U.N.E.S.C.O., amongst other things, sets and monitors the realisation of international educational standards; gathers and disseminates information of educational, scientific or cultural interest; provides to member States advisory services and technical assistance and assists in the setting up of educational, scientific and cultural institutions and centres; organises congresses, seminars and symposia; and provides subsidies to certain non-governmental organisations.[2]

Within the framework of its standard-setting function, U.N.E.S.C.O. has adopted the following international instruments (some of which will be examined in detail in Chapter 4) aimed at the realisation of human rights in general and the right to education in particular:

Convention against Discrimination in Education 1960

Recommendation against Discrimination in Education 1960

Protocol Instituting a Conciliation and Good Offices Commission to be responsible for seeking a settlement of any disputes which may arise between States parties to the Convention against Discrimination in Education 1962

Recommendation concerning the Status of Teachers 1966

Declaration of the Principles of International Cultural Co-operation 1966

Declaration of Guiding Principles on the Use of Satellite Broadcasting for the Free Flow of Information, the Spread of Education and Greater Cultural Exchange 1972

Convention concerning the Protection of the World Cultural and Natural Heritage 1972

Revised Recommendation concerning Technical and Vocational Education 1974

Recommendation concerning Education for International Understanding, Co-operation and Peace and Education relating to Human Rights and Fundamental Freedoms 1974

Recommendation on the Status of Scientific Researchers 1974

Recommendation on the Development of Adult Education 1976

Declaration on Fundamental Principles concerning the Contribution of the Mass Media to Strengthening Peace and International Understanding, to the Promotion of Human Rights and to Countering Racialism, Apartheid and Incitement to War 1978

International Charter of Physical Education and Sport 1978

Declaration on Race and Racial Prejudice 1978

Apart from the promulgation of international agreements containing world-wide educational standards, U.N.E.S.C.O. has organised since the adoption of the *Convention against Discrimination in Education 1960* a series of regional conferences on educational planning at the ministerial level. Since 1960, these conferences have encouraged the elaboration and implementation of educational policies and plans with a view to ensuring equality of educational opportunity and treatment in education, and identifying the link between education and economic and social development. These periodic regional meetings have brought together the education ministers of Europe, Africa, Asia, Latin America and the Caribbean, and the Arab States in order to reaffirm the right of everyone to education and the objective of educational democratisation, to assess achievements and difficulties, and to study trends, problems, solutions and prospects for educational development.[3]

Oversight of the implementation of the standards contained in the foregoing conventions and recommendations into the national laws and policies of Member States is undertaken by U.N.E.S.C.O.'s Committee on Conventions and Recommendations in Education pursuant to reporting and complaints procedures. In 1978, the Executive Board of U.N.E.S.C.O. adopted a complex complaints procedure prescribing the manner in which U.N.E.S.C.O. would receive and deal with communications alleging breaches of human rights and, in particular, the right to education.[4]

I.L.O.

The International Labour Organization was established by the Paris Peace Conference under Part XIII of the *Treaty of Versailles* in 1919. Although the I.L.O. predates the United Nations, it, like U.N.E.S.C.O., is a specialised agency of the U.N. The I.L.O. is based in Geneva and the principle of tripartitism is reflected in the composition of its various structures. Both the Governing Body, the chief executive organ of the I.L.O., and the International Labour Conference, its legislative and policy-making organ, are comprised of representatives of governments, workers and employers.

The I.L.O. was created primarily to assist in the task of improving the conditions of labour among the nations of the world. To this end, the I.L.O. has since in its inception developed international labour standards which are to be found in international conventions and recommendations.[5] As is the case with U.N.E.S.C.O., I.L.O. conventions are designed to be ratified as international treaties requiring ratifying nations to discharge legal obligations as a matter of international law. Like U.N.E.S.C.O., the I.L.O. has developed procedures for regular supervision of the discharge of these obligations. The major monitoring body is the Committee of Experts on the Application of I.L.O. Conventions and Recommendations. Once again, as is the case with U.N.E.S.C.O., recommendations do not give rise to international obligations. They merely provide guidelines for national policies and action. By virtue of their adoption by the International Labour Conference, however, the Recommendations often represent an international consensus on their subject matter and are regularly incorporated into national labour laws.

Meeting in Philadelphia in May, 1944, the General Conference of the I.L.O. adopted the *Declaration Concerning the Aims and Purposes of the International Labour Organization*, Principle III(j) of which recognises the solemn obligation of the ILO to further among the nations of the world programmes which will achieve "equality of educational and vocational opportunity". Educational and vocational training issues have been addressed in somewhat more detail in the *Social Policy (Basic Aims and Standards) Convention 1962* which was adopted by the General Conference of the I.L.O. on 22 June 1962.[6] Article 14 proclaims that "[i]t shall be an aim of policy to abolish all discrimination among workers . . . in respect of . . . opportunities for vocational training . . .". Article 15 is of sufficient importance to set out its text in full:

(1) Adequate provision shall be made to the maximum extent possible under local conditions, for the progressive development of broad systems of education, vocational training and apprenticeship, with a view to the effective preparation of children and young persons of both sexes for a useful occupation.

(2) National laws or regulations shall prescribe the school-leaving age and the minimum age for and conditions of employment.

(3) In order that the child population may be able to profit by existing facilities for education and in order that the extension of such facilities may

not be hindered by a demand for child labour, the employment of persons below the school-leaving age during the hours when the schools are in session shall be prohibited in areas where educational facilities are provided on a scale adequate for the majority of the children of school age.

Throughout its history, the I.L.O. has been concerned to ensure that the minimum ages prescribed for child labour are closely related to the age for completion of compulsory education. The possibility of children being in legal employment while under a legal obligation to attend school is removed by providing that the age of admission to employment should not be lower than the age of completion of compulsory schooling.[7] Some of the I.L.O. conventions which seek to address the subject of age for employment include the following:

Minimum Age (Industry) Convention 1919 (ILO Convention No. 5), revised 1937 (No. 59)

Minimum Age (Sea) Convention 1920 (ILO Convention No. 7), revised 1936 (No. 58)

Minimum Age (Agriculture) Convention 1921 (ILO Convention No. 10)

Minimum Age (Non-Industrial Employment) Convention 1932 (ILO Convention No. 33), revised 1937 (No. 60)

Minimum Age (Fishermen) Convention 1959 (ILO Convention No. 112)

Minimum Age (Underground Work) Convention 1965 (ILO Convention No. 123)

The *Convention concerning Minimum Age for Admission to Employment 1973* (Convention No. 138)[8] adopted by the General Conference of the I.L.O. is intended to establish a general international agreement on minimum age of admission, applicable to all forms of work and employment. The *Convention* is to replace the above-mentioned I.L.O. treaties which are economic sector-based. The *Convention* states in its Preamble that it is intended to "gradually replace the existing [I.L.O. conventions] applicable to limited economic sectors, with a view to achieving the total abolition of child labour . . .". Article 2 of the

Convention provides that the minimum age for admission to employment "shall not be less than the age of completion of compulsory schooling".

The I.L.O. has also adopted numerous recommendations concerning vocational training which include:

Vocational Training Recommendation, 1939 (No. 57)

Apprenticeship Recommendation, 1939 (No. 60)

Vocational Guidance Recommendation, 1949 (No. 87)

Vocational Training (Agriculture) Recommendation, 1956 (No. 101)

Vocational Training Recommendation, 1962 (No. 117)

The International Labour Conference has also adopted the *Vocational Rehabilitation and Employment (Disabled Persons) Convention 1983* (No. 159).

Other U.N. Instrumentalities Active in the Educational Field

In 1946, the United Nations Economic and Social Council ('ECOSOC') recommended to the United Nations General Assembly that a United Nations International Children's Emergency Fund (commonly referred to later as 'U.N.I.C.E.F.') be created to help mend the lives of children whose countries had been ravaged by World War II. On 11 December 1946, the General Assembly created U.N.I.C.E.F. pursuant to Resolution 57(1).[9] Although U.N.I.C.E.F. has continued to assist children who have been affected by war, drought, famine and other conflicts and emergencies, its activities were soon broadened. Health and nutrition programmes were instituted to combat high infant mortality rates, ill-health and hunger amongst the children of developing countries. Since 1961, U.N.I.C.E.F. aid has been committed in increasing amounts not only to child welfare and family planning but to education and vocational training as well.[10]

The Economic and Social Council also established in 1946 the Commission on the Status of Women which is primarily responsible for monitoring and encouraging implementation of the international law on women's rights. To fulfil its mandate, the Commission prepares recommendations and reports for ECOSOC on promoting women's rights in the political, economic, civil, social and educational fields. Improvement of the status and role of women in education, science and culture, and the elimination of discrimination against women in the educational field have been at the forefront of the Commission's agenda. The Commission has also examined reports prepared by U.N.E.S.C.O. on particular aspects of the education of girls and women, and adopted recommendations to member States on such subjects as the access of girls and women to primary, secondary and higher education; to technical and vocational education; and to the teaching profession.[11]

International Conferences and other Initiatives of the United Nations Recognising the Right to Education

Since the early 1960s, the United Nations and its agencies have undertaken a variety of initiatives which generally recognise the right to education and particularly address the chronic problem of illiteracy. In the 1960s, the United Nations General Assembly and the Economic and Social Council in partnership with U.N.E.S.C.O. developed an intensive *World Campaign for Universal Literacy*. The Economic Commission for Africa and the Economic Commission for Asia and the Far East were also active in the campaign.[12] In Resolutions 1937 (XVIII) of 11 December 1963 and 2043 (XX) of 8 December 1965, the General Assembly addressed recommendations concerning the eradication of illiteracy to member States and to U.N.E.S.C.O., and in Resolution 2192 (XXI) of 15 December 1966 the General Assembly invited Member States, international organisations and private institutions to provide continuing and effective financial, material and technical support for the *World Campaign for Universal Literacy*.[13]

The first United Nations-sponsored International Conference on Human Rights was convened in Teheran in May, 1968. International concern about continuing widespread illiteracy resulted in the adoption by the Conference of Paragraph 14 of the *Proclamation of Teheran*[14] which stated:

> The existence of over seven hundred million illiterates throughout the world is an enormous obstacle to all efforts at realizing the aims and purposes of the Charter of the United Nations and the provisions of the Universal Declaration of Human Rights. International action aimed at eradicating illiteracy from the face of the earth and promoting education at all levels requires urgent attention.

In its Resolution XII of 12 May 1968, the Conference invited the governments of all countries to allocate more resources to combat illiteracy and to intensify their co-operation and support for appropriate educational programmes. The Conference also invited the United Nations General Assembly to draw the attention of human rights organs to the importance of combating illiteracy as a means of ensuring the effective enjoyment of human rights, and urged the United Nations and its specialised agencies, especially U.N.E.S.C.O., to do their utmost to stimulate efforts for enhancing the contribution which literacy could make to economic and social development.[15]

It was perhaps more than a happy coincidence, then, that the United Nations General Assembly designated 1970 as "International Education Year" in Resolution 2412 (XXIII) of 17 December 1968. The General Assembly recommended in Resolution 2412 that Member States take stock of the situation concerning education and training in their countries and initiate action and studies linked to the objectives and themes of the International Education Year. The International Education Year was essentially an opportunity for reflection and action by Member States with a view to improving and expanding their educational systems.

In 1972, the United Nations itself entered the educational sector as a player when the General Assembly adopted Resolution 2951 (XXVII) of 11 December 1972, pursuant to which it was decided to establish an international university under the auspices of the United Nations to be known as the United Nations University. The General Assembly also prescribed objectives and principles to guide the United Nations University, some of which included research into pressing global problems of hunger, human welfare, economic and social development, peaceful coexistence, and human rights, as well as scientific and technological research and its application to developmental issues. The United Nations University is located in Tokyo.[16]

By 1986, the number of illiterate persons in the world had risen from some 700 million at the time of the Teheran Conference in 1968 to an estimated 889 million adults. This increase occurred despite the establishment through U.N.E.S.C.O. in the 1980's of four regional programmes to support national efforts to achieve universal primary education and eliminate adult illiteracy.[17] At its twenty-third session, held in 1986, the General Conference of U.N.E.S.C.O. expressed deep concern about the illiteracy problem, and appealed to the United Nations to proclaim and observe an "International Literacy Year" as a means of stimulating greater efforts to spread literacy and education.[18] In approving the U.N.E.S.C.O. appeal in Resolution 41/118 of 4 December 1986, the General Assembly encouraged U.N.E.S.C.O. to elaborate a plan of action which would assist member States in eradicating illiteracy by the year 2000. The General Assembly proclaimed the year 1990 as International Literacy Year in its Resolution 42/104 of 7 December 1987 which also recognised the elimination of illiteracy as a prerequisite for ensuring the right to education and, as such, a priority issue to be addressed particularly by U.N.E.S.C.O. Article 28(3) of the *Convention on the Rights of the Child*, adopted by the U. N. General Assembly on 20 November 1989, builds upon this initiative in calling on States Parties to "promote and encourage international co-operation in matters relating to education, in particular with a view to contributing to the elimination of ignorance and illiteracy throughout the world . . .". In response to the General Assembly's invitation and in acknowledgment of Article 28(3), the General Conference of U.N.E.S.C.O. adopted at its 25th session in 1989 the *Plan of Action for the Eradication of Illiteracy by the Year 2000.*

The first World Conference on Education for All was held in Jomtien, Thailand in March 1990 to help mark International Literacy Year. The convening of the Conference also marked the acknowledgment by the world community that previous concerted efforts to reduce illiteracy rates had failed. Indeed, the *Preamble* of the *World Declaration on Education for All* which was adopted by the Conference observed that despite notable efforts by countries around the globe to ensure the right to education for all, the following realities persist:

- more than 100 million children, including at least 60 million girls, have no access to primary schooling;

- more than 100 million children and countless adults fail to complete basic education programmes . . .

- more than 960 million adults, two-thirds of whom are women, are illiterate, and functional illiteracy is a significant problem in all countries, industrialized and developing . . .

According to U.N.E.S.C.O. statistics on 1990 literacy rates,[19] African, Asian and Latin American literacy rates are lagging behind those of the industrialised North:

North America, Europe, and Australia and New Zealand	95% or over
Sub-Saharan Africa	47%

Caribbean and Latin America	85%
Arab States	51%
South East Asia	80%
Eastern Asia	76%
Southern Asia	46%

Although the industrialised countries of the northern hemisphere had relatively few illiterates, they did have a significant proportion of "functional illiterates" - those without sufficient literacy and numeracy skills to be able to participate adequately in employment, educational and social opportunities.[20]   By 1990, the right to education for all had become only a theoretical entitlement in many developing States which had been crippled by the debt crisis and forced to curtail governmental spending. Speaking in 1990, U.N.E.S.C.O. Director-General Federico Mayor observed:

> The past few years have witnessed an unprecedented halt in the growth of basic educational services and a stagnation and deterioration of educational quality . . . In nearly half the developing countries the goal of universal primary education is now receding rather than drawing nearer.[21]

Such was the contextual background to the World Conference on Education for All which was convened jointly by U.N.E.S.C.O., U.N.I.C.E.F., the United Nations Development Programme and the World Bank. Delegates from 155 States, including policy-makers and specialists in education and other major sectors, together with officials and specialists representing some 20 inter-governmental bodies and 150 non-governmental organisations, adopted by acclamation at the closing plenary session of the Conference on 9 March 1990 the texts of two documents - the *World Declaration on Education for All* and the *Framework for Action to Meet Basic Learning Needs*. As stated by Wadi Haddad, Executive Secretary of the Inter-Agency Commission for the World Conference on Education for All, these two documents " . . . represent a worldwide consensus on an expanded vision of basic education and a renewed commitment to ensure that the basic learning needs of all children, youth and adults are met effectively in all countries".[22]

Although some of the provisions of the *Declaration*   and *Framework for Action* will be mentioned in later parts of this monograph, a number of the more important preambular and operative provisions of these documents should now be noted. Although these provisions are not legally binding, they are aspirational in the sense of informing the development of national laws and policies. The fifth preambular provision of the *Declaration* acknowledges "that, overall, the current provision of education is seriously deficient and that it must be . . . made universally available". Education is reaffirmed as a fundamental and universal right for all in the first preambular paragraph. The penultimate preambular paragraph recognises that basic education is an essential prerequisite to strengthening higher levels of education, including science and technology, and thus to self-reliant development. In terms of the operative provisions of the *Declaration,* Article 1(1) states in part:

> Every person - child, youth and adult - shall be able to benefit from educational opportunities designed to meet their basic learning needs. These needs comprise both essential learning tools (such as literacy, oral expression, numeracy, and problem-solving) and the basic learning content (such as knowledge, skills, values, and attitudes) required by human beings to be able to survive, to develop their full capacities, to live and work in dignity, to participate fully in development, to improve the quality of their lives, to make informed decisions, and to continue learning.

Article 5 of the *Declaration* notes that the main delivery system for the basic education of children outside the family is primary schooling which must be universal and ensure that the basic learning needs of all children are satisfied. Article 1(4) and Article 5 respectively recognise that basic education and literacy are necessary skills in themselves as well as the foundation for other life skills. Paragraph 45(g) of the *Framework for Action* observes that substantial bilateral and multilateral assistance will be required to reduce significantly the world's large number of illiterates by implementing basic education programmes in regions with high illiteracy rates. Several of the more notable and ambitious goals that countries are urged by Paragraph 8 of the *Framework for Action* to strive for during the 1990s are universal access to, and completion of, primary education by the year 2000, reduction of the adult illiteracy rate to one-half its 1990 level by the year 2000 and a significant reduction of the current disparity between male and female illiteracy rates.

The reduction of illiteracy rates and the expansion of access to basic education were also squarely on the agenda of the United Nations-sponsored World Conference on Human Rights which met in Vienna in June, 1993. The Conference adopted by consensus the *Vienna Declaration and Programme of Action* which reaffirm the universal character of human rights and the obligation of States to take measures concerning special groups such as children. Paragraph 47 of Part 4 (headed "The rights of the child") of Division IIB of the *Vienna Declaration and Programme of Action* calls on States to, *inter alia*, integrate the *Convention on the Rights of the Child* into national action plans which place particular priority on reducing illiteracy and providing access to basic education.

Notes

1   Constitution of the United Nations Educational, Scientific and Cultural Organization 4 U.N.T.S 275.

2   United Nations *United Nations Action in the field of Human Rights* (1988) p. 29, para. 230.

3   1980 Report submitted to the United Nations General Assembly by the Director-General of UNESCO A/35/148, paras. 9 and 10.

4   The communications procedure would also appear to cover complaints by parents and guardians and members of minority groups: M. Tardu *Human Rights: the International Petition System* (1980) Vol. 3, Part II, Booklet IV, 13-14.

5   See generally E. Osieke *Constitutional Law and Practice in the International Labour Organisation* (1985).

6   Convention No. 117 entered into force on 23 April 1964. Its full text may be found at 494 *United Nations Treaty Series* 249.

7   Geraldine Van Bueren *The International Law on the Rights of the Child* (1995) 265.

8   1015 *United Nations Treaty Series* 297.

9   United Nations *United Nations Action in the Field of Human Rights* (1980) 209.

10   United Nations *United Nations Action in the Field of Human Rights* (1980) 209.

11   United Nations *United Nations Action in the Field of Human Rights* (1980) 146.

12   United Nations *United Nations Action in the Field of Human Rights* (1980) 199.

13   Ibid.

14   Adopted at the twenty-seventh plenary meeting of the International Conference on Human Rights on 13 May 1968.

15   United Nations (N.Y.) *United Nations Action in the Field of Human Rights* (1980) 199.

16   Id. 199-200.

17   Major Project in the field of Education in Latin American and Caribbean; Regional Programme for the Eradication of Illiteracy in Africa; Asia-Pacific Programme for Education for All; Regional Programme for the

Universilization and Renewal of Primary Education and the Eradication of Illiteracy in the Arab States by the Year 2000.

18   United Nations *United Nations Action in the Field of Human Rights* (1988) 169.

19   T. Skutnabb-Kangas *Language, Literacy and Minorities* (1990) (Minority Rights Group Report) 7.

20   Id. 5.

21   U.N.I.C.E.F. *The World Summit for Children* (1990) 14.

22   Inter-Agency Commission *World Declaration on Education for All and Framework for Action to Meet Basic Learning Needs* (1990) Preface.

4 International Recognition of the Right to Education under Conventional and Customary Law

> Everything begins with education, for neither nature nor society can be made to serve their useful purpose without it. This is the reason for the priority which it is universally accorded.[1]

Introduction

The human right to education features prominently in the hierarchy of human rights in so far as it has been recognised in international and regional instruments and by customary law. Each level or source of recognition will be examined in turn in this chapter.

Recognition of the Right to Education by International Instruments

The right to education has been specifically recognised and reaffirmed in some detail by four major international human rights instruments - the *Universal Declaration of Human Rights* of 1948, the *U.N.E.S.C.O. Convention against Discrimination in Education* of 1960, the *International Covenant on Economic, Social and Cultural Rights* of 1966 and the *Convention on the Rights of the Child* of 1989. The right to education has also been recognised in numerous other instruments dealing with particular groups or subject matter. These instruments will be catalogued in this section.

Mainstream Recognition

The *Charter of the United Nations* was adopted by the United Nations Conference on International Organization held at San Francisco and entered into force on 24 October 1945. The *Charter* is an international treaty establishing the organisational structure and guiding principles of the United Nations. Its provisions have the force of positive international law and create duties that all Member States must fulfil in good faith.[2] Article 55(b) of the *Charter* requires the United Nations to promote "international cultural and educational co-operation" in order to create conditions of stability and well-being which are necessary for peaceful relations among nations. Article 73 imposes on those members of the United Nations which have assumed responsibility for the administration of non-self-governing trust territories an obligation to promote the well-being of the inhabitants of these territories by, *inter alia*, ensuring their "educational advancement". Although the U.N. *Charter* does not in itself guarantee a right to education, it does provide a basis for its future development by conventional and customary law.

A general right to education was directly and specifically articulated for the first time in the *Universal Declaration of Human Rights* in 1948. Article 26(1) states:

> Everyone has the right to education. Education shall be free, at least in the elementary and fundamental stages. Elementary education shall be compulsory. Technical and professional education shall be made generally available and higher education shall be equally accessible to all on the basis of merit.

Article 26(1) must be read in conjunction with Article 2 of the *Universal Declaration* which states that "[e]veryone is entitled to all the rights and freedoms set forth in this Declaration, without distinction of any kind, such as race, colour, sex, language, religion, political or other opinion, national or social origin, property, birth or other status".

The *Universal Declaration* was unanimously adopted by the United Nations General Assembly on 10 December 1948 to give content to the human rights provisions of Article 55 of the U. N. *Charter* and to provide, in its own words, "a common standard of achievement for all peoples and all nations". The inclusion of the right to education in Article 26(1) was not a source of contention and the debate was, therefore, brief.[3] In terms of the wording of Article 26(1), there would appear to be no clear distinction between elementary and fundamental education. Elementary education would arguably include elements of fundamental education such as literacy, numeracy and tuition in the basic knowledge and skills essential for functioning in society. As these elements may differ from society to society, the concept of fundamental education is probably best left to be defined by the individual nations themselves.[4]   Higher education is to be available to all on the basis of merit rather than wealth or station.   The obligation to supply free education to children implies that each nation should establish a free public education system in order to place education within the reach of the great majority of children.[5]

Compulsory elementary education appears to be based on the notion that every person has an irrevocable entitlement to a period of education at public expense. The apparent inconsistency between the right to education and the compulsory nature of elementary education can be accommodated if the term 'compulsory' is intended to imply that no person or body can prevent children from receiving a basic education.   This imposes an obligation on the State to ensure that children receive at least an elementary education in circumstances of parental neglect or ignorance, for example.[6]

Bearing in mind the non-binding, aspirational nature of the *Universal Declaration* at the time of its adoption, it is still rather remarkable that these *desiderata* were articulated when relatively few nations possessed adequate secondary and higher education systems.[7]   It would appear, however, that the *Declaration's* limitation of free education to elementary education now falls short of the practice of many countries where secondary and even higher education are free.[8]   The term 'free' must be understood to mean that the delivery of elementary education itself would be free of charge but it is not as certain that other expenses of the student such as transportation costs, books and school uniforms would be covered. The position in terms of the constitutional jurisprudence of the United States appears to be that charges related to the central educational mission of the school are unconstitutional under state constitution education clauses, but incidental charges are allowed.[9]

The educational provisions of the *Universal Declaration* have been reaffirmed, amplified and made more detailed by later United Nations instruments including the *International Covenant on Economic, Social and Cultural Rights* (hereinafter referred to as the "*I.C.E.S.C.R.*") which was adopted by the United Nations General Assembly on 16 December 1966. Unlike the *Universal Declaration*, the *I.C.E.S.C.R.* is an international agreement which imposes legally binding obligations on those nations which ratify or accede to it. A number of provisions of the *I.C.E.S.C.R.* refer to education.   Article 6(2) obliges States Parties to devise and implement "technical and vocational guidance and training programmes" to achieve the fuller realisation of the right to work. Article 10(1) proclaims that the widest possible protection and assistance should be accorded to the family while it is responsible for the care and education of dependent children. Article 14 concerns developing countries and provides:

> Each State Party to the present Covenant which, at the time of becoming a Party, has not been able to secure in its metropolitan territory or other territories under its jurisdiction compulsory primary education, free of charge, undertakes, within two years, to work out and adopt a detailed plan of action for the progressive implementation, within a reasonable number of years, to be fixed in the plan, of the principle of compulsory education free of charge for all.

Article 14 would also apply to countries which originally introduced free primary education but have reverted to the imposition of school fees prior to becoming a party to the *I.C.E.S.C.R.* [10]   Working in the climate of the 1960s "Development Decade", the drafters of Article 14 were aware of the link between free and compulsory primary education and economic development.

Article 13 of the *I.C.E.S.C.R.* expands upon the content attributed to the right to education by Article 26(1) of the *Universal Declaration*. Article 13 is exclusively devoted to the right to education and, in its day, contained the most extensive and detailed provisions on this subject to be incorporated in an international legal instrument. This was due largely to the fact that U.N.E.S.C.O., with which the drafters consulted, favoured detailed provisions on the right to education.[11]   As a whole, Article 13 seeks to promote inexpensive, egalitarian and comprehensive education for all.

In line with Article 26(1) of the *Universal Declaration*, Article 13(1) proclaims that the "States Parties . . . recognize the right of everyone to education" while Article 13(2)(a) requires compulsory primary education available free to all. As such, Article 13 implicitly endorses the concept of equality of educational opportunity which is reinforced by the non-discrimination language contained in Article 2(2) of the *ICESCR*. As one commentator has observed, the right to education is the only human right for which international law stipulates a corresponding duty in the form of compulsory education until the end of primary education.[12] Compulsory education is an important means by which the State protects children from their parents and economic exploitation.[13]   As we saw in Chapter 3, the prohibition of child labour through a fixed minimum age for admission to employment is a complementary standard to that of compulsory primary education.

Unlike Article 26(1), Article 13 makes specific reference to secondary education. Article 13(2)(b) reads:

> Secondary education in its different forms, including technical and vocational secondary education, shall be made generally available and accessible to all by every appropriate means, and in particular by the progressive introduction of free education.

It would appear that secondary education is not required to be compulsory. Article 13(2)(c) essentially repeats the provisions of Article 26(1) of the *Universal Declaration* concerning higher education but does go further in one respect by calling for the "progressive introduction of free education" at this level as well. Article 13(2)(e) constitutes a new provision in calling for the active pursuit of the development of a system of schools at all levels, the establishment of an adequate fellowship system and the continuous improvement of the material conditions of teaching staff.

Implementation of the right to education as contained in Article 13 is progressive in nature and requires positive State action, as States Parties to the *I.C.E.S.C.R.* are obligated to improve the existing conditions concerning education to the maximum of their available resources. This is made clear by Article 2(1) of the *I.C.E.S.C.R.* which provides that "[e]ach State Party . . . undertakes to take steps, individually and through international assistance and co-operation . . . to the maximum of its available resources, with a view to achieving progressively the full realization of the rights recognized in the present Covenant by all appropriate means . . .". The U.N. Committee on Economic, Social and Cultural Rights has rejected the notion that the implementation of these rights may be deferred indefinitely. The Committee has insisted that the obligation to "take steps" is serious and that the poverty of States is not a valid reason for inaction since diligent governments should solicit resources from the international community.[14] The Committee has stated:

> . . . while the full realization of the relevant rights may be achieved progressively, steps towards that goal must be taken within a reasonably short time after the Covenant's entry into force for the States concerned. Such steps should be deliberate, concrete and targeted as clearly as possible towards meeting the obligations recognized in the Covenant.[15]

The interpretative guidelines of *The Limburg Principles on the Implementation of the International Covenant on Economic, Social and Cultural Rights* [16] specifically relating to Article 2(1) of the *I.C.E.S.C.R.*

are also informative in terms of the implementation of the obligation assumed by States Parties under Article 13. Principle 21 states:

> The obligation "to achieve progressively the full realization of the rights" requires States parties to move as expeditiously as possible towards the realization of the rights. Under no circumstances shall this be interpreted as implying for States the right to defer indefinitely efforts to ensure full realization. On the contrary all States parties have the obligation to begin immediately to take steps to fulfil their obligations under the Covenant.

Principles 23 and 25 of the *Limburg Principles* offer little comfort to developing States. Principle 23 provides that "[t]he obligation of progressive achievement exists independently of the increase in resources; it requires effective use of resources available". Principle 25 acknowledges that "States parties are obligated, regardless of the level of economic development, to ensure respect for minimum subsistence rights for all". It is arguable that fundamental education - literacy, numeracy and basic life skills - would be considered a minimum subsistence right and, as such, must be given sufficient priority in terms of the governmental allocation of scarce resources.

The *Convention on the Rights of the Child*, adopted by the United Nations General Assembly on 20 November 1989, contains a number of provisions concerning education. Article 23(3) refers to the obligation of States Parties to ensure that the disabled child has effective access to education and training. Article 40(4) concerns the availability of guidance, education and vocational training programmes as alternatives to institutional care in the juvenile justice context. Article 32(1) recognises the right of the child to be protected from performing any work that is likely to be hazardous or to interfere with the child's education. Article 28, together with Article 29 concerning the aims of education which will be dealt with in Chapter 5, represents the most comprehensive formulation of the right to education at the international level. Article 28(1) provides:

> States Parties recognize the right of the child to education, and with a view to achieving this right progressively and on the basis of equal opportunity, they shall, in particular:
>
> (a) make primary education compulsory and available free to all;
>
> (b) encourage the development of different forms of secondary education, including general and vocational education, make them available and accessible to every child, and take appropriate measures such as the

introduction of free education and offering financial assistance in case of need;

(c) make higher education accessible to all on the basis of capacity by every appropriate means;

(d) make educational and vocational information and guidance available and accessible to all children;

(e) take measures to encourage regular attendance at schools and the reduction of drop-out rates.

Neither the *Convention on the Rights of the Child* nor the *I.C.E.S.C.R.* makes any reference to pre-school education. This is a rather disappointing omission as the opportunity to participate in pre-school education has been recognised by U.N.E.S.C.O. as important because children's attitudes on such matters as race are often formed in the pre-school years.[17] During the technical review of the *Draft Convention on the Rights of the Child*, U.N.E.S.C.O. expressed concern that Article 28(1)(a) made no mention of early childhood care and education.[18] During the second reading of the *Convention*, U.N.E.S.C.O. sought to amend what is now Article 28 by incorporating a legal duty on States Parties to "facilitate the provision of early childhood care and education, using all possible means, in particular for the disadvantaged child, in order to contribute to the young child's growth, development and to enhance his or her later success at other levels of education".[19] U.N.E.S.C.O.'s proposed amendment failed due to the opposition of many States to increasing their educational expenditure and, consequently, international law does not impose on States any duty to provide any type of pre-school education.[20] Nevertheless, references to pre-school education may be found in both legally binding and non-binding international instruments. Consider Article 10 of the *Central American Convention on the Unification of the Fundamental Norms of Education* of 1962, Article 10(a) of the *Convention on the Elimination of All Forms of Discrimination against Women* of 1979, Article 1 of the U.N.E.S.C.O. *International Charter of Physical Education and Sport* of 1978 and Paragraph B.3 of the *Charter of the Rights of the Arab Child* adopted by the League of Arab States. Paragraph 24 of the U.N.E.S.C.O. *Recommendation Concerning Education for International Understanding, Co-operation and Peace and Education Relating to Human Rights and Fundamental Freedoms 1974* urges Member States to encourage, as part of pre-school education, activities which correspond to the purposes of the *Recommendation*.

The use of the term 'progressively' in the introductory part of Article 28(1) must be read in conjunction with Article 4 which obliges States Parties to undertake measures to implement the economic, social and cultural rights recognised by the *Convention* to the maximum extent of their available resources. During the drafting of the *Convention*, a number of delegations, including those from China and Bangladesh, expressed concern about the different levels of economic development amongst States and their impact on the ability to provide free education.[21]   Although Article 28(1)(a) repeats the wording of Article 13(2)(a) of the *I.C.E.S.C.R.*, the obligation imposed is arguably weaker than that imposed by the latter instrument. This is due to the absence in the *Convention* of an equivalent provision to Article 14 of the *I.C.E.S.C.R.* which obliges States Parties who have not already implemented free and compulsory primary education to adopt within two years a detailed plan of action for the implementation of such system. The *Convention* fails to specify any time-frame.

Article 28(1)(b) is based on the wording of Article 13(2)(b) of the *I.C.E.S.C.R.* Article 28(1)(b) is weaker than its counterpart, however, in two respects. First, States Parties to the *Convention* are merely required to "encourage the development of different forms of secondary education" whereas under the *I.C.E.S.C.R.* "[s]econdary education in its different forms . . . shall be made generally available . . .".[22]   Secondly, the introduction of free secondary education is accorded a lower priority in the *Convention* than it is under the *I.C.E.S.C.R* presumably because many States still cannot afford to offer it free. The Japanese delegation was only prepared to accept the wording of Article 28(1)(b) on the understanding that it would not impose any legal obligation on the States Parties to implement a system of free secondary education.[23]

Article 28(1)(c) also appears to be a step backwards from existing standards concerning higher education in its failure to include the phrase "the progressive introduction of free education" as it appears in Article 13(2)(c) of the *I.C.E.S.C.R.* Despite the urging of U.N.E.S.C.O. and the United Nations Secretariat that the wording of Article 28(1)(c) should also include a reference to "the progressive introduction of free education" for the sake of consistency with Article 13(2)(c) of the *I.C.E.S.C.R.*,[24] the wording remained unchanged in order to accommodate the concerns of various delegations whose nations' policies only went so far as providing financial assistance for students pursuing higher education.[25] Regrettably, then, much of Article 28 appears to derogate from the international standards previously embodied in the various formulations of the right to education.   Article 28(1)(d) and Article 28(1)(e) are, however, new provisions. In terms of Article 28(1)(e) concerning the encouragement of regular school attendance and the reduction of drop-out rates, it would appear from the *travaux préparatoires* that these aims are intended to be achieved by positive rather than punitive measures.[26] It was estimated at about the time the *Convention on the Rights of the Child* was adopted by the U.N. General Assembly in 1989 that of the 100 million six-year-olds who would begin school in 1990, over 40 million would drop out before completing primary education.[27]

International Instruments Concerning Particular Groups and Topics

Apart from mainstream recognition canvassed in the previous sub-section, the right to education has also been recognised by international instruments which seek to regulate specific topics of international concern. The various instruments adopted by the General Conference of U.N.E.S.C.O. will be examined in the initial part of this sub-section.

The *Convention against Discrimination in Education*, adopted by the General Conference of U.N.E.S.C.O. on 14 December 1960,[28] is the first international instrument to prescribe comprehensive international standards for public education. The *Convention* seeks particularly to eliminate discrimination and ensure equal treatment and equality of opportunity to education at all levels. Discrimination in education had been investigated as one of a number of studies of discrimination in various fields by the Sub-Commission on the Prevention of Discrimination and Protection of Minorities under the authorisation of the Commission on Human Rights. Special Rapporteur Charles Ammoun's 1957 report entitled *Study of Discrimination in Education*[29] proposed the drafting of an international convention on the elimination of discrimination in education and set out the fundamental principles on which such a convention would be based. These principles were incorporated and expanded in the *Convention against Discrimination in Education*.[30] To accommodate concerns expressed by several U.N.E.S.C.O. Member States with federal systems of government concerning their competence to ratify a convention which covered a matter within the jurisdiction of their states or provinces, the U.N.E.S.C.O. General Conference adopted at the same time as the *Convention* a non-binding *Recommendation against Discrimination in Education*. The content of the *Recommendation*, which applies to all U.N.E.S.C.O. Member States which have not become a party to the *Convention*, is virtually identical to that of the *Convention*. [31]

It is clear from the preambular paragraphs of the *Convention* that it is based on Articles 2 and 26 of the *Universal Declaration of Human*

Rights which deal respectively with the principle of non-discrimination and the right of every person to education and which, when read together, prohibit discrimination in education. The Preamble of the *Convention* also adverts to Article I.2.(b) of U.N.E.S.C.O.'s Constitution which charges U.N.E.S.C.O. with the task of "instituting collaboration among the nations to advance the ideal of equality of educational opportunity . . .". At the time of the adoption of the *Convention* in 1960, young women and members of minority groups were denied access to universities in many countries[32] and racially segregated school systems existed in countries such as South Africa and the United States.[33]

For the purposes of the *Convention*, the term 'education' refers to all types and levels of education including access to education, the quality of education, and the conditions under which it is delivered. The democratisation of education is achieved by three critical operative provisions. Article 1(1) broadly defines the term 'discrimination' for the purpose of the *Convention* in such a way as to catch both direct and indirect discrimination. 'Discrimination' includes "any distinction, exclusion, limitation or preference which, being based on race, colour, sex, language, religion, political or other opinion, national or social origin, economic condition or birth, has the *purpose or effect* of nullifying or impairing equality of treatment in education . . .".[34] Article 1(1) also explicitly considers as discriminatory the deprivation of any person or group of persons of access to education, the subjection of any person or group to education of an inferior standard and, subject to certain exceptions to be discussed in later chapters, the creation and maintenance of separate educational systems.[35] Article 3 of the *Convention* obliges States Parties to eliminate and prevent discrimination in education in law and in fact. In particular, Article 3 obliges States Parties to abrogate any laws or administrative practices which involve educational discrimination, to ensure that there is no discrimination in the admission of pupils to educational institutions, and not to allow any differences of treatment by the public authorities between nationals, except on the basis of merit or need, in the setting of school fees and the granting of financial assistance to pupils. Article 3 also proscribes discrimination, based solely on the ground that pupils belong to a particular group, in the granting of assistance by the public authorities to educational institutions.

Article 4 states in part:

> The States Parties . . . undertake furthermore to formulate, develop and
> apply a national policy which, by methods appropriate to the circumstances

and to national usage, will tend to promote equality of opportunity and of treatment in the matter of education and in particular:

(a)   To make primary education free and compulsory; make secondary education in its different forms generally available and accessible to all; make higher education equally accessible to all on the basis of individual capacity . . .

(b)   To ensure that the standards of education are equivalent in all public education institutions of the same level . . .

(d)   To provide training for the teaching profession without discrimination.

The clause "by methods appropriate to the circumstances and to national usage" appearing in the *chapeau* of Article 4 is an acknowledgment, according to one commentator, of the fact that many States view the measures required to ensure equality of opportunity as complex and involving implementation of a broad range of policies necessitating considerable expenditure over a prolonged period.[36] Article 4(a) essentially reaffirms the provisions of Article 26(1) of the *Universal Declaration of Human Rights* but does add a reference to secondary education.

On 10 December 1962, after considerable debate amongst member States, the General Conference of U.N.E.S.C.O. adopted the *Protocol Instituting a Conciliation and Good Offices Commission to be Responsible for Seeking a Settlement of any Disputes which may arise between States Parties to the Convention against Discrimination in Education 1962.*[37] The *Protocol* facilitates the implementation of the *Convention against Discrimination in Education* by setting up an inter-State complaints procedure. Articles 1 and 2 of the *Protocol* create a permanent eleven-member Conciliation and Good Offices Commission to be responsible for seeking the amicable settlement of disputes between States Parties to the *Convention* concerning the application or interpretation of the latter instrument. Pursuant to Article 12 of the *Protocol*, if a State Party to the *Protocol* considers that another State Party is not giving effect to a provision of the *Convention*, it may bring the matter to the attention of that State. Within three months of receiving the complaint, the respondent State must afford the complainant State a written explanation concerning the matter including any remedies pursued. If the matter is not satisfactorily adjusted within six months of the receipt of the complaint, either State Party may refer the matter to the Commission which, under Article 17, is required to ascertain the facts and make available its good offices to the States concerned with a view to reaching an amicable solution on the basis of respect for the *Convention.*

Apart from the *Convention against Discrimination in Education* the General Conference of UNESCO has addressed discrimination issues in the field of education in various non-binding recommendations and declarations. UNESCO has been particularly concerned about racism based on its constitutional mandate contained in Article 1 of its Constitution and a 1948 request by the United Nations Economic and Social Council that it "consider the desirability of initiating and recommending the adoption of a programme of disseminating scientific facts designed to remove what is commonly known as racial prejudice".[38] On 19 November 1974, the General Conference of U.N.E.S.C.O. adopted the *Recommendation Concerning Education for International Understanding, Co-operation and Peace and Education Relating to Human Rights and Fundamental Freedoms 1974.* Paragraph 7 recommends that each Member State of U.N.E.S.C.O. formulate and apply national policies aimed at strengthening the contribution of education, *inter alia,* "to the establishment of social justice, to respect for and application of human rights and fundamental freedoms, and to the eradication of the prejudices, misconceptions, inequalities and all forms of injustice which hinder the achievement of these aims". Principle 11 urges Member States to take steps to ensure that the principles of the *International Convention on the Elimination of All Forms of Racial Discrimination* of 1965 become an integral part of the educational curriculum at all levels. Member States are also invited by Principle 39 to "ensure that educational aids, especially textbooks, are free from elements liable to give rise to misunderstanding, mistrust, racialist reactions, contempt or hatred with regard to other groups or peoples". To achieve the purposes of Principle 39, U.N.E.S.C.O. has facilitated the international exchange and critical examination of history and geography textbooks with a view to the elimination of any references to racism or ethnocentrism.[39] In its *Declaration on Race and Racial Prejudice* adopted by the U.N.E.S.C.O. General Conference on 27 November 1978, the Conference proclaimed that "States . . . as well as . . . the entire teaching profession, have a responsibility to see that the educational resources of all countries are used to combat racism . . .".[40]

The significant role of the mass media in the education of young people in a spirit of mutual respect and understanding has been acknowledged by Article IV of the *Declaration on Fundamental Principles Concerning the Contribution of the Mass Media to the Strengthening of Peace and International Understanding, to the Promotion of Human Rights and the Countering of Racialism, Apartheid and Incitement to War* adopted by the U.N.E.S.C.O. General Conference on 28 November 1978. The General Conference of U.N.E.S.C.O. has also adopted the *Second Medium-Term Plan (1984-1989) Education for All* which includes comprehensive and co-ordinated scientific research on racial discrimination. This initiative builds upon the *Programme of Action for the Second Decade to Combat Racism and Racial Discrimination*, in which U.N.E.S.C.O. is requested to continue "its work . . . on the factors of influence in the maintenance, transmission and alteration of prejudices and on the causes and effects of the various forms of racism and racial and ethnic discrimination . . .".[41] The *Second Medium-Term Plan* also addresses issues concerning the democratisation of education, equality of educational opportunity for girls and women and educational obstacles confronted by the disabled, refugees and migrant workers.

Another important U.N.E.S.C.O. instrument is the *Recommendation concerning the Status of Teachers* of 1966. This recommendation was adopted by a special inter-governmental conference convened jointly by the I.L.O. and U.N.E.S.C.O. It will be recalled that Article 13(2)(e) of the *International Covenant on Economic, Social and Cultural Rights* refers to the continuous improvement of the material conditions of teaching staff. Amongst other things, the *Recommendation concerning the Status of Teachers* seeks to establish minimal working conditions, prohibits any form of discrimination in the preparation and employment of teachers and recognises the role to be played by teachers' organisations in the determination of educational policy. A Joint I.L.O./U.N.E.S.C.O. Committee has been set up to consider the implementation of the *Recommendation.* Article 7 of the *World Declaration on Education for All* adopted by the World Conference on Education for All states in part that "the terms and conditions of service of teachers and their status, which constitute a determining factor in the implementation of education for all, must be urgently improved in all countries in line with the joint I.L.O./U.N.E.S.C.O. Recommendation Concerning the Status of Teachers (1966)".

The right to education has been mentioned in various international instruments regulating the treatment of stateless and refugee persons and the victims of armed conflict. Article 22 of the *Convention relating to the Status of Refugees* of 1951 and Article 22 of the *Convention relating to the Status of Stateless Persons* of 1954 respectively provide that the Contracting States shall accord to refugees and stateless persons "the same treatment as is accorded to nationals with respect to elementary education" and, in respect of all other types and levels of education, "treatment as favourable as possible and, in any event, not less favourable than that accorded to aliens generally in the same circumstances". The human rights of those persons caught up in armed conflict are protected by a branch of international law known as international humanitarian law. The *Geneva Convention Relative to the Protection of Civilian Persons in Time of War of August 12, 1949* contains a number of provisions which refer to education. Article 24 provides that the Parties to the conflict shall take the necessary measures to ensure that the education of children under fifteen, who are orphaned or are separated from their families as a result of the war, is facilitated in all circumstances and entrusted to persons of a similar cultural tradition. Article 94 provides in part:

> The Detaining Power shall encourage intellectual, educational and recreational pursuits, sports and games amongst internees . . .

> All possible facilities shall be granted to internees to continue their studies or to take up new subjects. The education of children and young people shall be ensured; they shall be allowed to attend schools either within the place of internment or outside . . .

In 1977, the international community agreed to adopt two new instruments of humanitarian law - the *Protocol Additional to the Geneva Conventions of 12 August 1949, and Relating to the Protection of Victims of International Armed Conflicts (Protocol I)* and the *Protocol Additional to the Geneva Conventions of 12 August 1949, and Relating to the Protection of Victims of Non-International Armed Conflicts (Protocol II)*. Article 78(2) of the former instrument, which deals with international armed conflicts, provides that the education of each evacuated child, including religious and moral education according to parental preference, shall be provided with the greatest possible continuity. Article 4(3)(a) of the latter instrument, which deals with internal armed conflicts, similarly provides that children shall receive an education, including religious and moral education, in keeping with the wishes of their parents.

It will be recalled that Article 1(1) of the *Convention against Discrimination in Education* of 1960 defines the term 'discrimination' to include, *inter alia*, "any distinction . . . based on race". Pursuant to Article 5(e)(v) of the *International Convention on the Elimination of All Forms of Racial Discrimination*, adopted by the United Nations General Assembly in Resolution 2106 A (XX) of 21 December 1965, States Parties "undertake to prohibit and to eliminate racial discrimination in all its forms and to guarantee the right of everyone . . . to equality before the law, notably in the enjoyment of . . . the right to education and training".

Article 7 reinforces Article 5(e)(v) by requiring States Parties "to adopt immediate and effective measures, particularly in the fields of teaching, education, culture and information, with a view to combating prejudices which lead to racial discrimination . . . ". Article 3(1) of the non-binding *Declaration on the Elimination of All Forms of Racial Discrimination*, proclaimed by the United Nations General Assembly in Resolution 1904 (XVIII) of 20 November 1963, had previously urged United Nations Member States to undertake particular efforts "to prevent discrimination based on race, colour or ethnic origin, especially in the fields of . . . education, religion, employment, occupation and housing".

The right to education and its importance to social progress and development have been mentioned in a number of non-binding instruments adopted by the United Nations. In the *Declaration on Social Progress and Development*, proclaimed by the General Assembly in Resolution 2542 (XXIV) of 11 December 1969, the eradication of illiteracy and the guarantee of the right to free compulsory education at the elementary level as well as the right to free education at all levels are mentioned in Article 10(e) as goals to be attained in the raising of the standards of living of all members of society. Similarly, Article 7 of the *Programme of Action* of the World Conference on Agrarian Reform and Rural Development hosted by the United Nations Food and Agriculture Organization in Rome in July, 1979, recommends that governments give high priority to the achievement of universal literacy and numeracy and free primary education for all children including those in rural areas. More recently, Article 8(1) of the *Declaration on the Right to Development* adopted by the General Assembly in Resolution 41/128 of 4 December 1986 provides that "States should undertake, at the national level, all necessary measures for the realization of the right to development and shall ensure, *inter alia*, equality of opportunity for all in their access to . . . education . . .".

The right to education has been included in various declarations concerning religious and belief minorities. Article XXI of the *Universal Islamic Declaration of Human Rights* adopted on 19 September 1981 provides that "[e]very person is entitled to receive education in accordance with his [or her] natural capabilities". Article 5 of the *Declaration on the Elimination of All Forms of Intolerance and of Discrimination Based on Religion or Belief*, proclaimed by the United Nations General Assembly in Resolution 36/55 of 25 November 1981, canvasses the respective rights of parents and their children in the context of religious and moral education.

Many of the international instruments which seek to protect or recognise the rights (including the right to education) of *specific groups* take the form of a declaration. A declaration is a species of international instruments commonly referred to as "soft law"; by contrast, "hard law" comprises conventions which are legally, as opposed to merely morally, binding. Typically, a declaration proclaims a set of principles, ideals or standards generally accepted by the international community which are intended to inform national policies. Initially, however, a declaration does not contain binding legal obligations. The operative provisions of a declaration can eventually crystallise into customary law as did certain provisions of the *Universal Declaration of Human Rights*. Alternatively, these provisions can be incorporated later into a legally binding international agreement. This occurred with certain provisions of the *Declaration of the Rights of the Child* which were later embodied in the *Convention on the Rights of the Child.*

Educational rights have been recognised in two United Nations declarations concerning disabled persons. Principle 2 of the *Declaration on the Rights of Mentally Retarded Persons* proclaimed by the General Assembly in Resolution 2856 (XXVI) of 20 December 1971 states that "[t]he mentally retarded person has a right to . . . such education, training, rehabilitation and guidance as will enable him to develop his ability and maximum potential". Similarly, Principle 6 of the *Declaration on the Rights of Disabled Persons* proclaimed by the General Assembly in Resolution 3447 (XXX) of 9 December 1975 affirms the right of disabled persons to "education, vocational training and rehabilitation . . . and other services which will enable them to develop their capabilities and skills to the maximum".

The right to education features prominently in three United Nations declarations concerning children and youth. Principle 5 of the *Declaration of the Rights of the Child* adopted by the General Assembly on 20 November 1959[42] states that the physically or mentally handicapped child shall be given the special treatment, education and care required by his or her particular condition. Principle 9, a forerunner of Article 32(1) of the *Convention on the Rights of the Child*, forbids the employment of a child in any occupation which would prejudice his or her health or education. The most important operative provision of the *Declaration of the Rights of the Child* concerning education is Principle 7. Consistently with Article 26(1) of the *Universal Declaration of Human Rights* and Article 13(2)(a) of the *International Covenant on Economic, Social and Cultural Rights*, Principle 7 provides in part that "[t]he child is entitled to receive education, which shall be free and compulsory, at least in the elementary stages". As such, Principle 7 represents the first specific global reference to the right *of the child* to receive education.[43] The words "free and compulsory" imply the establishment and maintenance of a public education system and a State responsibility to ensure primary school attendance in circumstances, for example, of parental neglect. Although free education at all levels was a goal to strive for, many States were unable to achieve it at that time. Reference to the 'fundamental' stage of education which appears in Article 26(1) of the *Universal Declaration* was omitted in Principle 7 because fundamental education usually refers to adult education.

On 7 December 1965, the United Nations General Assembly proclaimed in Resolution 2037 (XX) the *Declaration on the Promotion among Youth of the Ideals of Peace, Mutual Respect and Understanding between Peoples*. Principle II thereof urges that "[a]ll means of education . . . should foster among [the young] the ideals of peace, humanity, liberty and international solidarity and all other ideals which help to bring peoples closer together . . .". High on the agenda of the heads of State and Government who attended the *World Summit for Children* held at United Nations headquarters in New York on 30 September 1990 were the necessity to reduce illiteracy and to improve equality of educational opportunity. At the conclusion of the *Summit*, the *World Declaration on the Survival, Protection and Development of the Child* was adopted, Principle 20(6) of which reads:

> We will work for programmes that reduce illiteracy and provide educational opportunities for all children, irrespective of their back-ground and gender; that prepare children for productive employment and lifelong learning opportunities, i. e. through vocational training; and that enable children to grow to adulthood within a supportive and nurturing cultural and social context.

The *World Summit for Children* also adopted a non-binding *Plan of Action for Implementing the World Declaration on the Survival, Protection and Development of the Child* which, *inter alia*, sets as two of its goals access to, and completion of, basic education for 80% of school- age children, and the reduction of adult illiteracy by one-half.[44]

The right to education has also been recognised by instruments seeking to address human rights issues concerning women. Article 9 of the *Declaration on the Elimination of Discrimination Against Women* proclaimed by the United Nations General Assembly in Resolution 2263 (XXII) of 7 November 1967 enjoins that "[a]ll appropriate measures shall be taken to ensure to girls and women, married or unmarried, equal rights with men in education at all levels". Article 9 particularly insists on equal conditions of access to, and study in, all types of educational institutions as well as the same choice of curricula, teaching staff with qualifications of the same standard and school premises and equipment of the same quality. Similarly, an entire provision of the *Convention on the Elimination of All Forms of Discrimination Against Women*, which was adopted by the United Nations General Assembly in Resolution 34/180 of 18 December 1979, is devoted to the right to education. Article 10 essentially reaffirms Article 9 of the *Declaration* and adds some new provisions such as the necessity to reduce female student drop-out rates. Thus, what was only a programmatic statement of principle in Article 9 of the *Declaration* has been converted into a binding legal obligation in Article 10 of the *Convention*.

Recognition of the Right to Education by Regional Human Rights Instruments

There have also been significant efforts made at the regional level to recognise and secure the right to education, most notably in Europe, Africa and Latin America. Each region will be considered in turn.

Europe

Although the original text of the European *Convention for the Protection of Human Rights and Fundamental Freedoms* of 1950[45] contained no provision concerning the right to education, Article 2 of the *First Protocol*[46] to the European *Convention* adopted by the Council of Europe on 20 March 1952 states that "[n]o person shall be denied the right to education". The *First Protocol* is the first internationally binding instrument after the *Universal Declaration of Human Rights* to explicitly refer to a right to education. Article 2 is unique in the sense that it is the only regional or international human rights provision to adopt a negative formulation of the right to education. This was due to the fact that in 1952 all the Member States of the Council of Europe had a general education system and thus it was regarded as unnecessary to require them to establish such a system.[47] Indeed, the text was also changed from its original form - "Every person has the right to education" - to its present form to avoid what some States anticipated might be excessively burdensome positive obligations.[48] Article 2 extends to all forms of education provided or permitted by the State, although its primary focus is on elementary education.[49] Although the term 'education' includes higher education, it does not extend to vocational training.[50]

The European Commission of Human Rights and the European Court of Human Rights have been called on from time to time to interpret the meaning and content of the right to education as contained in Article 2 of the *First Protocol*. According to the European Court in the *Belgian Linguistic Case*,[51] the rights protected by Article 2 include a right of access to existing educational institutions, a right to an effective education and a right to the official recognition of the studies a student has successfully completed. The Court also held in the same case that States Parties to the *First Protocol* are not required by Article 2 to establish at their own expense, or to subsidise, education of any particular type or at any particular level. Refusal of a subsidy to pupils at a private school has been held, therefore, not to breach Article 2.[52] Therefore, unlike most other international and regional provisions on the right to education which generally impose a positive obligation on States, Article 2 merely imposes a negative obligation on a State Party not to take steps to interfere with the right.

The right to education is not explicitly referred to in the *European Social Charter* signed by the members of the Council of Europe at Turin on 18 October 1961. The *Charter* focuses instead on the right to vocational guidance and training which can be considered a minor, albeit important, aspect of the right to education. The Contracting Parties are obliged under Article 9 to provide a free vocational guidance service to school children, young persons and adults alike. Article 10 requires the Parties to provide a system of apprenticeship and technical and vocational training and "to grant facilities for access to higher technical and university education, based solely on individual aptitude". Pursuant to Article 7(3), a provision reminiscent of Article 32(1) of the *Convention on the Rights of the Child*, the Contracting Parties undertake "to provide that persons who are still subject to compulsory education shall not be employed in such work as would deprive them of the full benefit of their education".

The European Court of Justice has recently expanded Community law into the educational field through the use of the combined effect of Articles 7 and 128 of the *Treaty of Rome* of 25 March 1957[53] establishing the European Economic Community. Article 7 of the *Treaty of Rome* prohibits discrimination on the ground of nationality while Article 128 provides in part that "[t]he Council [of Europe] shall . . . establish general principles for the implementation of a common policy of occupational training capable of contributing to the harmonious development both of national economies and of the Common Market". Those general principles are to be found in Council Decision 63/266.[54] A general right under Community law to non-discrimination in the conditions of access to vocational training has been found in the conjunction of Articles 7 and 128.[55]   Community law thus has the potential to have a direct influence on the execution of national educational policy in the vocational training field.[56]   The European Court of Justice has, for example, ruled on the financing of education in Belgium.[57]   Greater respect for the discretionary competence of Member States in the educational field may be forthcoming as a result of the *Treaty on European Union and Economic and Monetary Union* (otherwise known as the *Maastrict Treaty*) signed on 7 February 1992.[58] Some of the main innovations introduced by the *Maastrict Treaty* include the development of quality education, language teaching, vocational training policy and greater mobility for students and teachers. The *Treaty* also acknowledges respect for the responsibility of Member States for the content of teaching and the organisation of educational systems and for their cultural and linguistic diversity. Consequently, no harmonisation of laws and regulations of Member States in these areas is required.

     The right to education has been formulated in more positive terms viv-à-vis Article 2 of the *First Protocol* by a number of non-binding resolutions and declarations adopted by the European Parliament during the 1980s. In its "Freedom of Education in the European Community" Resolution of 14 March 1984, the European Parliament called for recognition within the European Community of the principle that "[e]very child and young person shall have the right to education and teaching without any discrimination based on sex, race, philosophical or religious beliefs, nationality, social class or economic standing". Similarly, Article 16 of the *Declaration of the European Parliament of Fundamental Rights and Freedoms*, adopted by the European Parliament on 12 April 1989, proclaims that "[e]veryone shall have the right to education and vocational training appropriate to their abilities".

Africa

The *Charter of the Organization of African Unity* (otherwise known as the *Charter of Addis Ababa*) was adopted by a conference of African Heads of States and Governments in Addis Ababa, Ethiopia, on 25 May 1963. Article 1(1) thereof established the *Organization of African Unity* while Article 2(2)(c), contrary to the more recent European experience reflected in the *Maastrict Treaty* of 1992, stressed the need for Member States to co-ordinate and harmonise their general policies in the field of educational and cultural co-operation to help achieve the basic aims of the O.A.U. The latter provision has been reaffirmed recently by the *Treaty Establishing the African Economic Community* adopted by the O.A.U. on 3 June 1991, Article 68(1) of which provides that "Member States shall strengthen co-operation among themselves in the field of education and training and co-ordinate and harmonize their policies in this field".

It was not until 1981, however, that the O.A.U. explicitly recognised the right to education within a human rights instrument. Article 17(1) of the *African Charter on Human and Peoples' Rights*,[59] which was adopted by the O.A.U. in Nairobi, Kenya on 27 June 1981, provides simply that "[e]very individual shall have the right to education". The most comprehensive formulation of the right to education in a regional African human rights instrument is to be found in the *African Charter on the Rights and Welfare of the Child* [60] which was adopted by the O.A.U. on 11 July 1990. The *Children's Charter* imposes legally binding obligations on those African States which ratify it and also creates the Committee on the Rights and Welfare of the Child to monitor its implementation. Article 11(1) thereof states that "[e]very child shall have the right to education". Article 11(3)(a)(b) and (c) essentially replicate Article 28(1)(a)(b) and (c) of the *Convention on the Rights of the Child* in calling for the provision of free and compulsory basic education, the development of universal secondary education in its different forms and universal accessibility to higher education on the basis of capacity. Unlike the *Convention*, however, no mention is made of the right to vocational guidance and training.

The right to education has also been mentioned in various non-binding declarations adopted by the League of Arab States and the Organization of the Islamic Conference. Article XXI of the *Universal Islamic Declaration of Human Rights* adopted at Paris on 19 September 1981 states that "[e]very person is entitled to receive education in accordance with his [or her] natural capabilities". Article 9(b) of the *Cairo Declaration on Human Rights in Islam* adopted by the Organization of the Islamic Conference on 5 August 1990 provides in part that "[e]very human being has the right to receive both religious and worldly education from the various institutions of education and guidance, including the family, the school, the university, the media . . .". The League of Arab States has "confirmed and guaranteed" in Article B.3. of the *Charter of the Rights of the Arab Child* "the child's right for free education both in the pre-schooling, the basic and compulsory education periods . . .".

Latin America

The right to education is most comprehensively dealt with by the Latin American regional human rights system. The right to education features prominently in the *Charter of the Organization of American States* of 1948 as amended by the *Protocol of Buenos Aires* of 1967.[61]   Article 31(h) of the *Charter* identifies as 'basic' the goal of "rapid eradication of illiteracy and expansion of educational opportunities for all" in order to accelerate the economic and social development of Member States.   Article 48 reinforces Article 31(h) in providing that "Member States will give special attention to the eradication of illiteracy . . .".   The most important pronouncements on the right to education in the *Charter*, however, are to be found in Article 47 which states:

> The Member States will exert the greatest efforts, in accordance with their constitutional processes, to ensure the effective exercise of the right to education, on the following bases:
>
> (a) Elementary education, compulsory for children of school age, shall also be offered to all others who can benefit from it. When provided by the State it shall be without charge;
>
> (b) Middle-level education shall be extended progressively to as much of the population as possible; and
>
> (c) Higher education shall be available to all, provided that, in order to maintain its high level, the corresponding regulatory or academic standards are met.

Article 47(a) of the O. A. S. *Charter* essentially repeats the prescription of free and compulsory elementary education contained in Article 26(1) of the *Universal Declaration of Human Rights* of 1948. Chapter XIV of the *Charter* is devoted to the Inter-American Council for Education, Science, and Culture whose purpose, according to Article 99, is "to promote friendly relations and mutual understanding between the peoples of the Americas through educational, scientific and cultural cooperation and exchange between Member States . . .". To accomplish this purpose, the Inter-American Council is charged by Article 100(c) to support efforts of the Member States to improve and extend education at all levels.

At the same Ninth International Conference of American States which adopted the O.A.S. *Charter*, the *American Declaration of the Rights and Duties of Man* was proclaimed on 2 May 1948.[62] The *American*

Declaration, similar in design and purpose to the *Universal Declaration of Human Rights*, appears in the Final Act of the Conference held in Bogotá, Colombia in April-May, 1948. Article XII of the *American Declaration* elaborates upon the educational provisions of the O.A.S. *Charter*. Article XII recognises that "[e]very person has the right to an education . . . [which] includes the right to equality of opportunity in every case . . .". Article XII also guarantees the right of every person to a free primary education, although the issue of its compulsory nature is not addressed.[63]

In terms of Latin American conventional recognition of the right to education, Article 1 of the *Central American Convention on the Unification of the Fundamental Norms of Education* [64] (hereinafter referred to as the *"Central American Convention"*) adopted by the O.A.S. on 22 June 1962 proclaims that "[a]ll persons in Central America have the right to the benefits of education". The adoption of the *Central American Convention* followed the Conference on Education and Economic and Social Development in the Latin American Countries held at Santiago, Chile in March 1962. The *American Convention on Human Rights* [65] (otherwise known as the *Pact of San José*) was adopted by the O.A.S. on 22 November 1969 at the conclusion of the Inter-American Specialized Conference on Human Rights held at San José, Costa Rica. The *American Convention* does not attempt to deal with economic, social and cultural rights and thus no mention is made of the right to education.[66] Article 26 does, however, require States Parties to "adopt measures . . . with a view to achieving progressively . . . the full realization of the rights implicit in the economic, social, *educational*, scientific, and cultural standards set forth in the Charter of the Organization of American States . . ." (emphasis supplied).

The recent *Additional Protocol to the American Convention on Human Rights in the Area of Economic, Social and Cultural Rights* [67] (otherwise known as the *"Protocol of San Salvador"*), adopted by the O.A.S. at San Salvador, El Salvador on 14 November 1988, does contain an explicit recognition of the right to education. Article 13 closely resembles Article 13 of the *International Covenant on Economic, Social and Cultural Rights*. Article 13(1) recognises that "[e]veryone has the right to education" while Article 13(3)(a), consistently with the international instruments, guarantees to the child the right to free compulsory elementary education. The provisions concerning secondary and higher education contained respectively in Article 13(3)(b) and (c) mirror closely Article 13(2)(b) and (c) of the *International Covenant*. Pursuant to Article 19 of the *Protocol of San Salvador*, the Inter-American Council for Education, Science, and Culture (created under Chapter XIV of the O.A.S. *Charter*) is responsible for vetting periodic reports submitted by the States Parties on the measures which they have taken to progressively implement the right to education within their respective jurisdictions.

Recognition of the Right to Education Under Customary Law

Considering the widespread recognition of the right to education by both international and regional human rights treaties, it is pertinent to consider whether the right has become a binding rule of customary international law.

Customary international law develops from generally accepted practices which nations follow out of a sense of legal obligation.[68]   Article 38(1)(b) of the *Statute of the International Court of Justice* instructs the Court to apply "international custom, as evidence of a general practice accepted as law" in the resolution of disputes submitted to it.   The two critical elements for the existence of a customary norm of international law are a uniform practice adhered to generally by States and their belief that the practice is required by international law (the so-called *opinio juris* requirement).   Unlike treaties and conventions, a rule of customary law binds even those States which have never formally recognised it.[69] National and international courts have relied on international treaties and declarations as well as national constitutions and laws to assist them in determining whether a practice has crystallised into a customary norm. The International Court of Justice has, for example, relied directly upon United Nations instruments to establish the existence of a customary rule of international law in its *Western Sahara* Advisory Opinion.[70]

Certain aspects of the right to education including the right to free public primary education and the right to equality of educational opportunity have arguably joined the corpus of customary international law.[71]   Widely ratified and adopted human rights conventions and declarations, both international and regional, together with national laws concerning the right to education support this conclusion.   It will be recalled from earlier in this chapter that the content of the right to education is most comprehensively and universally dealt with by the following provisions:

Article 26   *Universal Declaration of Human Rights*

Articles 1, 3 and 4 *Convention against Discrimination in Education*

Article 13   *International Covenant on Economic, Social and Cultural Rights*

Article 28   *Convention on the Rights of the Child*

Those Member States of the United Nations which adopted the *Universal Declaration of Human Rights* in 1948 understood the instrument to contain non-binding aspirational principles to guide them in the formulation of national laws and policies.[72]   They viewed it as a preliminary stage leading ultimately to a comprehensive and legally binding International Bill of Rights in the form of a multilateral convention. Nearly fifty years on, a strong argument can be made that the *Universal Declaration* represents binding customary rules of international law. The drafting history of the *Universal Declaration* reveals a high degree of agreement in the discussion of the right to education.[73] The continual adherence to the provisions of the *Declaration* by States which joined the United Nations after 1948 and the incorporation of its principles into the constitutions of numerous States have prompted courts and prominent scholars to conclude that they now represent customary norms.[74]

As of 1995, 84 States had become a party to the *Convention against Discrimination in Education.*[75] The *International Covenant on Economic, Social and Cultural Rights* has been ratified or acceded to by 131 States.[76] As of 1996, the *Convention on the Rights of the Child* had been ratified or acceded to by 185 States.[77]   The rapid acceptance of the *Children's Convention* by almost all of the nations in just six years provides cogent evidence of the general acceptance amongst States of the right to education.[78]   The customary status of the right to education is reinforced by its recognition at the regional level in the European *Convention for the Protection of Human Rights and Fundamental Freedoms* (Article 2 of *Protocol I* thereof), the *African Charter on Human and Peoples' Rights* (Article 17(1)) and the *Additional Protocol to the American Convention on Human Rights in the Area of Economic, Social and Cultural Rights* (Article 13). The constitutional laws of States, as reflective of State practice, also provide compelling evidence that the right to education has evolved into a customary norm. The right to education is recognised in the Constitutions of some 52 States while many more recognise it in their ordinary legislation.[79]

It can be asserted with confidence that at least two educational principles have now acquired the status of customary norms - the right to free public primary education and the right to equality of educational opportunity. The following instruments all prescribe free public elementary/primary education:

Article 26(1) *Universal Declaration of Human Rights*

Article 4(a) *Convention against Discrimination in Education*

Article 13(2) *International Covenant on Economic, Social and Cultural Rights*

Article 28(1)(a) *Convention on the Rights of the Child*

Article 47(a) *O. A. S. Charter*

Article 13(3)(a) *Additional Protocol to the American Convention on Human Rights in the Area of Economic, Social and Cultural Rights*

Considering the widespread uniformity of language of these international and regional instruments, customary international law would now appear to require access for all children to a free elementary education.[80]

The right to equality of educational opportunity or the right to gain access to and enjoy educational programmes without discrimination has also featured prominently in international and regional instruments. Article 28(1) of the *Convention on the Rights of the Child*, for example, provides that "States Parties recognize the right of the child to education . . . on the basis of equal opportunity . . .". The *Convention against Discrimination in Education* reaffirms the commitment of the *Universal Declaration of Human Rights* to the principle of non-discrimination in the educational sphere. The following international and regional instruments also seek to guarantee the right to equality of educational opportunity through a combination of provisions relating to a general right to non-discrimination and specifically to the right education:

Articles 2 and 26 *Universal Declaration of Human Rights*

Articles 2(2) and 13 *International Covenant on Economic, Social and Cultural Rights*

Articles 2 and 17 *African Charter on Human and Peoples' Rights*

Article 14	European *Convention for the Protection of Human Rights and Fundamental Freedoms* (combined with Article 2 of *Protocol I* thereof)
Articles 3 and 13	*Additional Protocol to the American Convention on Human Rights in the Area of Economic, Social and Cultural Rights*

Apart from the above-mentioned international instruments, the national laws of many States specifically mention equality of opportunity in the exercise of the right to education.[81]

Notes

1   René Maheu (former Director-General of UNESCO) as quoted in M. El Fasi "The Right to Education and Culture" (1968) 9 *Journal of the International Commission of Jurists* 33, 38.

2   L. Sohn "The Human Rights Law of the Charter" (1977) 12 *Texas International Law Journal* 129, 131.

3   K. Halvorsen "Notes on the Realization of the Human Right to Education" (1990) 12 *Human Rights Quarterly* 341, 350.

4   P. Arajärvi "Article 26" in A. Eide (ed.) *The Universal Declaration of Human Rights: A Commentary* (1992) 405, 408-9.

5   F. Volio "The Child's Right to Education: A Survey" in G. Mialaret *The Child's Right to Education* (1979) 19, 25.

6   Id. 23.

7   D. Ray and N. Tarrow *Human Rights and Education* (1987) 10.

8   M. El Fasi "The Right to Education and Culture" (1968) 9 *Journal of the International Commission of Jurists* 33, 34.

9   M. Yudof "Articles 13 and 14 - Right to Education" in H. Hannum and D. Fischer (eds) *U.S. Ratification of the International Covenants on Human Rights* (1993) 235, 242.

10   G. Van Bueren *The International Law on the Rights of the Child* (1995) 235.

11   *U.N. Annotations* 112, para. 36.

12   M. Nowak "The Right to Education" in A. Eide (ed.) *Economic, Social and Cultural Rights* (1995) 189, 204.

13   Id. 205.

14   P. Thornberry "International Standards" in *Education Rights and Minorities* (1994) (Minority Rights Group Report) 10, 11.

15   Paragraph 2 of General Comment 3 (1990): The nature of States parties' obligations, reproduced in *Manual on Human Rights Reporting*, HR/PUB/91/1, UN Sales No. E.91.XIV.1, 43-7.

16   U.N. Doc. E/CN.4/1987/17, Annex.

17   See Paragraph 24 of the UNESCO *Recommendation Concerning Education for International Understanding, Co-operation and Peace and Education Relating to Human Rights and Fundamental Freedoms 1974.*

18   Commission on Human Rights *Technical Review of the Text of the Draft Convention on the Rights of the Child* E/CN.4/1989/WG.1/CRP.1 (15 October 1988) p. 33.

19   Commission on Human Rights *Report of the Working Group on a Draft Convention on the Rights of the Child* E/CN.4/1989/48 (2 March 1989) p. 80, para. 459. A Venezuelan proposal had also sought to make reference to the "overall care for the child of pre-school age": see id. p. 79, para. 458.

20   G. Van Bueren "Education: Whose Right is it Anyway?" in L. Heffernan (ed.) *Human Rights: A European Perspective* (1994) 340, 341.

21   Commission on Human Rights *Report of the Working Group on a Draft Convention on the Rights of the Child* E/CN.4/1985/64 (3 April 1985) p. 11, para. 58; Commission on Human Rights *Report of the Working Group on a Draft Convention on the Rights of the Child* E/CN.4/1986/39 (13 March 1986) Annex IV, p. 3 (Paper submitted by the Permanent Representative of Bangladesh).

22   The obligation in this respect is also weaker than that imposed by Article 4(a) of the *Convention against Discrimination in Education.* See *Technical Review*, op. cit., p. 33 for the critical comment by UNESCO in this regard. See also Commission on Human Rights *Report of the Working Group on a Draft Convention on the Rights of the Child* E/CN.4/1989/48 (2 March 1989) p. 82, para. 463 (UNESCO suggestion that the words "encourage the development of" be deleted so as not to derogate from existing standards).

23   Commission on Human Rights *Report of the Working Group on a Draft Convention on the Rights of the Child* E/CN.4/1985/64 (3 April 1985) p. 13, para. 74; Commission on Human Rights *Report of the Working Group on a Draft Convention on the Rights of the Child* E/CN.4/1989/48 (2 March 1989) p. 82, para. 464.

24   Commission on Human Rights *Technical Review of the Text of the Draft Convention on the Rights of the Child: Additional Comments and Clarifications by the Secretariat* E/CN.4/1989/WG.1/CRP.1/Add.1 (14 November 1988) p. 9, para. 35; Commission on Human Rights *Report of the Working Group on a Draft Convention on the Rights of the Child* E/CN.4/1989/48 (2 March 1989) pp. 79-80, para. 459.

25   Commission on Human Rights *Report of the Working Group on a Draft Convention on the Rights of the Child* E/CN.4/1989/48 (2 March 1989)

p. 82, paras. 465-6 (see particularly the comments of the representatives of the United Kingdom, the Netherlands and Finland).

26 Commission on Human Rights *Report of the Working Group on a Draft Convention on the Rights of the Child* E/CN.4/1989/48 (2 March 1989) p. 82, para. 467.

27 UNICEF *The World Summit for Children* (1990) 32.

28 429 U.N.T.S. 93 (entry into force 22 May 1962). As of 1995, 84 States had become parties to the *Convention* : "International Instruments Relating to Human Rights" (1995) 16 *Human Rights Law Journal* 75, 88.

29 United Nations publication, Sales No. E.57.XIV.3.

30 H. Cullen "Education Rights or Minority Rights?" (1993) 7 *International Journal of Law and the Family* 143, 148.

31 United Nations *United Nations Action in the Field of Human Rights* (1988) p. 167, para. 32.

32 Consider, for example, the former Japanese policy of denying financial assistance to students of the Korean minority wishing to pursue university studies: Y. Iwasawa "Legal treatment of Koreans in Japan: The Impact of International Human Rights Law on Japanese Law" (1986) 8 *Human Rights Quarterly* 131, 175.

33 Nowak, op. cit., 202.

34 Emphasis supplied by author.

35 Article 2(a) of the *Convention* provides that separate educational institutions for pupils of the two sexes shall not be deemed discriminatory under the *Convention* provided certain conditions are met.

36 G. Van Bueren *The International Law on the Rights of the Child* (1995) 246.

37 Entry into force 24 October 1968.

38 United Nations *United Nations Action in the Field of Human Rights* (1988) p. 80, para. 45.

39 United Nations *United Nations Action in the Field of Human Rights* (1980) p. 199

40 Article 5(2).

41 United Nations *United Nations Action in the Field of Human Rights* (1988) p. 80, para. 46.

42 General Assembly Resolution 1386, U.N. GAOR, 14th Sess., Supp. No. 16, at 19, U.N. Doc. A/4354 (1959).

43 Article 26(1) of the *Universal Declaration of Rights*, it will be recalled, stated that "*Everyone* has the right to education" (emphasis supplied).

44 See Principle 20 of the *Plan of Action*.

45 Signed in Rome, Italy by the Council of Europe on 4 November 1950; entry into force 3 September 1953.

46 Entry into force 18 May 1954.

47 G. Van Bueren "Education: Whose Right is it Anyway?" in L. Heffernan (ed.) *Human Rights: A European Perspective* (1994) 339, 341.

48   A. Robertson   "The European Convention on Human Rights: Recent Developments"   (1951) 28 *British Yearbook of International Law*   359, 362.

49   *X v UK No 5962/72*, 2 DR 50 (1975).

50   *X v UK No 8844/80*, 23 DR 228 (1980).

51   *Belgian Linguistic Case (No. 1)*, Judgment of 9 February 1967, Series A, No. 5, (1979-80) 1 EHRR 241;   *Belgian Linguistic Case (No. 2)*, Judgment of 23 July 1968, Series A, No. 6; (1979-80) 1 EHRR 252.

52   *App. 10476/83, W and KL v Sweden*, 11 December 1985, (1986) 45 DR 143.

53   298 U.N.T.S. 11.

54   OJ Eng. Spec. Ed. 1963/4 p. 25.

55   See the relevant cases identified and discussed in M. Gould "Children's Education and the European Court of Justice" in D. Freestone (ed.) *Children and the Law* (1990) 172.

56   Case 293/83, *Gravier v City of Liège* [1985] ECR 593.

57   Case 42/87, *Commission v Belgium* [1989] 1 CMLR 457.

58   (1992) 31 I.L.M. 247.

59   June 27, 1981, O.A.U. Doc. CAB/LEG/67/3 Rev. 5, reprinted in (1982) 21 *International Legal Materials* 58.

60   July 11, 1990, O.A.U. Doc. CAB/LEG/24.9/49.

61   *Charter of the Organization of American States* signed at Bogotá, Colombia on 30 April 1948; entry into force 13 December 1951, No. 1609, (1952) 119 U.N.T.S. 3, as amended by the *Protocol of Amendment to the Charter of the Organization of American States* (*"Protocol of Buenos Aires"*) signed 27 February 1967; entry into force 27 February 1970, No. 1609, (1970) 721 U.N.T.S. 324.

62   O.A.S. Off. Rec., O.E.A./Ser., L/V/II, 23, Doc. 21, Rev. 2 (English 1975).

63   Article XXXI of the *American Declaration* contains the following rather remarkable provision: "It is the *duty* of every person to acquire at least an elementary education" (emphasis supplied).

64   770 U.N.T.S. 219 (entry into force 31 October 1963).

65   O.A.S. Off. Rec., O.E.A./Ser. K/XVI/1.1, Document 65, Rev. 1, Corr. 2 of 7 January 1970; (1970) 9 *International Legal Materials* 673.

66   Article 12(4) of the *American Convention* does refer, however, to the right of parents to control their children's religious and moral education.

67   (1989) 28 *International Legal Materials* 156.

68   *Restatement (Third) of Foreign Relations Law of the United States* 702 cmt. a (1987).

69   Article 38 of the *Vienna Convention on the Law of Treaties*.

70   (1975) *I.C.J. Rep.*   12 (the right of self-determination for non-self-governing territories has become a rule of customary law).

71   See C. de la Vega "The Right to Equal Education: Merely a Guiding Principle or Customary International Legal Right? (1994) 11 *Harvard Black Letter Law Journal* 37; C. Christopher "*Plyler v. Doe* and the

Right of Undocumented Alien Children to a Free Public Education" (1984) 2 *Boston University International Law Journal* 513; S. Knight "Proposition 187 and International Human Rights Law: Illegal Discrimination in the Right to Education" (1995) 19 *Hastings International and Comparative Law Review* 183.

72   H. Lauterpacht *International Law and Human Rights* (1950) 397.

73   K. Halvorsen "Notes on the Realization of the Human Right to Education" (1990) 12 *Human Rights Quarterly* 341, 350.

74   *Filartiga v Peña-Irala*, 630 F.2d 876, 883 (2d Cir. 1980); L. Sohn "The New International Law: Protection of the Rights of Individuals Rather than States" (1982) 32 *Am. U. Law Review* 1, 17. ("The Declaration, as an authoritative listing of human rights, has become a basic component of international customary law, binding on all states, not only on members of the United Nations.")

75   "International Instruments Relating to Human Rights" (1995) 16 *Human Rights Law Journal* 75, 88.

76   United Nations *Multilateral Treaties Deposited with the Secretary-General: Status as of 31 December 1994* (1994) 107.

77   (1996) 17 *Human Rights Law Journal* 72.

78   S. Knight, op. cit., 183, 190.

79   C. de la Vega, op. cit., 37, 48. See also Chapter 2 of this work.

80   S. Knight, op. cit., 197.

81   C. de la Vega, op. cit., 48, citing G. Kurian (ed.) *World Education Encyclopedia* (1988). See also Chapter 2 of this work.

5 The Classification and Aims of the Right to Education

[W]e declare our firm belief in the principles enunciated in the Universal Declaration of Human Rights that everyone has the right to education; that education shall be directed to the full development of the human personality and to the strengthening of respect for human rights and fundamental freedoms. It shall promote understanding, tolerance and friendship among the nations, racial or religious groups, and shall further the activities of the United Nations for the maintenance of peace.[1]

Classification of the Right to Education

Today it is common to distinguish three generations of human rights: the first generation of civil and political rights, the second generation of economic, social and cultural rights, and the third generation of group or peoples' rights.

Historically the first generation of human rights preceded the second and third generations. The rights enumerated in such eighteenth century instruments as the *Virginia Declaration of Rights* of 1776, the *American Declaration of Independence* of 1776 and the *Declaration of the Rights of Man* proclaimed by the French National Assembly in 1789 were essentially freedoms concerning areas of human conduct which were regarded as beyond the scope of State intervention. In the heyday of *laissez-faire*, individual autonomy and liberty were emphasised; the State was perceived as a servant of free enterprise and as a potential threat to its freedom and the liberty of the people. Governmental mandates were limited accordingly to defence, foreign relations and the administration of criminal and civil justice. Prominent amongst those civil liberties enshrined in these eighteenth century instruments were the freedom from arbitrary arrest, freedom of opinion and religious belief, and freedom of expression. These classical civil liberties are today catalogued in the *International Covenant on Civil and Political Rights* which also contains in Articles 21 and 22 respectively the right of peaceful assembly and the right to freedom of association.

71

Unlike first generation rights which seek to restrict governmental action and interference in human affairs, second generation rights require governments to take positive action by conferring benefits upon eligible individuals. Economic and social rights coincided with the nineteenth century emergence of socialism which perceived the State as a beneficial institution whose main purpose was to secure the economic and social well-being of the entire community through governmental intervention and regulation. The *laissez-faire* theory of the State was gradually superseded by the perception of the State as a "benevolent provider". The demand for rights in the twentieth century increasingly became a claim upon the State for basic welfare services and entitlements. The historical culmination of the evolution of second generation rights is represented by the *International Covenant on Economic, Social and Cultural Rights* which recognises such rights as the right to work (Article 6), the right to social security (Article 9), the right to adequate food, clothing and housing (Article 11), the right to physical and mental health (Article 12) and the right to education (Article 13). The implementation of such rights, by their very nature, requires entitlement criteria as well as resource distribution and political control mechanisms.[2]   The emergence of third generation group rights coincided with the consolidation of the voting strength of the bloc of non-aligned Member States of the United Nations in the General Assembly in the 1960s. Common Article 1 of the *International Covenant on Civil and Political Rights* and the *International Covenant on Economic, Social and Cultural Rights* concerning the right of all peoples to self-determination and the *African Charter on Human and Peoples' Rights* exemplify the recognition of binding third generation group rights.

The classification of a right into one of the three generations may be useful in ascertaining the legal claims of the holder of the right and the corresponding obligations of the State.[3]   The way in which the right to education is framed in various international and regional human rights instruments would tend to suggest that the right partakes of the qualities of both the first and second generations. As such, the right to education nicely illustrates the distinction between liberty rights (restraining interference by others including the State) and welfare rights (requiring the State to provide certain goods or services).

The right to education is primarily a second generation right as that right is recognised by Article 28(1) of the *Convention on the Rights of the Child*, Article 13(1) and (2) of the *International Covenant on Economic, Social and Cultural Rights*,   Article 13(1) and (3) of the *Additional Protocol to the American Convention on Human Rights in the Area of Economic, Social and Cultural Rights* and Article 4(a) of the *Convention against Discrimination in Education.* As a second generation right, the right to education is based on the socialist philosophy that human rights can only be completely guaranteed by positive State action. Consequently, the right to education obliges a State to develop and maintain a system of schools within its available resources.[4] Article XVIII of the *Universal Islamic Declaration of Human Rights*, for example, states that "[e]very person has the right to . . . education . . . consistent with the resources of the community". Similarly, Article XII of the *American Declaration of the Rights and Duties of Man* refers to "the resources that the state or the community is in a position to provide" in the context of the right to education and its implementation.[5]

The right to education as it has been formulated in international and regional instruments also can be considered a first generation right to the extent that they impose a duty on the State to respect the parental right to ensure education and teaching in conformity with their own religious and moral convictions. Protection of this parental right from undue State interference may be found in Article 18(4) of the *International Covenant on Civil and Political Rights*, Article 13(3) of the *International Covenant on Economic, Social and Cultural Rights*, Article 2 of *Protocol I* to the *European Convention for the Protection of Human Rights and Fundamental Freedoms*, Article 13(4) of the *Additional Protocol to the American Convention on Human Rights in the Area of Economic, Social and Cultural Rights*, and Article 12(4) of the *American Convention on Human Rights*.

The Aims of Education

The debate concerning the aims and objectives of education long preceded the adoption of the modern human rights instruments. While Jean-Jacques Rousseau proclaimed in *Emile* the emancipation of the child as the major aim of education, other philosophers and statesmen preferred a duty perspective. Horace Mann once said that "[t]he will of God . . . places the right of every child that is born into the world to such a degree of education as will enable him, and, as far as possible, will predispose him, to perform all domestic, social, civil, and moral duties".[6] Article 108 of the *Treaty of Paris, Poland-Danzig* signed on 9 November 1920[7] stated that "[i]nstruction on the duties of citizenship shall form part of the school curriculum".

It is now common for provisions of international and regional human rights instruments which recognise the right to education also to articulate the basic aims or goals sought to be realised by the exercise of the right. These provisions furnish common goals to be pursued by the educational systems of all countries. These goals are often based on religious or moral values and political imperatives.[8]   The most detailed and comprehensive provision on the aims of education in international law can now be found in Article 29(1) of the *Convention on the Rights of the Child.* The exercise of the right to education is not intended merely to acquire information and knowledge but to achieve a variety of objectives which will enure to the benefit not only of individuals but to the communities within which they live.   As one commentator has aptly remarked, "[t]he right to education, while primarily an individual right, can be understood within its social function of developing people as full citizens of their society".[9]   It is not, therefore, a question of merely communicating knowledge through instruction but also of assisting individuals to make maximum use of their capabilities.[10]

Although international law prescribes in detail the many and varied aims of education, it fails to provide any guidance as to the relative importance of each aim. It must be assumed, therefore, that all educational aims are of equal value and that it is not open to a State Party to selectively implement only some of the aims which are included in conventions which it has ratified.[11]   Some commentators have regarded the prescription of educational goals as rather presumptuous and smacking of benevolent paternalism.[12]   In their view, how a child's potential is to be developed is essentially a value-laden exercise.   For example, Article 12(3) of the *Central American Convention on the Unification of the Fundamental Norms of Education* of 1962 proclaims as one of the aims of education in Central America the preparation of citizens "for the effective exercise of democracy as a political system and a way of life".   Similarly, Article 13(2) of the *Additional Protocol to the American Convention on Human Rights in the Area of Economic, Social and Cultural Rights* of 1988 states in part that "education ought to enable everyone to participate effectively in a democratic and pluralistic society".

Although the aims of education tend to vary according to the historical, political, cultural, religious or national context,[13]   the international and regional[14] instruments have frequently and consistently prescribed four basic aims:

(a)   the full development of the individual's personality, talents and abilities[15]

binding instruments:

Universal Declaration of Human Rights, Article 26(2)

Convention against Discrimination in Education, Article 5(1)(a)

International Covenant on Economic, Social and Cultural Rights, Article 13(1)

Central American Convention on the Unification of the Fundamental Norms of Education, Articles 2 and 12(2)(4)

Additional Protocol to the American Convention on Human Rights in the Area of Economic, Social and Cultural Rights, Article 13(2)

Convention on the Rights of the Child, Article 29(1)(a)

African Charter on the Rights and Welfare of the Child, Article 11(2)(a)

non-binding instruments:

Declaration of the Rights of the Child, Principle 7

United Nations *Declaration on the Promotion Among Youth of the Ideals of Peace, Mutual Respect and Understanding Between Peoples* of 1965, Principle VI

U.N.E.S.C.O. *Recommendation Concerning the Status of Teachers 1966,* Principle 1

United Nations Food and Agriculture Organization *Declaration of Principles and Programme of Action of the World Conference on Agrarian Reform and Rural Development* of 1979, Section VII

European Parliament "Freedom of Education in the European Community" Resolution of 14 March 1984, Principle 5

Preamble of the *World Declaration on Education for All* adopted by the World Conference on Education for All in 1990

Cairo Declaration on Human Rights in Islam of 1990, Article 9(b)

(b)   the strengthening of respect for human rights and fundamental freedoms

binding instruments:

Charter of the United Nations, Article 55(c)

Universal Declaration of Human Rights, Article 26(2)

Convention against Discrimination in Education, Article 5(1)(a)

International Convention on the Elimination of All Forms of Racial Discrimination of 1965, Article 7   ("States Parties undertake to adopt immediate and effective measures, particularly in the fields of teaching, education, culture and information, with a view to combating prejudices which lead to racial discrimination . . .")

International Covenant on Economic, Social and Cultural Rights, Article 13(1)

Additional Protocol to the American Convention on Human Rights and Fundamental Freedoms in the Area of Economic, Social and Cultural Rights, Article 13(2)

Convention on the Rights of the Child, Article 29(1)(b)   (also includes a reference to the development of respect for the principles enshrined in the Charter of the United Nations)

African Charter on the Rights and Welfare of the Child,   Article 11(2)(b)

non-binding instruments:

Declaration on the Promotion Among Youth of the Ideals of Peace, Mutual Respect and Understanding Between Peoples, Principles III and VI

U.N.E.S.C.O. *Recommendation Concerning the Status of Teachers,* Principle 1

U.N.E.S.C.O. *Recommendation Concerning Education for International Understanding, Co-operation and Peace and Education Relating to Human Rights and Fundamental Freedoms 1974,* Principles 7, 11 and 18(c)

European Parliament "Freedom of Education in the European Community" Resolution of 14 March 1984, Principle 5

Cairo Declaration on Human Rights in Islam, Article 9(b)

(c) **the enabling of all persons to participate effectively and responsibly in a free society**[16]

binding instruments:

Central American Convention on the Unification of the Fundamental Norms of Education, Article 12(1)

International Covenant on Economic, Social and Cultural Rights, Article 13(1)

Convention on the Rights of the Child, Article 29(1)(d)

Additional Protocol to the American Convention on Human Rights in the Area of Economic, Social and Cultural Rights, Article 13(2)

African Charter on the Rights and Welfare of the Child, Article 11(2)(d)

non-binding instruments:

American Declaration of the Rights and Duties of Man, Article XII

Declaration of the Rights of the Child, Principle 7

(d) **the promotion of understanding, tolerance and friendship among all nations, racial, ethnic or religious groups and the furtherance of the activities of the United Nations for the maintenance of peace**[17]

binding instruments:

Universal Declaration of Human Rights, Article 26(2)

Convention against Discrimination in Education, Article 5(1)(a)

International Convention on the Elimination of All Forms of Racial Discrimination, Article 7

International Covenant on Economic, Social and Cultural Rights, Article 13(1)

Additional Protocol to the American Convention on Human Rights in the Area of Economic, Social and Cultural Rights, Article 13(2)

Convention on the Rights of the Child, Article 29(1)(d)   (adds references to "equality of sexes" and friendship among "all peoples" and "persons of indigenous origin")

non-binding instruments:

American Declaration of the Rights and Duties of Man, Article XII

Declaration of the Rights of the Child, Principle 10

Declaration on the Promotion Among Youth of the Ideals of Peace, Mutual Respect and Understanding Between Peoples, penultimate preambular paragraph and Principle VI

Recommendation Concerning Education for International Understanding, Co-operation and Peace and Education Relating to Human Rights and Fundamental Freedoms 1974, Principles 4(b), 6, 7, 17 and 18(b)

United Nations *Declaration on the Elimination of All Forms of Intolerance and of Discrimination Based on Religion or Belief* of 1981, Article 5(3)

Preamble of the *World Declaration on Education for All*

Apart from these four basic aims of education, other aims are mentioned, albeit less frequently, by the various instruments. These include:

- **the inter-generational transmission of cultural heritage:** *Declaration of the Rights of the Child,* Principle 7; *Central American Convention on the Unification of the Fundamental Norms of Education,* Article 12(7); *Recommendation Concerning Education for International Understanding, Co-operation and Peace and Education Relating to Human Rights and Fundamental Freedoms 1974,* Principles 4(b) and 18(f); Preamble of the *World Declaration on Education for All*; *African Charter on the Rights and Welfare of the Child,* Article 11(2)(c);

- **the development of national consciousness:** *Central American Convention on the Unification of the Fundamental Norms of Education,* Article 4; *Convention on the Rights of the Child,* Article 29(1)(c);

- **contribution to the economic and social development of the community:** *American Declaration of the Rights and Duties of Man,* Article XII; *Central American Convention on the Unification of the Fundamental Norms of Education,* Articles 2, 8 and 12(1); *Recommendation Concerning Education for International Understanding, Co-operation and Peace and Education Relating to Human Rights and Fundamental Freedoms 1974,* Principle 18(d); *Declaration of Principles and Programme of Action of the World Conference on Agrarian Reform and Rural Development,* Section VII; Preamble of the *World Declaration on Education for All*;

- **the development of a sense of moral duty and social responsibility:** *Declaration of Geneva* of 1924, Principle V; *Declaration of the Rights of the Child,* Principles 7 and 10; *Declaration on the Promotion Among Youth of the Ideals of Peace, Mutual Respect and Understanding Between Peoples,* Principle VI; *Recommendation Concerning Education for International Understanding, Co-operation and Peace and Education Relating to Human Rights and Fundamental Freedoms 1974,* Principles 4(e), 5 and 18(d); *Declaration on* *the Elimination of All Forms of Intolerance and of Discrimination Based on Religion or Belief,* Article 5(3); *Cairo Declaration on Human Rights in Islam,* Articles 7(b) and 9(b); *African Charter on Human and Peoples' Rights* of 1981, Article 17(3) ("The promotion and protection of morals and traditional values recognized by the community shall be the duty of the State."); *African Charter on the Rights and Welfare of the Child,* Article 11(2)(c);

- **the development of the individual's critical ability and judgment:** *Declaration of the Rights of the Child,* Principle 7; *Central American Convention on the Unification of the Fundamental Norms of Education,* Article 12(4); *Recommendation Concerning Education for International Understanding, Co-operation and Peace and Education Relating to Human Rights and Fundamental Freedoms 1974,* Principle 5;

- **the development of respect for the natural environment:** *Recommendation Concerning Education for International Understanding, Co-operation and Peace and Education Relating to Human Rights and Fundamental Freedoms 1974,* Principle 18(e); *Convention on the Rights of the Child,* Article 29(1)(e);[18] Preamble of the *World Declaration on Education for All; African Charter on the Rights and Welfare of the Child,* Article 11(2)(g);

- **the development of the sense of dignity of the human personality:** *International Covenant on Economic, Social and Cultural Rights,* Article 13(1);

- **the raising of the educand's standard of living:** *American Declaration of the Rights and Duties of Man,* Article XII;

- **the strengthening of the educand's faith in God:** *Cairo Declaration on Human Rights in Islam,* Article 9(b);

- **the preservation of national independence:** *African Charter on the Rights and Welfare of the Child,* Article 11(2)(e);

- **the ability to communicate with others:** *Recommendation Concerning Education for International Understanding, Co-operation and Peace and Education Relating to Human Rights and Fundamental Freedoms 1974,* Principle 4(d);

- **the attainment of social justice, freedom and peace:** *Charter of the Organization of American States* of 1948, Article 3(m); *Recommendation Concerning Education for International Understanding, Co-operation and Peace and Education Relating to Human Rights and Fundamental Freedoms 1974,* Principles 6, 7 and 18(b); *Additional Protocol to the American Convention on Human Rights in the Area of Economic, Social and Cultural Rights,* Article 13(2);

- **the promotion of the child's understanding of primary health care:** *African Charter on the Rights and Welfare of the Child,* Article 11(2)(h).

Occasionally the aims of education are formulated rather widely and perhaps even vaguely. Article 100(g) of the *Charter of the Organization of American States*, for example, entrusts the Inter-American Council for Education, Science, and Culture with promoting "the education of the American peoples with a view to harmonious international relations and a better understanding of the historical and cultural origins of the Americas, in order to stress and preserve their common values and destiny". The *Charter of the Rights of the Arab Child* of the League of Arab States contains a panoply of educational aims ranging from social change and positive contributions to society to the promotion of self-discipline and a strong work ethic and the attainment of a good standard of living.

Apart from Article 11(2) of the *African Charter on the Rights and Welfare of the Child* adopted by the Organization of African Unity in July, 1990, Article 29(1)(c) of the *Convention on the Rights of the Child* of 1989 is the most recent attempt to formulate innovative educational aims particularly from the child's perspective.[19] The latter provision, based largely on proposals submitted by Algeria and the Four Directions Council,[20] provides:

States Parties agree that the education of the child shall be directed to . . . the development of respect for the child's parents, his or her own cultural identity, language and values, for the national values of the country in which the child is living, the country from which he or she may originate, and for civilizations different from his or her own.

Regrettably, Article 29(1) fails to make explicit reference to the social, spiritual and moral development of the child as an educational aim worthy of fulfilment.[21] It is also possible that some educational aims may conflict with each other, thereby causing problems in realising them. Multicultural pluralistic societies are finding it increasingly difficult to strike a balance between cultural and minority values and national and majoritarian values.[22] Indeed, the tension between these values was noted during the drafting of the *Convention on the Rights of the Child.* [23]

Educational aims have also been enshrined in national constitutions and ordinary legislation. Article 117 of the Constitution of Nicaragua of 1986, for example, states that education should promote, *inter alia*, national values and culture, and scientific research with a view to securing scientific and technological advances. A most comprehensive formulation of educational aims in national legislation is to be found in the Constitution of the Philippines of 1987, Article XV, Section 2 of which provides:

> (1) Education . . . shall be committed to the total spiritual, intellectual, social, cultural, scientific and physical development of man, thus making him a God-fearing, peace-loving and work-oriented citizen of the nation;
>
> (2) All schools . . . shall inculcate patriotism and nationalism . . . and shall teach the rights and duties of citizenship, and the cultures of the Muslims, Christians, and tribal peoples . . . to develop, promote and enhance unity in diversity;
>
> (7) The education . . . shall develop consciousness and appreciation of one's ethnic identity and shall provide a better understanding of each other's cultural heritage for the attainment of national unity and harmony;

The Tunisian basic education curriculum has been reviewed recently to include references in all textbooks to the values of tolerance, love for peace, conflict resolution, responsibility and solidarity.[24] This review was a result of Tunisia's ratification of the *Convention of the Rights of the Child.*

Notes

1   N. Mandela "No Easy Walk to Freedom" (1953 Address) in W. Laqueur and B. Rubin (eds) *The Human Rights Reader* (1989) 317, 319.

2   W. Foster and G. Pinheiro "Constitutional Protection of the Right to an Education" (1987-88) 11 *Dalhousie Law Journal* 755, 766.

3   M. Nowak "The Right to Education" in A. Eide (ed.) *Economic, Social and Cultural Rights* (1995) 189, 196.

4   Ibid.

5   Consider also the combined effect of the following provisions: Articles 4 and 28 of the *Convention on the Rights of the Child*; Articles 2(1) and 13 of the *International Covenant on Economic, Social and Cultural Rights*; Articles 1 and 13 of the *Additional Protocol to the American Convention on Human Rights in the Area of Economic, Social and Cultural Rights*.

6   L. Cremin (ed.) *The Republic and the School: Horace Mann on the Education of Free Men* (1957) 63.

7   6 L.N.T.S. 190.

8   Nowak, op. cit., 193.

9   H. Cullen "Education Rights or Minority Rights?" (1993) 7 *International Journal of Law and the Family* 143, 144.

10   F. Volio "The Child's Right to Education: A Survey" in G. Mialaret (ed.) *The Child's Right to Education* (1979) 19, 24.

11   G. Van Bueren *The International Law on the Rights of the Child* (1995) 253.

12   See, for example, J. N. Turner "The Rights of the Child Under the U. N. Convention" (1992) 65 *Law Institute Journal* 38, 45; I. Snook *Education and Rights* (1979) 31.

13   Nowak, op. cit., 189.

14   Compared with human rights instruments concluded under the auspices of the United Nations and the Organization of American States, other regional instruments are vague in defining the aims of the right to education.

15   This includes all of the dimensions of the human experience: physical, intellectual, psychological and social. The aim is essentially that individuals will develop themselves to their maximum potential according to their abilities and talents.

16   Article 4(g) of the U.N.E.S.C.O. *Recommendation Concerning Education for International Understanding, Co-operation and Peace and Education Relating to Human Rights and Fundamental Freedoms 1974* defines the concept of a responsible life as "readiness on the part of the individual to participate in solving the problems of his community, his country and the world at large".

17   This particular aim of education presupposes that children should be exposed to a notion of tolerance that complements fixed beliefs that they may acquire from their parents or others close to them. Children should

become aware of the diversity of beliefs people hold and appreciate what it is to be part of a society where these differences exist: see P. Hobson and R. Cresswell "Parental Rights, Education and Liberal Tolerance" (1993) 14 *Discourse* 44, 50.

18　The *Convention on the Rights of the Child* incorporates for the first time in treaty form this educational aim.

19　One commentator considers that every school should treat Article 29(1) of the *Convention on the Rights of the Child* as its mission statement: J. N. Turner "Panic Over Children's Rights" (1996) 1 *Newcastle Law Review* 72, 90.

20　Commission on Human Rights *Report of the Working Group on a Draft Convention on the Rights of the Child* E/CN.4/1985/64 (3 April 1985) Annex II p. 3; Commission on Human Rights *Report of the Working Group on a Draft Convention on the Rights of the Child* E/CN.4/1988/28 (6 April 1988) p. 48, para. 235.

21　Such a proposal had been submitted in 1983 by the Baha'i International Community, a non- governmental organisation in consultative status with the United Nations Economic and Social Council: Commission on Human Rights *Report of the Working Group on a Draft Convention on the Rights of the Child* E/CN.4/1983/62 (25 March 1983) Annex II (E/CN.4/1983/WG.1/WP.2).

22　D. McGoldrick "The United Nations Convention on the Rights of the Child" (1991) 5 *International Journal of Law and the Family* 132, 148; S. Poulter *English Law and Ethnic Minority Customs* (1986) *passim.*

23　Commission on Human Rights *Report of the Working Group on a Draft Convention on the Rights of the Child* E/CN.4/1987/25 (9 March 1987) p. 10, para. 41; Commission on Human Rights *Report of the Working Group on a Draft Convention on the Rights of the Child* E/CN.4/1989/48 (2 March 1989) p. 85, paragraphs 478 and 479.

24　http://www.unicef.org/crc/success/mena.html.

6   Educational Rights of Minority Groups

Introduction

Minority rights have recently become a major issue in international human rights law. Apart from such long-standing conflicts involving the Sikhs in India, the Kurds in Turkey, the Tamils in Sri Lanka and the Basques in Spain, struggles over minority rights are also likely to occur in the newly emerging nations in Eastern Europe and the former Soviet Union where nationalistic sentiments suppressed during the Communist era have re-emerged.

Despite the many references to minorities contained in international legal instruments, there is no generally accepted definition of the term 'minority'. The Permanent Court of International Justice considered the concept of a minority in an advisory opinion of 31 July 1930 in the context of the emigration of the Greco-Bulgarian communities. Considering the Convention of 27 November 1919 between Bulgaria and Greece, the Court stated:

> The criterion to be applied to determine what is a community within the meaning of the articles of the Convention . . . is the existence of a group of persons living in a given country or locality, having a race, religion, language and traditions of their own, and united by the identity of such race, religion, language and traditions in a sentiment of solidarity, with a view to preserving their traditions, maintaining their form of worship, securing the instruction and upbringing of their children in accordance with the spirit and traditions of their race and mutually assisting one another.[1]

A contemporary definition of the term 'minority' has been proposed by Professor Francesco Capotorti, a Special Rapporteur of the United Nations Sub-Commission on Prevention of Discrimination and Protection of Minorities and author of the *Study on the Rights of Persons Belonging to Ethnic, Religious and Linguistic Minorities.*[2]   Professor Capotorti defined a minority as:

> . . . a group numerically inferior to the rest of the population of a State, in a
> non-dominant position, whose members - being nationals of the state -
> possess ethnic, religious or linguistic characteristics differing from those of
> the rest of the population and show, if only implicitly, a sense of solidarity,
> directed towards preserving their culture, traditions, religion or language.[3]

As one commentator has observed, international human rights law
is concerned with cohesive groups, the characteristics of which endure,
and who regard themselves - or are regarded by others - as different to the
mainstream of society.[4]   The law has generally concerned itself with
ethnic, religious, linguistic, national[5] and racial groups under the term
'minority'.   Ethnicity has become somewhat of a catch-all concept.   An
ethnic group is one which sees itself and/or is seen by others as being
distinctive within the territorial State by having amongst its members
certain common attributes such as history, culture, language, and religion.
As Richardson J. observed in the New Zealand case of *King-Ansell v
Police* :

> A group is identifiable in terms of its ethnic origins if it is a segment of the
> population distinguished from others by a sufficient combination of shared
> customs, beliefs, traditions and characteristics derived from a common . . .
> past, even if not drawn from what in biological terms is a common racial
> stock.   It is that combination which gives them a historically determined
> social identity in their own eyes and in the eyes of those outside the group.[6]

The vitality of customs and cultural traditions of minority groups
depends in no small measure upon the effectiveness of their transmission
from one generation to the next through the medium of education.[7]
Educationalists have emphasised the importance for the minority child of
the establishment and maintenance of a strong and positive cultural
identity.[8]   Indeed, a former United Nations Secretary-General has
observed that "[t]he person who can neither read nor write and who has
not received the most elementary instruction is impervious to any true
culture".[9]   Minority educational rights are also based on two *desiderata*
which are usually complementary but which may occasionally conflict
with each other.   *Equality of opportunity* requires the provision of
educational services which will enable minority group members to
maximise their individual talents and take their place within mainstream
society. *Pluralism* seeks to preserve minority identity and to celebrate the
diversity of cultures.[10]   Pluralism also enjoins that public institutions
reflect the fact that most societies contain many beliefs and cultures.[11]

A Brief History

International law has enjoyed a long tradition of protecting minority groups in its pursuit of both humanitarian and pragmatic motives. Religious minority groups were the first to be protected by treaty; national minority groups were protected subsequently by the League of Nations.[12] Treaties concerning the protection of particular minorities were concluded as an adjunct to peace treaties signed by the Allied and Associated Powers and the vanquished States in the aftermath of World War I. The League of Nations minorities system was the first to protect minorities as such, albeit in a limited manner. The post-World War I minorities treaties were prompted by the redrawing of European borders under the *Treaty of Versailles* which often placed minority groups within the borders of states of differing religious and ethnic composition.[13] These minorities treaties attempted to provide detailed guarantees of minority linguistic, cultural, religious and educational rights and the Permanent Court of International Justice was asked on several occasions to interpret these guarantees.[14]

The importance to minorities of the transmission of their culture and beliefs through education was fully recognised by the League of Nations. The *Treaty Between The Principal Allied and Associated Powers and Poland* signed on 28 June 1919,[15] the first of the series, contains provisions concerning minority education which recur in most of the other League minorities treaties. Articles 8 and 9 state:

Article 8

Polish nationals who belong to racial, religious or linguistic minorities shall enjoy the same treatment and security in law and in fact as the other Polish nationals. In particular they shall have an equal right to establish, manage and control at their own expense charitable, religious and social institutions, schools and other educational establishments, with the right to use their own language and to exercise their religion freely therein.

Article 9

Poland will provide in the public educational system in towns and districts in which a considerable proportion of Polish nationals of other than Polish speech are resident adequate facilities for ensuring that in the primary schools the instruction shall be given to the children of such Polish nationals through the medium of their own language. This provision shall not prevent the Polish government from making the teaching of the Polish language obligatory in the said schools.

In towns and districts where there is a considerable proportion of Polish nationals belonging to racial, religious or linguistic minorities, these minorities shall be assured an equitable share in the enjoyment and application of the sums which may be provided out of public funds under the State, municipal or other budget, for educational, religious or charitable purposes . . .

Article 9 essentially provided for public primary education in the minority language as the medium of instruction for all subjects except study of the Polish language. The Polish Government could insist that the official Polish language be taught in minority schools but could not require that the other subjects be taught only in that language.[16] The *Treaty of Paris, Poland-Danzig* signed on 9 November 1920[17] devoted an entire Section IV to "Education and Schools". Article 105 thereof prescribed that private schools would be subject to the laws of the State and would require State approval which would only be granted if the private school was not inferior to the state school in its educational programme and organisation. The inclusion of an educational component in the League's minorities treaties established a historical precedent which would ultimately inform United Nations standard-setting in this area.

International Recognition of the Educational Rights of Minorities

The immediate aftermath of World War II was marked by governmental wariness of minority rights. The conventional wisdom of that period regarded rights for particular groups as outdated in the new world order of universal individual human rights.[18] This development was reflected at the national level through the adoption of a philosophy of assimilation in the sphere of formal education.

The *Universal Declaration of Human Rights* of 1948 does not recognise or protect the rights of minorities as such. The text of the *Declaration* is couched largely in individualistic language and nowhere mentions the term 'minority'. A number of proposals concerning minority rights were considered, however, during the drafting of the *Declaration*.[19] The most detailed proposed minority provision stated:

In all countries inhabited by a substantial number of persons of a race, language or religion other than those of the majority of the population, persons belonging to such ethnic, religious or linguistic minorities shall have the right to establish and maintain, out of an equitable proportion of public funds for the purpose, their schools and cultural institutions, and to use their language before the courts and other authorities and organs of the State, and in the press and public assembly.[20]

Disputes concerning this and other minority provision proposals - particularly on the issues of non-discrimination and minority-language teaching - were so protracted that no formula could be agreed upon.[21] The only provisions of the *Declaration* of possible use to individual members of minority groups are the general non-discrimination provision of Article 2 and the reference in Article 26(2) to the role of education in promoting "understanding, tolerance and friendship among all nations, racial or religious groups". In the result, minorities as collective entities have no rights under the *Declaration* while individual minority group members only enjoy those rights which are extended to all individuals.

The interest of the United Nations in minority rights was revived in 1966 when the General Assembly adopted the *International Covenant on Civil and Political Rights.* Article 27 thereof states that "[i]n those States in which ethnic, religious or linguistic minorities exist, persons belonging to such minorities shall not be denied the right, in community with the other members of their group, to enjoy their own culture, to profess and practise their own religion, or to use their own language". The significance of Article 27 for minority education is unclear. Although the case-law of the Human Rights Committee set up under Article 28 of the *Covenant* has dealt with various aspects of Article 27, its deliberations have not focussed specifically on the educational sector. However, the Committee has directed questions on minority education from time to time to reporting governments. This would imply that the Committee is of the view that education is covered by the general wording of Article 27.[22] This view would be supported on the basis of the previously mentioned link between education and cultural survival and development. Despite the negative wording - "shall not be denied" - Professor Capotorti maintains that mere abstention by a State Party is not an adequate fulfilment of the Article 27 obligation; positive action, including special minority education measures, may be required.[23]

U.N.E.S.C.O. has made a major contribution in the field of minority education rights. Its *Convention against Discrimination in Education* of 1960 advocates the inclusion of such rights as an essential component of the right to education.[24] The *Convention* contains a comprehensive set of normative standards applicable to minority education which have been echoed in subsequent international and regional instruments. The relevant provisions of the *Convention* are as follows:

Article 2

When permitted in a State, the following situations shall not be deemed to constitute discrimination . . .

(b)   The establishment or maintenance, for religious or linguistic reasons, of separate educational systems or institutions offering an education which is in keeping with the wishes of the pupil's parents or legal guardians, if participation in such systems or attendance at such institutions is optional and if the education provided conforms to such standards as may be laid down or approved by the competent authorities, in particular for education of the same level;

(c)   The establishment or maintenance of private educational institutions, if the object of the institutions is not to secure the exclusion of any group but to provide educational facilities in addition to those provided by the public authorities, if the institutions are conducted in accordance with that object, and if the education provided conforms with such standards as may be laid down or approved by the competent authorities, in particular for education of the same level.

Article 5

1. The States Parties to this Convention agree that:

(c) It is essential to recognize the right of members of national minorities to carry on their own educational activities, including the maintenance of schools and, depending on the educational policy of each State, the use or the teaching of their own language, provided however:

(i)   That this right is not exercised in a manner which prevents the members of these minorities from understanding the culture and language of the community as a whole and from participating in its activities, or which prejudices national sovereignty;

(ii) That the standard of education is not lower than the general standard laid down or approved by the competent authorities; and

(iii) That attendance at such schools is optional.

Apart from breaking new ground, Article 5(1)(c) is also notable in its salutary requirement that minority members learn the 'mainstream' language and culture, and in acknowledging the inter-relationship between language, education and culture. Article 5(1)(c) does contain a number of shortcomings, however. The provision is unduly restrictive in scope in terms of contemporary developments as it only refers to "national minorities" - racial, ethnic religious or linguistic minorities are not referred to as such. Apparently, the States Parties did not want to extend the right to establish minority schools to immigrants.[25] There is no provision for State financing or other positive support of minority schools which represents somewhat of a retreat from the position under the League of Nations minorities treaties. The complete financing by the national minority of its own educational system may undermine the spirit of equality which otherwise pervades the *Convention* and constitute a contravention of a wide interpretation of Article 3(d) thereof which obliges States Parties "[n]ot to allow, in any form of assistance granted by the public authorities to educational institutions, any restrictions or preference based solely on the ground that pupils belong to a particular group". Moreover, Article 5(2) of U.N.E.S.C.O.'s *Declaration on Race and Racial Prejudice* of 27 November 1978 enjoins States to make "the resources of the educational system available to all groups of the population without racial restriction".[26] The inclusion within Article 5(1)(c) of the clause "depending on the educational policy of each State" to qualify the use or the teaching of the minority language in the national minority schools also dilutes the strength of the provision. Finally, the reference in Article 5(1)(c)(i) to "prejudices national sovereignty" is perhaps a product of outdated assumptions which, as we shall see shortly, have been reconsidered by, for example, the International Labour Organization.

Segregation in schools is one of the most graphic forms of discrimination against minorities in the educational sphere. Segregation involves refusal of access to majority schools. Two of the more outstanding recent examples include the education of non-whites in South Africa and the United States of America. As minority segregated schools tend to be inferior in standard (due to under-funding) and attendance at such schools is compulsory, segregated schooling essentially entails a denial of the opportunity to receive the same content and quality of education as the majority. Article 3 of the *Convention against Discrimination in Education* seeks, *inter alia*, to proscribe segregated schooling in various ways. Article 3 reads in part:

> In order to eliminate and prevent discrimination within the meaning of this Convention, the States Parties thereto undertake:

(a)   To abrogate any statutory provisions and any administrative instructions and to discontinue any administrative practices which involve discrimination in education;

(b)   To ensure, by legislation where necessary, that there is no discrimination in the admission of pupils to educational institutions;

(c)   Not to allow any differences of treatment by the public authorities between nationals, except on the basis of merit or need, in the matter of school fees and the grant of scholarships or other forms of assistance to pupils . . .

(d)   Not to allow, in any form of assistance granted by the public authorities to educational institutions, any restrictions or preference based solely on the ground that pupils belong to a particular group . . .

The freedom to establish private schools has not been recognised by conventions protecting civil and political rights but only as a State limitation clause concerning the right to education.[27] For example, Article 13(4) of the *International Covenant on Economic, Social and Cultural Rights* implies a duty of State non-interference:

No part of this article shall be construed so as to interfere with the liberty of individuals and bodies to establish and direct educational institutions, subject always to the observance of the principles set forth in paragraph 1 of this article and to the requirement that the education given in such institutions shall conform to such minimum standards as may be laid down by the State.

The scope of Article 13(4) is considerably wider than that of Article 5(1)(c) of the *Convention against Discrimination in Education* as the former provision is not confined to national minorities or, indeed, to any minorities. The freedom to establish and direct educational institutions belongs not only to minority groups but to private individuals and corporate legal entities. Article 13(4) presumably applies to all levels and types of education but is subject to two limitations. First, the education offered must adhere to the aims of education listed in Article 13(1). Secondly, it must conform to minimum educational standards laid down by the State, such as those concerning admission, the content of the curriculum, the qualifications of the teaching staff and the recognition of certificates. Note should also be taken of Article 13(3) of the *International Covenant* which, like Article 5(1)(b) of the *Convention*, obliges States Parties to have respect for the liberty of parents to choose for their children non-public schools which conform to State minimum educational standards.

Various provisions of the *Convention on the Rights of the Child* concern minority education issues. Article 29(1)(c) records the agreement of the States Parties that the education of the child shall be directed to "the development of respect for the child's parents, his or her own cultural identity, language and values, for the national values of the country in which the child is living, the country from which he or she may originate, and for civilizations different from his or her own". Article 29(2) is virtually identical to Article 13(4) of the *International Covenant on Economic, Social and Cultural Rights.* Article 29(2) reads:

> No part of this article or Article 28 shall be construed so as to interfere with the liberty of individuals and bodies to establish and direct educational institutions, subject always to the observance of the principles set forth in paragraph 1 of this article [concerning the aims of education] and to the requirements that the education given in such institutions shall conform to such minimum standards as may be laid down by the State.[28]

Article 30 of the *Convention on the Rights of the Child* builds on and extends Article 27 of the *International Covenant on Civil and Political Rights* by including indigenous children within its ambit. Article 30 states:

> In those States in which ethnic, religious or linguistic minorities or persons of indigenous origin exist, a child belonging to such minority or who is indigenous shall not be denied the right, in community with other members of his or her group, to enjoy his or her own culture, to profess and practise his or her own religion, or to use his or her own language.

Article 30 is based on a proposal submitted by the Four Directions Council - a non-governmental organisation striving to enhance the standards of protection for indigenous children.[29] Unfortunately, no provision of the *Convention on the Rights of the Child* explicitly recognises the right of minority groups to use their own language for the purposes of general teaching. The Four Directions Council had unsuccessfully sought the inclusion in what is now Article 30 of a provision recognising the right of indigenous children "[t]o be educated, at least at the primary level . . . in the language of his parents as well as an official language of the State".[30] At the 1987 session of the Working Group considering a draft convention on the rights of the child, the observer for Finland had strongly argued for the inclusion in the convention of the child's right to be educated in his or her own language.[31]　Article 30 fails, therefore, to recognise and develop the link between education, language and culture.

The most recent attempt by the United Nations to tackle the often thorny and controversial issues relating to minority rights is the adoption by the General Assembly of the *Declaration on the Rights of Persons Belonging to National or Ethnic, Religious and Linguistic Minorities* on 18 December 1992.[32]　The *Minorities Declaration* seeks to elaborate on the standards contained in Article 27 of the *International Covenant on Civil and Political Rights.* Sub-Articles (3) and (4) of Article 4 of the *Declaration* are most relevant to minority educational issues:

> Article 4(3)
>
> States should take appropriate measures so that, wherever possible, persons belonging to minorities have adequate opportunities to learn their mother tongue or to have instruction in their mother tongue.
>
> Article 4(4)
>
> States should, where appropriate, take measures in the field of education, in order to encourage knowledge of the history, traditions, language and culture of the minorities existing within their territory. Persons belonging to minorities should have adequate opportunities to gain knowledge of the society as a whole.

Article 4(3) is deficient in offering to minority persons instruction in their mother tongue and study of their mother tongue as alternatives which are qualified by the rather open-ended phrase "wherever possible". Article 4(4) represents a call to governments to revise the school curricula in order to enhance inter-cultural understanding.　Although the *Minorities Declaration* does not impose any legally binding obligations on United Nations member States, Article 4 does go significantly beyond the provisions on minority education contained in the *Convention on the Rights of the Child.* As one commentator has observed, the *Declaration* goes some way to remedying the early post-war neglect of minorities issues within the United Nations, and expresses global minimum standards for the protection and promotion of minority rights which will affect the content and design of United Nations minorities programmes for the foreseeable future.[33]　The World Conference on Human Rights held in Vienna in June, 1993 called on the United Nations Commission on Human Rights to examine ways to effectively protect and promote the rights of persons belonging to minorites as set out in the *Minorities Declaration*, and urged States and the international community to protect and promote such rights.[34]

The Recognition and Protection of Minority Educational Rights on a Regional Basis

Regional human rights instruments have also addressed minority educational issues, particularly the freedom to establish and direct non-State educational institutions. In Latin America, Article 13(5) of the *Additional Protocol to the American Convention on Human Rights in the Area of Economic, Social and Cultural Rights* of 1988 recognises "the freedom of individuals and entities to establish and direct educational institutions in accordance with the domestic legislation of the States Parties". Unlike the equivalent provisions of the international human rights instruments canvassed in the previous section, Article 13(5) does not make explicit reference to the requirement that the education given in such institutions conform to such minimum standards as may be prescribed by the State (although this would appear to be implicitly recognised by the clause "in accordance with the domestic legislation of the States Parties". As far as Africa is concerned, the *African Charter on Human and Peoples' Rights* of 1981 does not explicitly address minority educational issues. Article 17(1) simply states that "[e]very individual shall have the right to education". The only provision of the *Charter* which could be relevant in this context is the guarantee contained in Article 22 concerning the right of all peoples to their cultural development. This shortcoming is remedied by Article 11(7) of the *African Charter on the Rights and Welfare of the Child* of 1990 which recognises "the liberty of individuals and bodies to establish and direct educational institutions subject to the observance of the principles [concerning the aims of education set out in Article 11(2)] and the requirements [sic] that the education given in such institutions shall conform to such minimum standards as may be laid down by the State".

The *European Convention for the Protection of Human Rights and Fundamental Freedoms* of 1950 does not include any provision concerned specifically with minority group rights. The only explicit reference to minorities appears in Article 14 - the general non-discrimination provision - which states that "[t]he enjoyment of the rights and freedoms set forth in this Convention shall be secured without discrimination on any ground such as sex, race, colour, language, religion, political or other opinion, national or social origin, *association with a national minority*, property, birth or other status".[35]   Article 2 of the *First Protocol* does state, however, that:

> No person shall be denied the right to education. In the exercise of any functions which it assumes in relation to education and to teaching, the State shall respect the right of parents to ensure such education and teaching in conformity with their own religious and philosophical convictions.

The text of Article 2 does not make it clear whether there is a right to establish schools outside the State educational system. It has been argued, however, that Article 2 offers clear protection to belief minority parents as part of the general right to education[36] and that such a right does exist.[37] The requirements of the second sentence of Article 2 - that the State shall respect the religious and philosophical convictions of parents - arguably creates a pragmatic imperative to permit the operation of some private schools.[38]   Indeed, in the case of *Ingrid Jordebo Foundation of Christian Schools and Ingrid Jordebo v Sweden*[39] the European Commission of Human Rights appeared to accept the interpretation that Article 2 includes a right to start and run a private school. The State has the power and duty to regulate private as well as public education and may not use its regulatory power to make it impossible to establish private schools.[40]

Article 2 has also been interpreted by the European Court of Human Rights to require a commitment to pluralism in the educational process. In the case of *Kjeldsen, Busk Madsen and Pedersen v Denmark,*[41] the Court observed that Article 2 "aims . . . at safeguarding the possibility of pluralism in education . . . essential for the preservation of the 'democratic society' as conceived by the Convention . . .".[42]   Cultural and linguistic minorities, as opposed to belief minorities, must rely for the protection of their rights on a combination of the first sentence of Article 2 of the *First Protocol* and on Article 14 of the *European Convention.* Apart from a commitment to the principle of non-discrimination reflected in the *Belgian Linguistic Case*[43] and to pluralism in the educational process, the *European Convention* contains no explicit acknowledgment of, or positive protection for, minority educational rights.[44]   Attempts to bolster the positive recognition and promotion of minority educational rights within the framework of the *Convention* have so far failed.[45]

Minority educational rights have received greater consideration within the Council of Europe over the past decade. Principle 7 of the "Freedom of Education in the European Community" Resolution adopted by the European Parliament on 14 March 1984 provides in part that "[f]reedom of education and teaching shall include the right to establish a school and provide instruction . . .". Minority rights and minority educational rights have been firmly on the agenda of the Conference on Security and Co-operation in Europe (C.S.C.E.) since 1975. On 1 August 1975, the *Final Act of the Conference on Security and Co-operation in Europe* was adopted by thirty-five States, including the United States and the U.S.S.R., at Helsinki. The *Final Act* contains a declaration of principles under the heading "Questions relating to Security in Europe". Although the text of the *Final Act* contains a commitment to act in conformity with existing human rights obligations of the States signatories, the instrument does not have the status of a treaty and the understanding of the signatories was that it was not legally binding.[46] Indeed, the C.S.C.E. instruments merely represent a set of political obligations. Nonetheless, they do encourage C.S.C.E. States to consider, *inter alia*, a variety of measures to recognise and protect minority rights.

The most important reference to minorities in the Helsinki *Final Act* appears in Principle X of its Declaration of Principles:

> The participating States on whose territory national minorities exist will respect the right of persons belonging to such minorities to equality before the law, will afford them the full opportunity for the actual enjoyment of human rights and fundamental freedoms and will, in this manner, protect their legitimate interests in this sphere.

The *Final Act* also contains a section on "Co-operation and Exchanges in the Field of Education" which contains the following paragraph on national minorities:

> The participating States, recognizing the contribution that national minorities or regional cultures can make to co-operation among them in various fields of education, intend, when such minorities or cultures exist within their territory, to facilitate this contribution, taking into account the legitimate interests of their members.

The most important recent C.S.C.E. breakthrough on minority educational rights was produced at its Copenhagen Meeting of the Conference on the Human Dimension held in June, 1990. The *Copenhagen Declaration of the Conference on the Human Dimension* states in Principle 32 that:

> Persons belonging to national minorities have the right freely to express, preserve and develop their ethnic, cultural, linguistic or religious identity and to maintain and develop their culture in all its aspects, free of any

attempts at assimilation against their will. In particular, they have the right . . . to establish and maintain their own educational, cultural and religious institutions, organizations or associations, which can seek voluntary financial and other contributions as well as public assistance, in conformity with national legislation.

Significantly, Principle 32 does not guarantee any State funding for minority schools. Although only 'national' minorities are referred to (as is the case with the *Convention against Discrimination in Education*), the explicit reference to "ethnic, cultural, linguistic or religious identity" arguably requires an expansive interpretation of the term 'national'. According to Principle 34, the participating States will take account of the history and culture of national minorities in the context of the teaching of history and culture in educational establishments. The C.S.C.E Meeting of Experts on National Minorities held in Geneva on 19 July 1991 noted that some of the C.S.C.E. participating States had obtained positive results by, *inter alia*, the provision of financial and technical assistance to persons belonging to national minorities to enable them to exercise their right to establish and maintain their own educational institutions.

The right of minority groups to establish and direct educational establishments has also been recognised at the national level.   For example, Article 30(1) of the *Constitution of India* of 1949 provides that "[a]ll minorities, whether based on religion or language, shall have the right to establish and administer educational institutions of their choice". Article 30(2) states, moreover, that "[t]he State shall not, in granting aid to educational institutions, discriminate against any educational institution on the ground that it is under the management of a minority, whether based on religion or language". The latter provision effectively recognises the right of minorities to State support in the granting of aid to educational institutions.   In Denmark, members of the German minority group are granted the right to establish their own schools, and diplomas awarded by these schools, when their establishment has been authorised by the Danish Government, have the same validity as those awarded by State schools. Essential requirements for the establishment of private minority schools include approval by the Danish Government of the curriculum, and control of the academic qualifications of the supervising staff and of the suitability of the school premises in order to ensure that they meet the general standards for public schools.[47]

Inter-cultural (Multicultural) Education

As part of its constitutional mandate, U.N.E.S.C.O. has been involved since its inception in the advancement of "the mutual knowledge and understanding of peoples".[48] U.N.E.S.C.O. has enjoyed a long tradition of preserving and promoting cultures which has enured particularly to the benefit of minority cultures. Article I of U.N.E.S.C.O.'s *Declaration of the Principles of International Cultural Co-operation* of 1966 proclaimed that:

(1) Each culture has a dignity and value which must be respected and preserved . . .

(3) In their rich variety and diversity, and in the reciprocal influences they exert on one another, all cultures form part of the common heritage belonging to all mankind.

Article 4(g) of U.N.E.S.C.O.'s *Recommendation on Participation by the People at Large in Cultural Life and Their Contribution to It* of 1976 calls upon States to "protect, safeguard and enhance all forms of cultural expression such as national or regional languages, dialects, folk arts and traditions both past and present, and rural cultures as well as other social groups". Underlying these instruments is U.N.E.S.C.O.'s commitment to the belief that all children should be raised in an environment in which cultural differences are recognised and appreciated as a normal and natural feature of most societies. Paragraph 17 of U.N.E.S.C.O.'s *Recommendation Concerning Education for International Understanding, Co-operation and Peace and Education Relating to Human Rights and Fundamental Freedoms* of 1974 therefore provides:

Member States should promote, at various stages and in various types of education, study of different cultures, their reciprocal influences, their perspectives and ways of life, in order to encourage mutual appreciation of the differences between them. Such study should, among other things, give due importance to the teaching of foreign languages, civilizations and cultural heritage as a means of promoting international and inter-cultural understanding.

As we have seen earlier in this chapter, pluralism and multiculturalism have been recognised by the United Nations General Assembly in a general context in Article 27 of the *International Covenant on Civil and Political Rights* and Article 30 of the *Convention on the*

Rights of the Child. The importance of inter-cultural education has been reaffirmed most recently by the General Assembly in its *Declaration on the Rights of Persons Belonging to National or Ethnic, Religious and Linguistic Minorities* of 1992. Article 4(4) thereof states:

> States should, where appropriate, take measures in the field of education, in order to encourage knowledge of the history, traditions, language and culture of the minorities existing within their territory. Persons belonging to minorities should have adequate opportunities to gain knowledge of the society as a whole.

Article 4(4) therefore balances the need to give positive reinforcement to minority identity against the need to facilitate a degree of integration with the society at large.

The European Community has also considered inter-cultural education in the limited context of the education of the children of migrant workers. Article 3 of the *Council of the European Communities Directive on the Education of the Children of Migrant Workers 1977* states that "[m]ember States shall, in accordance with their national circumstances and legal systems, and in co-operation with States of origin, take appropriate measures to promote, in co-ordination with normal education, teaching of the mother tongue and culture of the country of origin" for such children.

The leading rationales supporting inter-cultural education are based on both individual and societal benefits. They include:

(a)   the instillation within minority children of pride in their own   culture which would enhance their self-image and sense of   identity;

(b)   the avoidance of bias and discrimination and the provision of   equality of educational opportunity;

(c)   the tuition of children in the composition of the society in which they live and of the wider world. As the 1977 United Kingdom Green Paper *Education in Schools* declared:

> Our society is a multicultural, multiracial one and the curriculum should reflect a sympathetic understanding of the different cultures and races that now make up our society . . . We also live in a complex, interdependent world, and many of our problems in Britain require international solutions. The curriculum should therefore reflect our need to know about and understand other countries.[49]

Minority Language Education

Introduction

The intimate inter-relationship between minority cultures and minority languages, and tuition in and of those languages, has been aptly identified by Professor Francesco Capotorti, Special Rapporteur of the United Nations Sub-Commission on Prevention of Discrimination and Protection of Minorities, in the following passage:

> In multi-ethnic and multilinguistic countries, the use of the languages of the various population groups in the educational system is a crucial test for determining the ability of these groups to maintain and develop their own characteristics, their own culture and their own traditions. The language of a minority group being an essential element of its culture, its capacity to survive as a cultural group is in jeopardy if no instruction is given in that language.[50]

The League of Nations treaties early on identified language as an integral part of minority identity. Articles 8 and 9 of the *Treaty Between The Principal Allied and Associated Powers and Poland* of 1919 recognised the right of Polish nationals who belonged to linguistic minorities to instruction through the medium of their own language.

The language chosen to teach the school curriculum can be a very sensitive issue to minority groups and an equally politically controversial topic amongst the wider community. Not surprisingly, as we shall observe shortly, international law has been comparatively slow to evolve standards in this area. Nevertheless, the issue of the educational lingustic rights of minorities is of immediate relevance to most societies in the world. The large majority of the world's nations are *de facto* multilingual in the sense that several native languages are spoken within their borders.[51] Although there are more than 40 officially bilingual or multilingual States, a majority of the nearly 200 States of the world are, despite their *de facto* multilingualism, officially monolingual in the sense that only one official language is recognised.[52] In most States, therefore, minority languages do not enjoy equal status with the official languages. Consequently, minority languages tend to be perceived as inferior in status and unsuitable for teaching and other academic work.[53] It has been argued that if a minority group is denied access to education in its mother tongue because that language is denied official recognition or is perceived as inferior, then that group will be significantly disadvantaged.

The teaching of minority languages in schools may take different forms and degrees. Such teaching may range through the following:

1)   the use of the mother tongue as the only medium of instruction in a non-State school;

2)   the use of the mother tongue as one of the mediums of instruction (along with the official language) in either a State or non-State school (sometimes referred to as "bilingual education");

3)   the development of a child's fluency as an integral part of the primary school curriculum in order to enhance existing language   skills (by timetabling a set number of hours each week for the teaching of the mother tongue);

4)   the teaching of the mother tongue as part of the foreign languages curriculum of secondary schools.

The Arguments: For and Against

The main arguments and difficulties which have been cited to reject the use or teaching of minority languages in schools include the following:

1) **the financial cost to governments** may prove to be prohibitive, especially where numerous minority languages exist within the country. Providing tuition of, or instruction in, minority languages may involve the construction of new classrooms, the printing of new textbooks and translation services, and the training of new staff. In countries where minority schools operate within the public school system, the State usually bears most of the costs. The economic position of the countries concerned will obviously have a bearing on these issues.[54]

2) **the threat to national unity.** In many post-colonial societies attempting to consolidate multi-ethnic communities created by the drawing of colonial borders, school language policy emphasises national integration at the expense of diversity.[55] In some of the developing countries where the language of one of the minority groups has been granted the status of the national or official language, that language has also been

designated as the sole language of instruction for primary education in order to foster a sense of national unity.[56] Some governments fear that the use of minority languages may strengthen the identity of minority groups and increase demands for political autonomy.[57] Reservations have also been expressed concerning the potentially harmful nature of separate or special teaching which is confined to ethnic minority pupils and which might serve to establish or confirm social divisions;[58]

3) **the shortage of trained teachers and suitable educational materials.**[59]

The arguments advanced in favour of the use of minority languages both as a medium of instruction and as the object of study include:

1) **the preservation of cultural heritage.** As Article 5 of the *World Declaration on Education for All* of 1990 succinctly states: "Literacy in the mother-tongue strengthens cultural identity and heritage". It has been said that "[t]he danger of language atrophy is that the culture itself is in mortal danger; for nobody will maintain that a group still has a living culture, in the full sense of the term, when it is forced to use another language in order to express to itself the realities which make up a large part of its daily life".[60] In *Mahe v Alberta* [61] the importance of minority language education to cultural survival was emphasised by the Supreme Court of Canada in its endorsement of the views which had previously been expressed by the Royal Commission on Bilingualism and Biculturalism in the following terms:

"Language is also the key to cultural development. Language and culture are not synonymous, but the vitality of the language is a necessary condition for the complete preservation of a culture . . . the aim must be to provide for members of the minority an education appropriate to their linguistic and cultural identity."

Thus, the teaching of minority languages helps to prevent the forced linguistic and cultural assimilation of minority groups.

2) **the promotion of tolerance and understanding between majority and minority groups;**[62]

3) **the maximisation of the talents and communication skills of the minority child;**

4) **linguistic (and cultural) pluralism enriches society as a whole.** Several languages disappear each year and the teaching of minority languages can assist in preventing language loss and retaining the world's linguistic diversity.[63] These views are based on the notion that languages are part of humanity's heritage and should therefore be cherished.

5) **the development of a positive self-image and sense of identity.** If schools do not teach minority languages, minority children may develop the impression that the educational system and wider community do not accept and value their language and culture. Such tuition is also necessary to enable minority children to know about and appreciate their group's history and culture and to have a sense of their position in the wider world.[64]

6) **the facilitation of greater communication between minority children and their parents, extended family and country of origin;**

7) **the development of valuable links with other countries in the trading, educational and cultural sectors;**[65]

8) **the enhancement of learning opportunities at the primary school level.** Recent research suggests that there are educational advantages to be gained in teaching children in the early years in their mother tongues for a part of the school day.[66]

Recognition of Minority Educational Linguistic Rights Under
International Law

There are relatively few international standards for the protection and promotion of the linguistic rights of minority groups in the educational sphere. Most of those standards which do exist are not legally binding.

It will be recalled that Articles 2(b) and 5(1)(c) of the *Convention against Discrimination in Education* of 1960 respectively provide for the establishment of separate educational institutions by linguistic and national minorities including "the use or the teaching of their own language". It is not so clear, however, whether Article 13 of the *International Covenant on Economic, Social and Cultural Rights* imposes a legal obligation on States Parties to provide education for linguistic minorities in their mother tongue. The *travaux préparatoires* appear to be silent on this point. It is at least arguable, however, that Article 13 does impose such a duty, bearing in mind that Article 2(2) of the *Covenant* prohibits discrimination on the basis of language and national origin.[67]

Article 27 of the *International Covenant on Civil and Political Rights* is equally vague on this matter. It states:

> In those States in which ethnic, religious or linguistic minorities exist, persons belonging to such minorities shall not be denied the right, in community with the other members of their group, to enjoy their own culture, to profess and practise their own religion, or to use their own language.

As no limitation is placed upon these minority rights, it would appear that prevention of the use of the mother tongue in school where there exists a reasonable level of minority community demand for it could constitute a violation of Article 27.[68]

The most recent development within the United Nations is the *Declaration on the Rights of Persons Belonging to National or Ethnic, Religious and Linguistic Minorities* of 1992. Article 4(3) thereof provides that "States should take appropriate measures so that, wherever possible, persons belonging to minorities have adequate opportunities to learn their mother tongue or to have instruction in their mother tongue". Article 4(3) does not impose any legally binding obligations but it does point the way for the evolution of binding universal norms. Article 4(3) is considerably weakened, however, by the inclusion of the qualifying phrase "wherever possible", the lack of definition of "appropriate measures" and the alternative formulation concerning tuition in, or tuition of, the mother tongue.

The Necessity to Learn the Official/Majority Language(s)

International law has recognised for many years the desirability - indeed, the necessity - for members of minority groups to learn the official national language(s) or at least the language of the dominant national group. Although Article 9 of the *Treaty Between The Principal Allied and Associated Powers and Poland* of 1919 obliged the Polish Government to provide minority language instruction in public primary schools when the numbers so warranted, it also explicitly acknowledged the right of the Government to require the teaching of the Polish language in those schools. To the same effect is Article 5(1)(c)(i) of the *Convention against Discrimination in Education* which recognises the right of members of national minorities to maintain their own schools and to use or teach their own language therein, provided that such rights are not exercised in a manner which prevents the members of such minorities from understanding the culture and language of the community as a whole. The *Declaration on the Rights of Persons Belonging to National or Ethnic, Religious and Linguistic Minorities* is less explicit on this point. Article 4(4) thereof merely states that "[p]ersons belonging to minorities should have adequate opportunities to gain knowledge of the society as a whole". It is arguable, however, that members of minority groups would not be able to acquire a sufficient level of knowledge of society as a whole without a basic knowledge of the official or dominant national language.

A variety of explanations have been advanced for this requirement. One commentator maintains that it is a question of reciprocity and the avoidance of "ethnic fundamentalism".[69] In fact, members of minority groups have little choice but to become bilingual if they live in a State where their mother tongue is not the official language. It is now generally agreed that when persons belonging to minority groups cannot pursue their education in their own language beyond the primary level, they should be taught the official language to facilitate entry into secondary schools and institutions of higher learning on an equal footing with all other pupils.[70] In the separate schools established for minorities in Austria, for example, instruction is given in the minority language in all grades but the language of the main population is extensively taught as a compulsory subject.[71] This is in marked contrast to the position of members of the majority group who do not need to know any other languages and only learn minority languages if they wish to.[72]   Nevertheless, Article 4(4) of the *Minorities Declaration* calls on States to take appropriate educational measures to encourage knowledge by the majority of minority languages existing within their territory.

Acquisition of a working knowledge of the official or dominant language by members of the minority group is also necessary for fuller intergration into society (as opposed to forced assimilation) and for equality of opportunity in terms of their participation in the political, economic and social life of their society.[73]   Minority children who do not acquire a sufficient knowledge of the majority language tend to be marginalised.[74]   This requirement of international law, then, appears to rest on a sound footing.

Minority Educational Linguistic Rights: Some Domestic Law Examples

The use of minority languages in public school systems tends to be protected and regulated by constitutional law, ordinary laws, administrative policy directives and/or treaties.[75]   This will, of course, vary from State to State.   According to a survey of various countries conducted by Professor Capotorti, arrangements to implement minority language teaching generally include the establishment of separate schools or the creation of separate sections or separate classes in the same school.   The use of minority languages in public school systems occurs predominantly at the primary school level;   the use of such languages in secondary schools or higher education is relatively rare.[76]   Lack of funds, unavailability of competent teaching staff and a desire not to fragment the educational system constitute the main reasons for exclusion of minority language teaching from the curriculum of secondary schools, particularly in the developing States.[77]

Pursuant to the *Treaty of Lausanne* of 1923, the use of the mother tongue in public primary schools in districts inhabited by Turkish and Greek minority groups is provided for in Greece and Turkey respectively. The same treaty also permits the establishment and maintenance within Turkey of private Greek minority primary and secondary schools in which instruction is provided in the Greek language.[78]   The former *Constitution of the U.S.S.R.* of 1977 provided in Article 45 that every citizen's right to education would be ensured by, *inter alia*, "the opportunity to attend a school where teaching is in the native language".   Article 350A of the *Constitution of India* of 1949 imposes a positive legal obligation on every State and local authority "to provide adequate facilities for instruction in the mother-tongue at the primary stage of education to children belonging to linguistic minority groups".

The Atlantic Coast Communities of Nicaragua receive exemplary minority protection under Nicaraguan law. Pursuant to Articles 90 and 121 of the *Constitution of Nicaragua* of 1986, the Nicaraguan State is obliged respectively to create special programmes to preserve and enhance their languages, art and culture and to permit them to have access in their region to education in their mother tongue. *The Atlantic Coast Autonomy Law* of 1987 grants autonomy to the Atlantic Coast Communities in various fields including education. Article 12(5) thereof states that "[t]he inhabitants of the Atlantic Coast Communities are entitled by law to be educated in their own languages, through programmes that take into account their historical heritage, their traditions and the characteristics of their environment, all within the framework of the national education system".

In some countries, the use of minority languages as languages of instruction depends on the number of pupils attending classes. In Austria, the *Burgenland Provincial School Act 1937* provides that a minority language will be the language of instruction if the last census has shown that 70 per cent of the school district population is composed of members of that linguistic minority. When the percentage is between 30 and 70 per cent, bilingual schools are to be established in which both the national language and the minority language are to be used as languages of instruction. If the percentage is less than 30 per cent, the State language is the only language of instruction, but the district school board must ensure that children belonging to the minority are taught their mother tongue.[79]

Minority Educational Linguistic Rights: Recent European Developments

The question whether members of a minority group have a right to mother-tongue tuition under the *European Convention for the Protection of Human Rights and Fundamental Freedoms* was considered in 1968 in the *Belgian Linguistic* cases.[80] French-speaking parents who were prevented from sending their children to a school where the language of instruction was French argued, *inter alia*, that this violated their rights under Article 14 (which prohibits discrimination on various grounds including "association with a national minority") and Article 2 of the *First Protocol* to the *Convention* which states in part that " . . . the State shall respect the right of parents to ensure such education and teaching in conformity with their own religious and philosophical convictions". The European Court held, however, that the *Convention* did not require States Parties to respect the *linguistic* preferences of parents. The Court stated:

> [Article 2] does not require of States that they should, in the sphere of education or teaching, respect parents' linguistic preferences, but only their religious and philosophical convictions. To interpret the terms 'religious' and 'philosophical' as covering linguistic preferences would amount to a distortion of their ordinary and usual meaning and to read into the Convention something which is not there.[81]

In the Court's view, Article 2 was never intended to secure a right for parents to have their children educated in a language other than the national language. In the absence of more explicit language, Article 14, when read in conjunction with Article 2, did not guarantee to minority group members the right to receive tuition in the language of his or her choice. The narrow effect the Court attributed to Article 14 was due to its endorsement of the Belgian Government's objective of securing unilingual regions throughout most of the country as a legitimate policy within its margin of appreciation. The disadvantage suffered by the French-speaking minority did not amount in law to arbitrary discrimination. The Court's reasoning has been criticised as pro-assimilationist and anti-pluralist in its orientation.[82] Indeed, the European Commission on Human Rights had found that several features of the Belgian educational linguistic policy were assimilationist in so far as they were designed to cause the French-speaking minorities in Dutch-speaking regions to abandon their language.[83]

The effect of the European Court's ruling in the *Belgian Linguistic* cases has been somewhat mitigated by more recent legislative and administrative developments within the European Community. These developments have been prompted in part by the mobility of the labour force within the Community and by the large number of citizens of those countries which comprise the E.C. who speak a language other than the official or dominant language.[84] According to its Preamble, the *Council of the European Communities Directive on the Education of the Children of Migrant Workers 1977* [85] was promulgated to improve the freedom of movement of workers within the European Economic Community and to acknowledge the desirability of a worker's children being taught their mother tongue "with a view principally to facilitating their possible reintegration into the Member State of origin". Article 3 of the *Directive* deals with the issue of mother-tongue teaching in the following terms:

> Member States shall, in accordance with their national circumstances and legal systems, and in co-operation with States of origin, take appropriate

measures to promote, in co-ordination with normal education, teaching of the mother tongue and culture of the country of origin for the children referred to in Article 1.

Article 1 defines the children to whom the *Directive* applies as those "children for whom school attendance is compulsory under the laws of the host State, who are dependants of any worker who is a national of another Member State, where such children are resident in the territory of the Member State in which that national carries on or has carried on an activity as an employed person". Although the benefits of the *Directive* are expressly confined to the children of nationals of the Member States of the European Communities, the text is silent on the issue of how much tuition such children are entitled to.

Pressure from speakers of minority languages during the 1980s led to the passing of several European Parliament resolutions aimed at securing their linguistic rights. The most significant of these resolutions - the 'Kuijpers' Resolution adopted on 30 October 1987 - "recommends to Member States that they carry out education measures including . . . arranging for pre-school to university education and continuing education to be officially conducted in the regional minority languages in the language areas concerned on an equal footing with instruction in the national languages . . .". Since European Parliament resolutions are not binding on Member States, their value lies more in creating a climate of awareness and discussion of the issues and in the potential they represent for influencing national policies.[86] The Conference on Security and Co-operation in Europe has also been involved recently in the formulation of non-binding standards in this area. Paragraph 34 of the *Declaration* of the Copenhagen Meeting of the Conference on the Human Dimension of the C.S.C.E. recites that "[t]he participating State will endeavour to ensure that persons belonging to national minorities . . . have adequate opportunities for instruction of their mother tongue or in their mother tongue . . . in conformity with applicable national legislation". Paragraph 32.3 also recognises the right of persons belonging to national minorities to conduct religious educational activities in their mother tongue. At a C.S.C.E. Meeting of Experts on National Minorities held in Geneva on 19 July 1991, the participating States noted that positive results had been obtained by some of them by, *inter alia*, the provision to persons belonging to national minorities of adequate types and levels of education in their mother tongue with due regard to the number, geographic settlement patterns and cultural traditions of these minorities.

The recognition of minority educational linguistic rights in Europe has been placed on a firmer footing with the adoption by the Committee of Ministers of the Council of Europe of the *European Charter for Regional or Minority Languages.*[87] The Preamble of the Charter declares that "the right to use a regional or minority language in private and public life is an inalienable right". For the purposes of the *Charter*, the term "regional or minority languages" means, according to Article 1(a), languages that are:

(i) traditionally used within a given territory of a State by nationals of that State who form a group numerically smaller than the rest of the State's population, and

(ii) different from the official language(s) of that State;

[but] does not include . . . the language of migrants.

Article 9 of the *Charter* provides for minority languages in the educational context in significant detail and covers all levels and types of education - pre-school, primary, secondary, technical and vocational, and higher education as well as adult and continuing education. Article 9(1)(b) states, for example, that the States Parties undertake within the territory in which such languages are used to:

(i) make available the whole of primary education in the relevant regional or minority languages; or

(ii) make available a substantial part of primary education in the relevant regional or minority languages; or

(iii) provide, within primary education, for the teaching of the relevant regional or minority languages as an integral part of the curriculum; or

(iv) apply the measures referred to under (i) to (iii) above at least to those pupils whose families so request and whose number is considered sufficient.

These various options, however, evidence a significant residual discretion left with governments in implementing minority educational linguistic rights. Article 9(1)(g) also obliges Parties to make arrangements to ensure the teaching of the history and culture which is reflected by the regional or minority languages. The *Charter* is to be implemented by a system of State reports to be reviewed by a Committee of Experts.[88]

The Council of Europe's *Framework Convention for the Protection of National Minorities* of 1994[89] recognises the right of persons belonging to national minorities to learn their minority language and, in minority areas, to endeavour to provide instruction in the minority language. The *Convention* also imposes obligations on States Parties to take measures in the educational field to foster understanding of minority culture and recognises the right of such persons to set up and manage their own private educational and training establishments.[90]

Conclusion

Apart from the European regional human rights régime, the existing international and regional human rights instruments do not sufficiently protect the linguistic rights of members of minority groups in the educational field.[91]   Acceptance by governments of an obligation to financially support minority language education has not been forthcoming. This is partly due to an assumption that mother-tongue teaching is primarily the responsibility of the minority communities themselves. Until such an obligation is accepted, governments might consider more modest support measures such as the free or subsidised use of school premises, grants or interest-free loans for books and equipment and assistance with teacher-training.

An international seminar on Human Rights and Cultural Rights[92] held in 1987 in Recife, Brazil acknowledged the need for specific international standards to protect and promote minority language rights. The seminar adopted the *Declaration of Recife* which identified "the need to provide explicit legal guarantees for linguistic rights to individuals and groups" and recommended that "steps be taken by the United Nations to adopt and implement a Universal Declaration of Linguistic Rights". A *Resolution on Linguistic Rights* was also adopted. It recognised, *inter alia*, the right of every child to learn the language of his or her group fully as well as the right to similarly learn at least one of the official languages of the country in which he or she is resident.   Considering the controversial nature of minority rights generally and the potential costs to be borne by governments in implementing such rights in the educational sphere, it may be some time before clear international norms emerge in this area.

Conclusion

A number of factors continue to impede the attainment of equality of opportunity for minority children in the educational context. Such factors include, but are not limited to, the level of socio-economic development and geographical location/concentration of the minority groups, their inferior social status and historical prejudices on the part of mainstream society, and their *de facto* segregation.[93]   Obviously, the provision of minority linguistic and cultural education is not resource-neutral. Human, financial and material resources are required. Qualified authors and translators of suitable textbooks must be found. Accessible schools may have to be provided in outlying regions where marginalised minorities often live.[94]   Persons (preferably from the minority group concerned) will have to be trained as teachers. The ability of the State and minority communities to supply these requirements will depend upon their own finite resources and other priorities.

Besides economic and financial constraints, the contemporary phenomenon of "mass education" is another important factor which stifles the development of minority educational rights. Many States are quite candid in citing as the primary aim of their educational system the promotion of national unity. The development of mass education for school-age children in pursuit of this aim has played an important role in promoting integration and uniformity within States.[95]   There is perhaps a superficial attraction in a philosophy of assimilation in the educational field with the aim being to improve race relations amongst the next generation by attempting to ensure that its members all have a uniform cultural background.[96]   But, as one commentator has pointed out, "such assimilationist policies can be used by governments not only to consign languages and linguistic systems to oblivion but also to suppress religious and cultural identities, ways of life and forms of knowledge".[97]   An outstanding example is to be found in Turkey where the State has imposed a highly centralised education system which places explicit emphasis on national unity at the expense of the recognition of the separate history and culture of the Kurdish people.[98]

As has been discussed earlier in this chapter, international human rights law recognises that education is not only a general and fundamental human right but an important constituent of minority rights. Unlike the right to education itself, however, minority educational rights tend to be dealt with more fully in "soft law" instruments such as United Nations General Assembly resolutions and instruments of the Conference on Security and Co-operation in Europe.[99]   The next stage of development will be to enshrine such rights within a convention on minority rights. Some of the rights which could be included within such a convention and related issues might include the following:

1) from the perspective of persons belonging to minority groups, a right to some tuition in, and of, their mother tongue as well as inclusion within the general curriculum of the history, traditions and culture of their groups. Reciprocally, members of minority groups have the right and responsibility to learn about the dominant culture and the national language;

2) from the perspective of persons belonging to the dominant national grouping, the State should undertake to adopt educational measures designed to encourage knowledge of, and respect for, the history, traditions, culture, contributions and language of at least the major national minorities;

3) educational programmes for minority groups should be developed and implemented in co-operation with them. The right of representatives of minority groups to participate in educational policy-making and curriculum development should be acknowledged. The C.S.C.E. Meeting of Experts on National Minorities held in Geneva on 19 July 1991 noted the positive results to be obtained from "advisory and decision-making bodies in which minorities are represented, in particular with regard to education";

4) teachers must be trained both as to the content of the curriculum and the attitudes they bring to the classroom. This includes the selection of teachers from minority groups, the inclusion of minority languages in teacher-training institutions, the education of non-minority teachers in understanding minority culture, and the promotion by teachers within their classrooms of a climate of mutual respect and exchange of cultural experiences.[100] As part of Viet Nam's effort to achieve universal primary education among its ethnic minorities, U.N.I.C.E.F. has recently supported the Government's development of training modules for pre-service and in-service training for teachers in ethnic minority schools.[101]

Notes

1   *P.C.I.J.*, Series B, No. 17, pp. 19, 21, 22 and 33.
2   E/CN.4/Sub.2/384/Rev.I.
3   Capotorti Report, Add. I, *The Concept of a Minority*;   U.N. Sales No.E.78.XIV.1.
4   P. Thornberry *Minorities and Human Rights Law* (1991) (A Minority Rights Group Report) 6.

5   A national group is one which sees itself as a distinct people or nation within a larger State, with long-established historical claims to territory within that State (e.g., the Kurds within Turkey).

6   [1979] 2 N.Z.L.R. 531, 543.

7   S. Poulter *English Law and Ethnic Minority Customs* (1986) 161.

8   G. Verma and C. Bagley *Race, Education and Identity* (1979).

9   B. Boutros-Ghali "The Right to Culture and the Universal Declaration of Human Rights" in *Cultural Rights as Human Rights* (Paris, U.N.E.S.C.O.,1970) (SHC.68/XIX.3/A), pp. 73-4.

10   H. Cullen "Education Rights or Minority Rights?" (1993) 7 *International Journal of Law and the Family* 143.

11   Id. 157.

12   P. Thornberry "Is There a Phoenix in the Ashes?: International Law and Minority Rights" (1980) 15 *Texas International Law Journal* 421.

13   H. Cullen, op. cit., 158.

14   See H. Cullen, op. cit., *passim* for a discussion of these decisions.

15   112 Great Britain T.S. 232.

16   J. Robinson *Were the Minorities Treaties a Failure?* (1943) 215-216.

17   6 L.N.T.S. 190.

18   P. Thornberry "International Standards" in *Education Rights and Minorities* (1994) (A Minority Rights Group Report) 10.

19   See P. Arajärvi "Article 26" in A. Eide *et al The Universal Declaration of Human Rights: A Commentary* (1992) 405, 406-407.

20   U.N. Doc. E/CN.4/AC.A/3/ADD. 1, p. 409.

21   K. Halvorsen "Notes on the Realization of the Human Right to Education" (1990) 12 *Human Rights Quarterly* 341, 354-355.

22   P. Thornberry "International Standards" in *Education Rights and Minorities* (1994) 11. Nevertheless, a proposal to permit such minorities within the framework of Article 27 " . . . to possess their national schools, libraries, museums and other cultural and educational institutions" was not accepted in the Commission on Human Rights: M. Bossuyt *Guide to the "Travaux Préparatoires" of the International Covenant on Civil and Political Rights* (1987) Martinus Nijhoff Publishers, Dordrecht, 494-5.

23   F. Capotorti, U.N. Special Rapporteur, *Study on the Rights of Persons Belonging to Ethnic, Religious and Linguistic Minorities* U.N. Sales No. E.91.XIV.2, United Nations, New York (1991).

24   H. Cullen, op. cit., 148.

25   Arajärvi, op. cit., 415.

26   U.N.E.S.C.O.'s *Revised Recommendation Concerning Technical and Vocational Education* of 1974 provides for participation by the representatives of different segments of society (and this presumably includes minority groups) in the formulation of policy concerning such education.

27   M. Nowak "The Right to Education" in A. Eide *Economic, Social and Cultural Rights* (1995) 189, 206.

28   Article 29(2) did not meet with the approval of some delegates who considered that the provision was not directly concerned with the protection of children's rights: Commission on Human Rights *Report of the Working Group on a Draft Convention on the Rights of the Child* E/CN.4/1985/64 (3 April 1985) p. 19, para. 102.

29   Commission on Human Rights *Report of the Working Group on a Draft Convention on the Rights of the Child* E/CN.4/1986/39 (13 March 1986) p. 13, para. 65.

30   Ibid.

31   Commission on Human Rights *Report of the Working Group on a Draft Convention on the Rights of the Child* E/CN.4/1987/25 (9 March 1987) p. 13, para. 55.

32   Adopted by United Nations General Assembly Resolution 47/135 of 18 December 1992. The addition of national minorities takes the text beyond Article 27 of the *International Covenant on Civil and Political Rights.* It will be recalled that Article 5(1)(c) of the *Convention against Discrimination in Education* had merely referred to national minorities.

33   P. Thornberry "International Standards" in *Education Rights and Minorities* (1994) (Minority Rights Group Report) 10, 12.

34   Paragraphs 25 and 26 of Section II B.2 of the *Vienna Declaration and Programme of Action.*

35   Emphasis supplied.

36   H. Cullen, op. cit., 150.

37   Opsahl in Robertson (ed.) *Privacy and Human Rights* (1973) 230.

38   D. Harris, M. O'Boyle and C. Warbrick *Law of the European Convention on Human Rights* (1995) 544.

39   (1987) No. 11533/85, 51 DR 125.

40   Id. 128.

41   Series A, No. 23, 1976; (1979-80) 1 E.H.R.R. 711.

42   Id. 729.

43   *Case Relating to Certain Aspects of the Laws on the Use of Languages in Education in Belgium* Series A, No. 6 (1968).

44   P. Thornberry "International Standards" in *Education Rights and Minorities* (Minority Rights Group Report) 10, 11.

45   Ibid.

46   I. Brownlie (ed.) *Basic Documents in International Law* (2nd ed., 1981) 320.

47   F. Capotorti *Study of the Rights of Persons Belonging to Ethnic, Religious and Linguistic Minorities* (1979) U.N. Doc. No. E/CN.4/Sub.2/384/Rev.1, p. 60.

48   See Chapter 3 for a discussion of U.N.E.S.C.O.'s Constitution.

49   Cmnd 6869 of 1977, para. 10.11.

50   Capotorti, op. cit. (1979), p. 84, para. 493.

51   T. Skutnabb-Kangas *Language, Literacy and Minorities* (Minority Rights Group Report) (1990) 6.

52   Ibid.
53   C. Jones and R. Warner "Language and Education" in *Education Rights and Minorities* (1994) 18.
54   Capotorti, op. cit. (1979), p. 84, para.495.
55   S. Graham-Brown "The Role of the Curriculum" in *Education Rights and Minorities* (Minority Rights Group Report) (1994) 27.
56   Capotorti, op. cit. (1979), p. 88, para. 515.
57   C. Jones and R. Warner, op. cit., 19.
58   See, for example, *Education For All: Report of the Committee of Inquiry into the Education of Children from Ethnic Minority Groups* (Swann Committee Report) (United Kingdom), Cmnd 9453 of 1985.
59   For a more detailed discussion of the difficulties involved in the use of minority languages in education, see *The Use of Vernacular Languages in Education*, Monographs on Fundamental Education, No. VIII (Paris U.N.E.S.C.O., 1953), pp. 50-54.
60   D. Opekokew and A. Pratt "The Treaty Right to Education in Saskatchewan" (1992) 12 *Windsor Yearbook of Access to Justice* 3, 11. The same authors have described the meaning of the term 'culture' (at id. 10) as follows:
           Culture is a way of being, thinking and feeling. It is a driving force animating a significant group of people united by a common tongue, and sharing the same customs, habits, and experiences. Culture is the sum of the characteristics particular to a group and common to its members.
61   (1990) 68 D.L.R. (4th) 69, 83.
62   The contribution of language education to cross-cultural learning and peaceful cohabitation was emphasised at a recent conference: see G. Alfredsson (Rapporteur), *Report from the Conference on the Strengthening of Human Rights and Inter-Ethnic Communication in Times of Political and Economic Transition: The Baltic Experience*, 1994.
63   Skutnabb-Kangas, op. cit., 6.
64   C. Jones and R. Warner, op. cit., 19.
65   S. Poulter *English Law and Ethnic Minority Customs* (1986) p. 172, para. 7.14.
66   *Linguistic Diversity and Mother Tongue Teaching* (N.U.T., 1982).
67   M. Yudof "Articles 13 and 14 - Right to Education" in H. Hannum (ed.) *U.S. Ratification of the International Covenants on Human Rights* (1993) 235, 239.
68   W. McKean *Equality and Discrimination in International Law* (1983) 145.
69   P. Thornberry "International Standards" in *Education Rights and Minorities* (1994) (Minority Rights Group Report) 10, 12.
70   Capotorti, op. cit. (1979), p. 87, para. 513.
71   Id. p. 88, para. 514.
72   C. Jones and R. Warner, op. cit., 19.

73   Skuttnabb-Kangas, op. cit., 5-6.
74   See Cullen, op. cit., 170 for a fuller discussion and example of this point.
75   Capotorti, op. cit. (1979), p. 85, para. 498.
76   Ibid.
77   Id. p. 88, para. 517.
78   Id. pp. 84-85, para. 497 and p. 87, para. 510.
79   Capotorti, op. cit. (1979), p. 87, para. 512.
80   *Cases Relating to Certain Aspects of the Laws on the Use of Languages in Education in Beligium.* Judgement of the European Court of Justice (23 July 1968). Series A, No. 6.
81   Id. p. 32, para. 6.
82   Cullen, op. cit., 157.
83   *Belgian Linguistic Cases.* Report of the Commission, Series B, No. 1, 329 and 335.
84   As of 1990, the number was estimated to be some 50 million people: see Skutnabb-Kangas, op. cit., 29.
85   Entry into force 25 July 1977 (77/486/EEC). Article 189(3) of the *Treaty of Rome* declares that "[a] directive shall be binding, as to the result to be achieved, upon each Member State to which it is addressed, but shall leave to the national authorities the choice of forms and methods".
86   Skutnabb-Kangas, op. cit., 29.
87   Opened for signature 2 October 1992 and subject to ratification by Member States of the Council of Europe.
88   See Articles 16-18.
89   (1995) 34 I.L.M. 351 (opened for signature 1 February 1995).
90   The relevant provisions of the *Framework Convention* are as follows:
      Article 12(1) The Parties shall, where appropriate, take measures in the field of education and research to foster knowledge of the culture, history, language and religion of their national minorities and of the majority.
      Article 12(3) The Parties undertake to promote equal opportunities for access to education at all levels for persons belonging to national minorities.
      Article 13(1) Within the framework of their education systems, the Parties shall recognise that persons belonging to a national minority have the right to set up and to manage their own private educational and training establishments.
      Article 13(2) The exercise of this right shall not entail any financial obligation for the Parties.
      Article 14(1) The Parties undertake to recognise that every person belonging to a national minority has the right to learn his or her minority language.
      Article 14(2) In areas inhabited by persons belonging to national minorities traditionally or in substantial numbers, if there is sufficient demand, the Parties shall endeavour to ensure, as far as possible and

within the framework of their education systems, that persons belonging to those minorities have adequate opportunities for being taught the minority language or for receiving instruction in this language.

Article 14(3) Paragraph 2 of this article shall be implemented without prejudice to the learning of the official language or the teaching in this language.

91   Skutnabb-Kangas, op. cit., 29.

92   The seminar was organised by U.N.E.S.C.O. and the International Association for Cross-cultural Communication.

93   See Capotorti, op. cit. (1979), p. 61, paras. 349 and 350 for more detail.

94   C. Beyani "The Prerequisites of Education" in *Education Rights and Minorities* (1994) (Minority Rights Group Report) 14, 15.

95   A. Phillips "Preface" in id. 5.

96   Poulter, op. cit., p. 161, para. 7.01.

97   S. Graham-Brown "The Role of the Curriculum" in *Education Rights and Minorities*, op. cit., 27.

98   Id. 31. Another graphic example is the Japanese assimilationist policy concerning its Korean minority: see Cullen, op. cit., 172.

99   P. Thornberry "International Standards" in *Education Rights and Minorities*, op. cit., 10, 13.

100   Graham-Brown, op. cit., 29.

101   http://www.unicef.org/crc/success/eap.html.

7 Educational Rights of Indigenous Peoples

Introduction

Until recently, indigenous peoples like the Aborigines of Australia, the Maoris of New Zealand, the Indians of North, Central and South America and the Kanaks of New Caledonia have been considered by international law as minority groups to the extent that they do no constitute a majority of the population of the State in which they reside. As such, they benefit from whatever protection is available to minority groups under domestic law and international instruments. As late as 1979, Professor Capotorti observed in his *Study on the Rights of Persons Belonging to Ethnic, Religious and Linguistic Minorities* that generally indigenous groups constituted the poorest of the minority groups in those countries in which they lived.[1] There is a growing tendency, however, to regard indigenous peoples as a separate topic. Indigenous groups themselves have tended to distance themselves from minorities in general, preferring instead to regard themselves as 'peoples'.

The Contribution of the International Labour Organisation to the Development of International Standards Concerning the Educational Rights of Indigenous Peoples

With the exception of the International Labour Organisation, few intergovernmental organisations have been concerned with indigenous rights in the post-World War II era of 'human' rights; perhaps the only notable exception is the Inter-American Indian Institute which was established in 1940 as a specialised agency of the Organization of American States.[2] In 1957, the I.L.O. adopted *Convention (No. 107) Concerning the Protection and Integration of Indigenous and Other Tribal and Semi-Tribal Populations in Independent Countries.*[3] As one commentator has observed, this instrument "reflects the prevailing assimilationist goals of its time, and it has long been seen as inadequate and inappropriate by indigenous peoples and their advocates".[4] For

121

example, Article 23(2) states that "[p]rovision shall be made for a progressive transition from the mother tongue . . . to the national language" while Article 24 identifies as an aim of primary education for the indigenous populations concerned[5] "[t]he imparting of general knowledge and skills that will help children to become integrated into the national community". Nevertheless, *Convention No. 107* was a significant development in its day in recognising the non-discrimination principle in the educational sector and in protecting and promoting the use of the indigenous mother tongue.

Articles 16 and 21 require States Parties to take measures to ensure that members of indigenous populations enjoy equality of opportunity in acquiring education (including vocational education) at all levels. Articles 23(1) and (3) respectively provide that indigenous children shall be taught to read and write in their mother tongue, and that appropriate measures shall be taken to preserve the mother tongue. The improvement of the level of education of indigenous populations is to be given "high priority" in plans for the economic development of areas inhabited by them (Article 6). States Parties must also take educational measures among other sections of the national community in order to eliminate prejudices that they may harbour concerning members of indigenous communities (Article 25).

Indigenous organisations have strongly rejected *Convention No. 107*. The instrument is rather paternalistic by modern standards and is devoted as much to the integration of indigenous communities as to the protection of their culture (which appears to be regarded as constituting a temporary obstacle to modernisation).[6] In 1986, a report prepared by José R. Martínez Cobo, Special Rapporteur of the United Nations Sub-Commission on Prevention of Discrimination and Protection of Minorities, entitled *Study of the Problem of Discrimination Against Indigenous Populations*[7] was released. The author identified the following shortcomings which existed in the educational systems of the various countries surveyed:

- in a large number of cases, there were still no schools in or near indigenous communities;

- there were too few teachers with the necessary knowledge of the relevant indigenous language and culture;

- in many cases, it was still not possible to learn to read and write in the indigenous mother tongue;

- insufficient stress was laid on instruction in the indigenous culture;

- in teaching the indigenous child the official language, insufficient care was being taken to prevent him or her from being cut off from the indigenous mother tongue;

- aid programmes for indigenous students were inadequate;

- the avowed purpose of educational materials for indigenous persons continued to be their systematic assimilation into mainstream society by forcing them to abandon their own culture;

- not enough was being done to combat prejudice against indigenous groups and to eliminate offensive references to them from school textbooks and to present therein accurate information concerning them;

- very little was being done in many countries to ensure that indigenous groups had the opportunity to participate in the establishment and operation of educational institutions that are active in indigenous communities.[8]

In addition to identifying these specific problems, the Special Rapporteur made the following general conclusions:

- the right of indigenous peoples to education has not been duly guaranteed and is not observed;

- States frequently do not recognise traditional indigenous education and often deliberately aim at doing away with it by replacing it with formal, alien and alienating educational processes;

- although there has been a significant improvement in the effective access of indigenous persons to public education of all kinds and at all levels, such education continues to be characterised by a marked tendency to deprive indigenous pupils of everything indigenous.[9]

Cobo concluded that this situation could in no circumstances be justified in the context of the growing acceptance by States of cultural and linguistic pluralism.[10]

The deficiencies of *Convention No. 107* and the Cobo findings prompted interest within the International Labour Organisation in a convention which advanced to a greater degree the aspirations of indigenous peoples. With the assistance of, amongst others, the Inter-American Indian Institute and U.N.E.S.C.O., the I.L.O. drafted *Convention (No. 169) Concerning Indigenous and Tribal Peoples in Independent*

Countries. The General Conference of the I.L.O. adopted *Convention No. 169* on 27 June 1989 which entered into force on 5 September 1991. Certain paragraphs of the Preamble of *Convention No. 169* are revealing in terms of the intent of the instrument. The fourth preambular paragraph refers to recent developments in international law and the situation of indigenous peoples which have made it appropriate to adopt new international standards in order to remove "the assimilationist orientation" of the earlier standards contained in *Convention No. 107* of 1957. The fifth preambular paragraph recognises the aspirations of indigenous peoples to exercise control over their own institutions and ways of life and to maintain and develop their identities, languages and religions within the States in which they live.

In terms of the operative provisions, an entire section - "Part VI - Education and Means of Communication" - is devoted to the educational rights of indigenous peoples. Article 26 repeats verbatim Article 21 of *Convention No. 107* but inserts the words "at least" before "an equal footing with the rest of the national community". This implicitly endorses the use of affirmative action measures in appropriate cases at the discretion of each State Party. Article 27 is a most important provision in according to indigenous peoples greater autonomy and self-determination in the educational sphere. Article 27 reads:

> 1. Education programmes and services for the peoples concerned shall be developed and implemented in co-operation with them to address their special needs, and shall incorporate their histories, their knowledge and technologies, their value systems and their further social, economic and cultural aspirations.
>
> 2. The competent authority shall ensure the training of members of these peoples and their involvement in the formulation and implementation of education programmes, with a view to the progressive transfer of responsibility for the conduct of these programmes to these peoples as appropriate.
>
> 3. In addition, governments shall recognise the right of these peoples to establish their own educational institutions and facilities, provided that such institutions meet minimum standards established by the competent authority in consultation with these peoples. Appropriate resources shall be provided for this purpose.

Article 27 is significant in at least four respects - first, it provides for a greater degree of participation by indigenous peoples in decisions which directly affect them; secondly, it prescribes a general framework for the content of indigenous educational programmes; thirdly, greater responsibility for, and control of, their educational programmes is to be handed over to indigenous peoples; and fourthly, unlike the European instruments on minority rights and U.N.E.S.C.O.'s 1960 *Convention against Discrimination in Education*, appropriate financial and other resources are to be provided by the State to enable indigenous communities to establish their own educational institutions.

Article 28 deals with the educational linguistic rights of indigenous persons and builds upon its counterpart provision - Article 23 - in *Convention No. 107.*   Article 28(1), like Article 23(1), requires that indigenous children be taught to read and write in their own indigenous language. Unlike Article 23(2) of *Convention No. 107* which provides for a progressive transition from the mother tongue to the national language, Article 28(2) merely requires that adequate measures be taken to ensure that indigenous persons have the opportunity to attain fluency in the national language. Whereas Article 23(3) merely required that appropriate measures be taken to preserve the mother tongue, Article 28(3) requires that measures be taken not only to preserve indigenous languages but to promote their development and practice as well.

Article 29 of *Convention No. 167* identifies as an aim of education for indigenous children the imparting of general knowledge and skills that will help them to participate fully and on an equal footing in their own community and in the national community. By contrast, Article 24 of *Convention No. 107* identified integration into the national community as the goal to be achieved by the imparting of such knowledge and skills. Clearly, the former provision is concerned less with integration and more with ensuring equality of opportunity. Finally, Article 31 essentially repeats Article 25 of *Convention No. 107* but does add a second sentence to the effect that efforts shall be made to ensure that history textbooks and other educational materials provide a fair and accurate portrayal of the cultures of indigenous peoples. In this context, it will be recalled that Article 7 of the *International Convention on the Elimination of All Forms of Racial Discrimination* of 1965 provides in part that "States Parties undertake to adopt immediate and effective measures, particularly in the fields of teaching, education, culture and information, with a view to combating prejudices which lead to racial discrimination . . .". More specifically, Principle 39 of U.N.E.S.C.O.'s *Recommendation Concerning Education for International Understanding, Co-operation and Peace and Education Relating to Human Rights and Fundamental Freedoms 1974* encourages Member States "to ensure that educational aids, especially textbooks, are free from elements liable to give rise to misunderstanding, mistrust, racialist reactions, contempt or hatred with regard to other groups or peoples". It is apparent, then, that *Convention No. 169* is less paternalistic and integrationist than its predecessor.

The Contribution of the United Nations to the Development of International Standards Concerning the Educational Rights of Indigenous Peoples

In response to the Cobo findings, the increasing disenchantment with *Convention No. 107* and growing pressure from non-governmental organisations (including indigenous groups), a pre-sessional Working Group on Indigenous Populations of the Sub-Commission on Prevention of Discrimination and Protection of Minorites was created by the United Nations in 1981. The Working Group reviews developments pertaining to the protection of the human rights of indigenous peoples and is also mandated to develop international standards for the protection of indigenous rights.[11]

The legal protection of indigenous peoples has been developing along separate lines from the protection of minorities since 1982 when work on the development of the United Nations *Draft Declaration on the Rights of Indigenous Peoples* was commenced by the Working Group on Indigenous Populations. After 13 years of work, with input from many indigenous representatives and organisations, the Working Group approved the *Draft Declaration* at its 1994 session and referred it to the Sub-Commission on Prevention of Discrimination and Protection of Minorities. At its 51st session in 1995, the Sub-Commission approved the *Draft Declaration* and referred it to the United Nations Commission on Human Rights. If and when approved by the Commission on Human Rights, the *Draft Declaration* will be referred to the Economic and Social Council and, from there, to the General Assembly. Upon its adoption by the General Assembly, the *Draft Declaration* will establish non-binding international standards for the rights of indigenous peoples. Amongst other things, the *Draft Declaration* encourages respect for indigenous identity and institutions and the principle of self-management, recognises the right of indigenous peoples to self-determination and their right not to be subjected to genocide, acknowledges their distinctive spiritual relationship to land, and envisages positive action by States to contribute to the maintenance of indigenous identity.

Three of the operative provisions of the *Draft Declaration* address the educational rights of indigenous peoples. Article 31 establishes the important principle that indigenous peoples have the right to self-government in matters relating to their internal and local affairs, including education. Articles 15 and 16 are more detailed:

Article 15

Indigenous children have the right to all levels and forms of education of the State. All indigenous peoples also have this right and the right to establish and control their educational systems and institutions providing education in their own languages, in a manner appropriate to their cultural methods of teaching and learning.

Indigenous children living outside their communities have the right to be provided access to education in their own culture and language.

States shall take effective measures to provide appropriate resources for these purposes.

Article 16

Indigenous peoples have the right to have the dignity and diversity of their cultures, traditions, histories and aspirations appropriately reflected in all forms of education and public information.

States shall take effective measures, in consultation with the indigenous peoples concerned, to eliminate prejudice and discrimination and to promote tolerance, understanding and good relations among indigenous peoples and all segments of society.

Article 15 prescribes four important principles - first, the right of indigenous children and peoples to education; secondly, the right of indigenous peoples to establish and control their own educational systems and institutions; thirdly, the right of such peoples to provide education in their own languages; and, fourthly, State support in the exercise of these rights. Article 15 is rather unique in two respects, however. First, unlike international and regional instruments canvassed in the previous chapter, Article 15 obliges States to take effective measures to provide appropriate resources to help achieve its purposes. "Appropriate resources" would presumably include financial, technical, material and human resources. Secondly, unlike Article 5(1)(c)(ii) of the *Convention against Discrimination in Education*, Article 13(4) of the *International Covenant on Economic, Social and Cultural Rights* and Article 29(2) of the *Convention on the Rights of the Child,* Article 15 does not refer to any requirement that the education given in indigenous educational institutions conform to minimum State standards.

The right of indigenous peoples to establish and control their own educational systems and institutions may well prove to be liberating. For example, amongst the Peruvian indigenous population, western-oriented education is regarded by many as the imposition of an alien language and culture which contributes to the loss of indigenous identity.[12] The Mapuche people of Chile have undergone a similar experience and Article 15 will assist in according greater respect for their "Mapuche Kimu" - an indigenous education system which encompasses traditional wisdom, values and techniques.[13]

Similarly, the right of indigenous peoples to provide tuition in their own languages will prevent a further loss of their identity. The policies formerly followed by a significant majority of States were based on the assumption that indigenous cultures and languages would disappear naturally or by assimilation into the national culture. Few States permitted the teaching of indigenous languages or their use as languages of instruction in the initial phases of education, fearing that it would result in linguistic insularity and excessive political and social fragmentation.[14] Contemporary experts have questioned the supposedly undesirable effects of incorporating indigenous languages into the school curriculum. Indeed, Article 15 of the *Draft Declaration* may signify increasing acceptance of the need to recognise the pluralingual and pluracultural nature of the countries inhabited by indigenous peoples. For several decades, it has been the policy of the Australian Government that Aboriginal children living in predominantly Aboriginal communities should receive their early education in their own language. Government funding has been provided in support of Aboriginal linguistic work and bilingual education programmes.[15] In Peru, the indigenous language known as 'Quechua' has been recognised since 1976 as an official language on the same footing as Spanish and has been taught at all levels of education on an obligatory basis.[16] The opening sentence of Article 16 of the *Draft Declaration* prescribes the general and minimum content of indigenous education. As a former Chairperson of the U.N. Working Group on Indigenous Populations has observed, "[t]raditional knowledge of values, autonomy or self-government, social organisation, managing ecosystems, maintaining harmony amongst peoples and respecting the land is embedded in arts, songs, poetry and literature which must be learned and renewed by each succeeding generation of indigenous children".[17]

Brief mention should also be made in this context to Article 30 of the *Convention on the Rights of the Child.* Article 30 provides in part that "[i]n those States in which . . . persons of indigenous origin exist, a child . . . who is indigenous shall not be denied the right, in community with other members of his or her group, to enjoy his or her own culture . . . or to use his or her own language". As was pointed out in Chapter 6, no provision of the *Convention on the Rights of the Child* explicitly recognises the right of indigenous peoples to use their own languages for the purposes of general teaching. The Four Directions Council, a non-governmental indigenous organisation, had unsuccessfully sought the inclusion in what is now Article 30 of a provision recognising the right of indigenous children "[t]o be educated, at least at the primary level . . . in the language of his parents as well as an official language of the State".[18] A valuable opportunity to develop the link between education, language and culture was missed. An indigenous representative has recently identified the serious consequences of such omission:

> The prohibition on indigenous languages in schools . . . [removes] the most fundamental vehicle of cultural transmission. Think how much of your own cultural transmission and the practice of your own culture depends on your native tongue, your mother tongue. To have it cut out is to be culturally orphaned; to be landed in a country with no familiar landmarks, and no point of orientation.[19]

Domestic Developments

Greater efforts are now being made in some countries to develop special programmes and materials for indigenous education. Those programmes and materials which have proved most successful in meeting the specific needs of indigenous persons have been developed with the direct participation of ethnologists, indigenous community leaders and other experts.[20] In some countries, teachers involved in indigenous education are being recruited, as far as possible, from indigenous communities and special training is provided for them, either within the communities themselves or at special teacher-training college programmes, in order to enable them to teach in their own communities.[21]

Some countries, including Canada and the United States of America, now recognise the right of indigenous communities to establish and operate their own educational institutions. In these two countries, indigenous schools are being operated and controlled locally on reserves by indigenous communities, with a portion of the funding being provided by the State.[22]   U. S. policy in this context is particularly forward-looking. Congressional recognition of the legitimacy of Indian self-determination and of the unique educational needs of Indian peoples including programmes to satisfy their linguistic and cultural aspirations, has resulted since the late 1960s in legislative and administrative measures supporting the education of Indian children in schools administered by Indian tribal organisations. The *Indian Self-Determination and Educational Assistance Act 1975* [23] directs the Secretary of the Interior, upon the request of any Indian tribe, to execute contracts with tribal organisations to administer Indian programmes previously administered by the Department of the Interior. The *Indian Education Act 1988* provides financial assistance to non-Indian schools to enable them to deliver culturally appropriate programmes and services for Indian students. Congress has also passed the *Native American Languages Act 1990* which implements a policy to protect Indian languages.   The preambular recitals of this piece of legislation refer to the unique status of Native American languages and cultures and the State responsibility to act together with Native Americans to ensure their survival. The Congressional view that "the traditional languages of Native Americans are an integral part of their cultures and identities and form the basic medium for the transmission, and thus survival, of Native American cultures, literatures, histories, religions, political institutions, and values" is also recorded.[24]

Conclusion

Although the development of the rights of indigenous peoples has recently proceeded along separate lines from the development of the rights of members of ethnic minority groups, the concluding comments articulated by the author at the end of the previous chapter on the rights of the latter generally apply as well to the situation of the former. Until the *Draft Declaration on the Rights of Indigenous Peoples* is adopted by the United Nations General Assembly, however, the protection of the educational rights of indigenous peoples will continue to lag behind the recognition afforded to the educational rights of minority groups generally.

Notes

1   (1979) U.N. Doc. No. E/CN.4/Sub.2/384/Rev.1, p. 88, para.516. See also Commission on Human Rights *Report of the Working Group on a Draft Convention on the Rights of the Child* E/CN.4/1989/48 (2 March 1989) p. 86, para. 487.

2   H. Hannum (ed.) *Documents on Autonomy and Minority Rights* (1993) 102.

3   Signed 26 June 1957; entry into force 2 June 1959. The text may be found at 328 U.N.T.S. 247. *Convention No. 107* was closed to further ratifications in 1991 when I.L.O. *Convention (No. 169) Concerning Indigenous and Tribal Peoples in Independent Countries* entered into force, and it will cease to be in force for those States which ratify the latter instrument.

4   Hannum, op. cit., 8.

5   *Convention No. 107* (as per its Article 1) applies to:

    (a) members of tribal or semi-tribal populations in independent countries whose social and economic conditions are at a less advanced stage than the stage reached by the other sections of the national community, and whose status is regulated wholly or partially by their own customs or traditions or by special laws or regulations;

    (b) members of tribal or semi-tribal populations in independent countries which are regarded as indigenous on account of their descent from the population which inhabited the country, or a geographical region to which the country belongs, at the time of conquest or colonization and which, irrespective of their legal status, live more in conformity with the social, economic and cultural institutions of that time than with the institutions of the nation to which they belong.

6   P. Thornberry *Minorities and Human Rights Law* (1991) (Minority Rights Group Report) 18.

7   E/CN.4/Sub.2/1986/7/Add.4.

8   Id. p. 10, paras. 97, 98, 106, 107 and 108.

9   Id. p. 9, paras. 89-91.

10   Id. p. 9, para. 92.

11   Hannum, op. cit., 102.

12   S. Graham-Brown "The Role of the Curriculum" in *Education Rights and Minorities* (1994) (Minority Rights Group Report) 27.

13   Paper entitled *Status of Mapuche Education in Chile,* 1993 World Indigenous Peoples' Conference: Education.

14   Cobo, op. cit., p. 11, para. 121.

15   Capotorti, op. cit., p. 86, para. 510.

16   Decree Law 21 156 (1976), Articles 1 and 2.

17   Erica-Irene Daes *Discrimination Against Indigenous Peoples: Study on the Protection of Cultural and Intellectual Property of Indigenous*

Peoples Economic and Social Council Paper E/CN.4/Sub.22/1993/28 (28 July 1993) para. 4.

18   Commission on Human Rights *Report of the Working Group on a Draft Convention on the Rights of the Child* E/CN.4/1986/39 (13 March 1986) p. 13, para. 65.

19   M. Dodson, Australian Aboriginal and Torres Strait Islander Social Justice Commissioner, *Cultural Rights and Educational Responsibilities*, The Ninth Frank Archibald Memorial Lecture delivered at the University of New England, Armidale, New South Wales on 5 September 1994, p. 10.

20   Cobo, op. cit., p. 10, paras. 100-101.

21   Id., p. 11, paras. 117-118.

22   Id., p. 11, para. 112.

23   Public Law 93-638, 4 January 1975, 88 Stat. 2203 (codified at 25 U.S.C.A. ss. 450-450n, 455-458e).

24   For greater detail, see D. Opekokew and A. Pratt "The Treaty Right to Education in Saskatchewan" (1992) 12 *Windsor Yearbook of Access to Justice* 3, 14-19.

PART III

HUMAN RIGHTS EDUCATION

8   Human Rights Education

> [I]t is impossible to defend human rights if they are unknown, and they cannot be known unless they are taught.[1]

Introduction

It has been claimed that those persons who are aware of their human rights are better able to claim them.[2]   As early as 1789, the French National Assembly recognised this in its *Declaration of the Rights of Man and of Citizens* when it proclaimed in its Preamble:

> The representatives of the people of France, formed into a National Assembly, considering that ignorance, neglect, or contempt of human rights, are the sole causes of public misfortunes and corruptions of Government, have resolved to set forth in a solemn declaration, these natural, imprescriptible, and inalienable rights: that this declaration being constantly present to the minds of the members of the body social, they may be for ever kept attentive to their rights and their duties . . .

The teaching of human rights has largely developed, however, since the founding of the United Nations, although civil liberties were taught within universities as a branch of constitutional law prior to World War II.

The purposes of human rights education have been variously stated: as an important means to create a universal human rights culture,[3]   a prerequisite for individuals and groups seeking respect for their rights and dignity,[4]   the promotion and application of human rights norms and the improvement of racial, ethnic and religious relations,[5]   and as a means to more fully realise human potential.[6]   The International Congress on Education for Human Rights and Democracy, convened by U.N.E.S.C.O. at Montreal in March, 1993, proclaimed that human rights education is itself a human right as well as a prerequisite for the realisation of other human rights, democracy and social justice.[7]

United Nations Recognition of the Right to Human Rights Education

Amongst the purposes of the United Nations listed in Article 1 of its *Charter* is the achievement of international co-operation "in promoting and encouraging respect for human rights". Article 55(c) of the *Charter* reinforces Article 1 by obliging the United Nations to "promote universal respect for, and observance of, human rights and fundamental freedoms for all without distinction".

The classical formulation of human rights education is contained, however, in the *Universal Declaration of Human Rights*. In its preambular proclamation, the United Nations General Assembly proclaimed the *Universal Declaration* "as a common standard of achievement for all peoples and all nations, to the end that every individual and every organ of society, keeping this Declaration constantly in mind, shall strive by teaching and education to promote respect for [the rights and freedoms contained in the *Declaration*]". In terms of its operative provisions, Article 26(2) states, *inter alia*, that "[e]ducation shall be directed to . . . the strengthening of respect for human rights".[8] In Resolution 217 D (III) of 10 December 1948, the General Assembly recommended that Member States use every means to publicise the text of the *Universal Declaration* and to cause it to be translated and disseminated principally in schools and other educational institutions. The Economic and Social Council subsequently invited U.N.E.S.C.O., in Resolution 314 (XI) of 24 July 1950, to encourage and facilitate teaching about the *Universal Declaration* in schools and adult education programmes.

Principle III of the *Declaration on the Promotion Among Youth of the Ideals of Peace, Mutual Respect and Understanding Between Peoples*, proclaimed by the United Nations General Assembly in Resolution 2037 (XX) of 7 December 1965, states that young people shall be brought up to respect fundamental human rights.[9] Article 7 of the *International Convention on the Elimination of All Forms of Racial Discrimination* is particularly important in this context. It reads:

> States Parties undertake to adopt immediate and effective measures, particularly in the fields of teaching, education, culture and information, with a view to combating prejudices which lead to racial discrimination and to promoting understanding, tolerance and friendship among nations and racial or ethnical groups, as well as to propagating the purposes and principles of the Charter of the United Nations, the Universal Declaration of Human Rights . . . and this Convention.

The topic of human rights education formed part of the agenda of the International Conference on Human Rights held in Teheran in 1968. On 12 May 1968, the Conference adopted Resolution XX entitled "Education of Youth in the Respect for Human Rights and Fundamental Freedoms".[10]   In the resolution, the Conference called upon all States "to ensure that all means of education should be employed so that youth grows up and develops in a spirit of respect for human dignity and for equal rights . . . without discrimination as to race, colour, language, sex or faith". U.N.E.S.C.O. was invited "to develop its programmes aimed at making children aware, from the time they start school, of respect for the dignity and rights of man and at making the principles of the Universal Declaration [of Human Rights] prevail at all levels of education . . .".

Paragraph 13 of the *Declaration on the Rights of Disabled Persons*[11] provides that "[d]isabled persons, their families and communities shall be fully informed, by all appropriate means, of the rights contained in this Declaration".   One year after the proclamation of the *Disabled Persons Declaration*, the United Nations Commission on Human Rights, in Resolution 1B (XXXII) of 11 February 1976, requested that the appropriate U.N. organs, specialised agencies and non-governmental organisations, as well as governments, promote within their respective spheres of competence a number of measures for the involvement of youth in human rights, including "[d]evelopment of a special curriculum on human rights for use in the various educational systems, whether at the primary, secondary or technical level . . . and study of the possibility of the introduction of a special curriculum on human rights in universities . . .".

Some of the various United Nations human rights instruments concerning specific groups contain provisions relevant to human rights education.   In striving to ensure to women equal rights with men in the educational field, Article 10 of the *Convention on the Elimination of All Forms of Discrimination against Women* of 1979 requires States Parties to take appropriate measures to eliminate "any stereotyped concept of the roles of men and women at all levels and in all forms of education . . . by the revision of textbooks and school programmes and the adaptation of teaching methods . . .". Similarly, in General Recommendation No. 19 on *Violence against Women*, the Committee on the Elimination of Discrimination against Women called for "preventive measures, including public information and education programmes to change attitudes concerning the roles and status of women".[12] In addition, Article 29(1)(b) of the *Convention on the Rights of the Child* of 1989 records the agreement of the States Parties that the education of the child shall be directed to "the development of respect for human rights and fundamental freedoms".

1993 proved to be a banner year for human rights education at the United Nations. In its Resolution 1993/56 of 9 March 1993, the Commission on Human Rights recommended that knowledge of human rights, both in its theoretical dimension and in its practical application, should be established as a priority in educational policies. One of the most important and comprehensive endorsements of human rights education is contained in the *Vienna Declaration and Programme of Action* adopted by the World Conference on Human Rights at Vienna in June, 1993. Paragraph 33 of the *Vienna Declaration* reads in part:

> The World Conference on Human Rights reaffirms that States are duty-bound, as stipulated in the Universal Declaration of Human Rights and the International Covenant on Economic, Social and Cultural Rights and in other international human rights instruments, to ensure that education is aimed at strengthening the respect of human rights and fundamental freedoms. The World Conference . . . emphasizes the importance of incorporating the subject of human rights education programmes and calls upon States to do so. . . [E]ducation on human rights and the dissemination of proper information, both theoretical and practical, play an important role in the promotion and respect of human rights with regard to all individuals without distinction . . . and this should be integrated in the education policies at the national as well as international levels.[13]

Nevertheless, it is conceded at the conclusion of Paragraph 33 that "resource constraints and institutional inadequacies may impede the immediate realization of these objectives". Consequently, Paragraph 34 urges governments "to increase considerably the resources allocated to programmes aiming at the establishment and strengthening of . . . human rights awareness through training, teaching and education".

The *Vienna Programme of Action* contains a section (IID.) devoted entirely to human rights education. Paragraph 78 notes the World Conference's view that human rights education is essential for fostering mutual understanding, tolerance and peace. In Paragraph 79, the World Conference calls on all States and institutions "to include human rights, humanitarian law, democracy and rule of law as subjects in the curricula of all learning institutions". States are urged by Paragraph 81 to "develop specific programmes and strategies for ensuring the widest human rights education". Paragraph 82, the final paragraph contained in the section, states in part:

Governments, with the assistance of intergovernmental organizations, national institutions and non-governmental organizations, should promote an increased awareness of human rights and mutual tolerance. The World Conference . . . underlines the importance of strengthening the World Public Information Campaign for Human Rights carried out by the United Nations. They should initiate and support education in human rights and undertake effective dissemination of public information in this field. The advisory services and technical assistance programmes of the United Nations system should be able to respond immediately to requests from States for educational and training activities in the field of human rights as well as for special education concerning standards as contained in international human rights instruments and in humanitarian law and their application to special groups such as military forces, law enforcement personnel, police and the health profession.

The final sentence of Paragraph 82 urged the consideration of the proclamation of a United Nations decade for human rights education.

Two further developments occurred in 1993 in the human rights education context. In Resolution 48/141 the United Nations General Assembly vested responsibility in the United Nations High Commissioner for Human Rights to co-ordinate relevant United Nations education and public information programmes in the human rights field. In its Resolution 48/127, the General Assembly, after noting its view in a preambular recital that "human rights education is a universal priority", requested the Commission on Human Rights to consider proposals for a United Nations decade for human rights education. In the same resolution, the General Assembly appealed to all governments to direct education to the strengthening of respect for human rights and urged governmental and non-governmental educational agencies to intensify their efforts to establish and implement programmes of human rights education, as recommended in the *Vienna Declaration and Programme of Action.* In Resolution 1994/51, the Commission on Human Rights endorsed the proposal for such a decade. The ten-year period beginning on 1 January 1995 was officially proclaimed the United Nations Decade for Human Rights Education by General Assembly Resolution 49/184. In the same resolution, the General Assembly requested the United Nations High Commissioner for Human Rights to co-ordinate the implementation of the *Plan of Action for the United Nations Decade for Human Rights Education, 1995-2005*[14] and urged governmental and non-governmental educational agencies to implement national programmes of human rights education. A plea was also made to non-governmental organisations, human rights advocates, educators, religious organisations and the media to increase their involvement in formal and non-formal human rights education.

The Contribution of the United Nations Specialised Agencies to Human Rights Education

Amongst the respective contributions of the various U.N. specialised agencies to the development of human rights education, those of the International Labour Organisation and U.N.E.S.C.O. stand out. In terms of the I.L.O., Article 3(b) of the *Convention Concerning Discrimination in Respect of Employment and Occupation (No. 111),1958*, obliges Member States to undertake "to promote such educational programmes as may be calculated to secure the acceptance and observance [of national policies aimed at equality of opportunity and treatment in employment and occupation]".   Articles 30 and 31 of the I.L.O. *Convention Concerning Indigenous and Tribal Peoples in Independent Countries (No. 169), 1989* are somewhat more detailed:

Article 30

(1) Governments shall adopt measures appropriate to the traditions and cultures of the peoples concerned, to make known to them their rights and duties, especially in regard to labour, economic opportunities, education and health matters, social welfare and their rights deriving from this Convention.

(2) If necessary, this shall be done by means of written translations and through the use of mass communications in the languages of these peoples.

Article 31

Educational measures shall be taken among all sections of the national community, and particularly among those that are in most direct contact with the peoples concerned, with the object of eliminating prejudices that they may harbour in respect of these peoples. To this end, efforts shall be made to ensure that history textbooks and other educational materials provide a fair, accurate and informative portrayal of the societies and cultures of these peoples.

It will be recalled[15] that one of the purposes of U.N.E.S.C.O. mentioned in Article I(1) of its *Constitution* [16] is "to contribute to peace and security by promoting collaboration among the nations through education, science and culture in order to further universal respect for . . . human rights . . .". It is not surprising, therefore, that initiatives to stimulate human rights teaching in schools have formed an integral part of U.N.E.S.C.O.'s educational programme for international understanding and teaching about the United Nations. Such initiatives have included studies of teaching methods and programmes, international and regional seminars and conferences, publications, the revision of textbooks,[17] and the provision of consultative services to Member States and to teacher-training institutions assisted under the United Nations Development Programme.[18] U.N.E.S.C.O. has also provided financial assistance to educational institutions in developing countries for the preparation of human rights programmes.

An early U.N.E.S.C.O. initiative took the form of a 1951 survey which provided the basis for a 1952 international seminar on human rights teaching held in the Netherlands. This resulted in the publication by U.N.E.S.C.O. in 1953 of *The Universal Declaration of Human Rights: A Guide for Teachers* which contained practical suggestions on human rights teaching. A flurry of initiatives in this area were undertaken by U.N.E.S.C.O. in the 1970s. Pursuant to Resolution 17 (XXIX) of 3 April 1973, the United Nations Commission on Human Rights requested U.N.E.S.C.O. "to . . . encourage teaching and research in human rights in universities . . .". A textbook entitled *The International Dimensions of Human Rights* was published in 1978 for use by university law and political science faculties. In November, 1974, the U.N.E.S.C.O. General Conference adopted the *Recommendation Concerning Education for International Understanding, Co-operation and Peace and Education Relating to Human Rights and Fundamental Freedoms 1974* which contains multiple references to human rights education. Paragraph 11 thereof urges Member States to "take steps to ensure that the principles of the Universal Declaration of Human Rights and of the International Convention on the Elimination of All Forms of Racial Discrimination become an integral part of the developing personality of each child, adolescent, young person or adult by applying these principles in the daily conduct of education at each level and in all its forms . . .". Paragraph 39 recommends that Member States should ensure that educational materials are free from elements liable to give rise to contempt or hatred with regard to other groups or peoples.[19]

Four initiatives undertaken by U.N.E.S.C.O. in 1978 bear mention. The International Congress on the Teaching of Human Rights, a joint initiative of U.N.E.S.C.O. and the Austrian Government, was held at Vienna in September, 1978. Pursuant to various recommendations adopted by the Congress, a meeting of experts prepared a Plan for the Development of the Teaching of Human Rights which was later approved by the U.N.E.S.C.O. General Conference. The Plan was essentially aimed at developing teaching materials and methods as well as the exchange of relevant information.[20] For the first time in 1978, a U.N.E.S.C.O. Prize for Human Rights Education was awarded "to encourage or stimulate new educational initiatives in human rights education".[21] Two declarations proclaimed in 1978 by the U.N.E.S.C.O. General Conference refer to human rights education. Article IV of the *Declaration on Fundamental Principles Concerning the Contributions of the Mass Media to Strengthening Peace and International Understanding, to the Promotion of Human Rights and to Countering Racialism, Apartheid and Incitement to War* acknowledges the essential role of the mass media "in the education of young people . . . in order to promote human rights".[22] Article 5(2) of the *Declaration on Race and Racial Prejudice* provides in part:

> States . . . and the entire teaching profession, have a responsibility to see that the educational resources of all countries are used to combat racism, more especially by ensuring that curricula and textbooks include scientific and ethical considerations concerning human unity and diversity . . . by training teachers to achieve these ends; by making the resources of the educational system available to all groups of the population without racial restriction or discrimination; and by taking appropriate steps to remedy the handicaps from which certain racial or ethnic groups suffer with regard to their level of education . . .[23]

Since 1980, U.N.E.S.C.O. has published a bulletin entitled *Teaching of Human Rights* which seeks to establish liaison between human rights teachers and researchers.[24] More recent U.N.E.S.C.O. initiatives include the International Congress on Human Rights Teaching, Information and Documentation held at Malta in September, 1987[25] and the 1993 International Congress on Education for Human Rights and Democracy held at Montreal.

Regional Human Rights Education

Various human rights education initiatives have been undertaken at the regional level, ranging from provisions contained in legally binding and non-binding instruments to the establishment of special institutes and programmes and the convening of conferences and seminars.

In terms of the Inter-American human rights system, Article 13(2) of the *Additional Protocol to the American Convention on Human Rights in the Area of Economic, Social and Cultural Rights* records the agreement of the States Parties that education should be directed towards the full development of human dignity and strengthening respect for human rights and fundamental freedoms. Although there are no relevant binding Asian standards, several references to human rights education appear in *The Bangkok Declaration* which was adopted on 2 April 1993 by Asian States at a regional meeting in the context of preparations for the 1993 Vienna World Conference on Human Rights. The final preambular recital stresses "the importance of education and training in human rights at the national, regional and international levels and the need for international co-operation aimed at overcoming the lack of public awareness of human rights". Operative Paragraph 27 of the *Declaration* reiterates "the need to explore ways to generate international co-operation and financial support for education and training in the field of human rights at the national level".

Human rights education has been dealt with more systematically within the African and European human rights systems. In terms of conventional recognition, Article 25 of the *African Charter on Human and Peoples' Rights* of 1981 imposes a duty on States Parties "to promote and ensure through teaching, education and publication, the respect of the rights and freedoms contained in the present Charter and to see to it that these freedoms and rights . . . are understood."[26] Human rights teaching in Africa has generally proceeded in the form of international symposia and seminars conducted by the United Nations, African jurists, universities and non-governmental organisations since 1961.[27] It was not until 1979 that the Senegalese Bar Association, inspired by the U.N.E.S.C.O.-sponsored International Congress on the Teaching of Human Rights held in Vienna the previous year, created the African Institute of Human Rights.[28] The Institute is a non-governmental organisation whose programme consists of:

- the dissemination of knowledge on human rights;

- the development of specialised education in human rights for the benefit of the professions, jurists and activists, whose vocation is teaching, defending and protecting those rights.

The Institute's activities include teaching and research sessions, conferences and seminars, exchanges with similar organisations and the publication of books and periodicals.[29] Another significant initiative in this area was the creation, with the assistance of U.N.E.S.C.O., of the

Institute of Human Rights and Peace which is affiliated with the Faculty of Law and Economics of the University of Dakar, Senegal. In collaboration with the United Nations, U.N.E.S.C.O., the World Health Organisation, the International Labour Organization and non-governmental organisations, the Institute's principal activities include:

- tuition in human rights particularly for judges, lawyers, professors, jurists, diplomats, doctors, members of national Red Cross and Red Crescent societies, members of military forces, politicians, trade unionists, journalists and teachers;

- research, documentation and dissemination of information on human rights;

- the organisation of national and international symposia and seminars on human rights.

The European counterpart to these African institutes is the International Institute of Human Rights located in Strasbourg. U.N.E.S.C.O. assists the Strasbourg Institute in the organisation of its annual training sessions, and especially in the programme that enables university teachers and professionals from the world over to acquire practical knowledge about the international protection of human rights.[30] Unlike the Inter-American and African systems, provisions on human rights education are not to be found as such in any legally binding European regional human rights instruments. Nevertheless, such provisions can be found in several non-binding instruments. For example, in its 1981 *Declaration regarding Intolerance - A Threat to Democracy*, the Committee of Ministers of the Council of Europe agreed in Paragraph IV(iii) thereof to urge Member States to promote through education an awareness of the requirements of human rights. Similarly in *Recommendation No. R(85)7 on Teaching and Learning About Human Rights in Schools, 1985*, the Committee of Ministers recommended that the governments of Member States, within their national educational systems, encourage teaching and learning about human rights. The Conference on Security and Co-operation in Europe has also considered human rights education issues from time to time in various documents. For example, Principle 13.6 of the *Concluding Document from the Vienna Meeting*[31] refers to the desirability of considering tuition in the protection and promotion of human rights within schools and other educational institutions. In October, 1993, the Heads of State and Government of the Member States of the Council of Europe, meeting at the Vienna Summit

Conference, adopted a *Declaration and Plan of Action on combating racism, xenophobia, antisemitism and intolerance.*[32]   As part of the *Plan of Action*, the Committee of Ministers were instructed to develop and implement a European Youth Campaign "to mobilise the public in favour of a tolerant society based on the equal dignity of all its members and against manifestations of racism, xenophobia, antisemitism and intolerance". It was envisaged that this would be achieved through, *inter alia*, the promotion of human rights education.[33]   Since its official opening in December, 1994, the European Youth Campaign has been implemented through the agency of national committees in almost 40 European countries. While the campaign was intended to be aimed at all sectors of society, it primarily involved young people in a wide range of activities at all levels.[34]

Human Rights Education: The Curriculum and Methods, Agents and Recipients of Dissemination

As we have seen earlier in this chapter, States have assumed a legal obligation under international human rights law to take appropriate measures to provide human rights education. While primary responsibility in this regard is vested in States, they will need to be assisted in their efforts by various organisations and individuals which will be mentioned shortly.

Possible topics for inclusion in a human rights education curriculum include:

- the dignity of human beings;

- equality of rights and opportunities;

- democracy and the rule of law;

- the human rights of women, children and persons with disabilities;

- the elimination of racial, ethnic and religious discrimination;

- the development of a sense of individual moral and social responsibility; and

- the improvement of inter-group relations through the teaching of different cultures and languages.[35]

According to the international and regional instruments, human rights education is to be provided at all levels of education in both formal and non-formal settings. In terms of the methods of teaching, such education may be delivered either as part of a course unit designed specifically for the purpose (such as units on human rights and equal opportunity law, humanitarian law and constitutional law) or as part of a wider discipline such as history or political science. Indeed, such interdisciplinary and multidisciplinary approaches to human rights education may benefit from the diversity of knowledge and methodologies developed in other branches of education.[36]

The more obvious candidates for human rights education would include:

- those involved in the administration of justice, such as judges, prosecutors, defence lawyers, police and prison guards;

- members of the health profession;

- members of the armed services;

- politicians and public servants;

- children and their parents;

- members of the mass media; and

- members of the teaching profession.

The delivery of human rights education will be achieved through the efforts of various organisations and individuals under the co-ordinated direction of the State. The partners in this venture will generally include:

- members of the teaching profession;

- universities and other institutions of higher learning. Many universities now provide tuition and research in human rights within law and medical faculties, political science departments and research centres. The contributions of such institutions and their libraries can also extend to the preparation of publications (such as textbooks, training manuals and periodicals) and bibliographies and the use of various information retrieval systems;

- non-governmental organisations, social justice groups, religious organisations and human rights activists;

- intergovernmental organisations. International intergovernmental organisations such as U.N.E.S.C.O., U.N.I.C.E.F., the International Labour Organization and the World Health Organization have played, and will continue to play, a significant role in promoting human rights education. National commissions supporting U.N.E.S.C.O. can play a pivotal role in the translation and dissemination of human rights teaching materials;

- members of the mass media. Through the electronic and print media, journalists can contribute indirectly to human rights education by covering human rights violations and exposing the perpetrators thereof.

Perhaps the most effective forum for human rights teaching is in the primary school system where such teaching may be conveniently incorporated into civic instruction classes. As one commentator has remarked, ". . . familiarization of human rights at an early age is the source of self-respect and respect for others".[37] Recent experience suggests that States Parties to the *Convention on the Rights of the Child* have undertaken practical and successful measures to fulfil their obligations under Article 42 "to make the principles and provisions of the Convention widely known, by appropriate and active means, to adults and children alike". In Burkina Faso, for example, an advocacy kit on children's rights has been produced and distributed nationwide to teachers to educate school children about their rights.[38] In Colombia, the Government's public awareness campaign concerning the *Convention on the Rights of the Child* entitled "There Are No Small Rights" is being conducted through the schools and the media. Several States Parties are conducting training programmes for teachers, and educators in the Dominican Republic are now relying on the "Teachers' Guide on the Rights of Children".[39] In 1991, Denmark also launched a campaign to convey the principles of the *Convention* to the public by producing and distributing materials on children's rights to students enrolled in the first to the tenth grades.[40]

International Technical Co-operation and Monitoring

It will be recalled that Article 13(1) of the *International Covenant on Economic, Social and Cultural Rights* provides that education shall be directed, *inter alia*, to the strengthening of respect for human rights.

Pursuant to Article 2(1) of the *Covenant*, each State Party "undertakes to take steps, individually and through international assistance and co-operation, especially economic and technical . . . with a view to achieving progressively the full realization of the rights recognized in the . . . Covenant . . .". International assistance and technical co-operation would presumably extend, therefore, to the delivery of human rights education. Paragraph 82 of the *Vienna Programme of Action* adopted by the 1993 World Conference on Human Rights provides in more direct terms that "[t]he advisory services and technical assistance programmes of the United Nations system should be able to respond immediately to requests from States for educational and training activities in the field of human rights . . .". In operative Paragraph 6 of Resolution 48/127 (1993), the United Nations General Assembly invited the U.N. specialised agencies and United Nations programmes to develop suitable activities in their respective fields of competence to further the objectives of human rights education. It is anticipated that U.N.E.S.C.O., U.N.I.C.E.F., the World Health Organisation and the International Labour Organisation would have particularly significant contributions to make in this regard.

As regards international monitoring, the reporting guidelines adopted by the monitoring bodies set up under the *International Covenant on Economic, Social and Cultural Rights*, the *Convention on the Rights of the Child*, the *Convention on the Elimination of All Forms of Discrimination Against Women* and the *International Convention on the Elimination of All Forms of Racial Discrimination* appear to require information concerning human rights education.[41] These monitoring bodies have occasionally expressed dissatisfaction with the quality, and lack, of information concerning human rights education provided in State reports. For example, the Committee on the Elimination of Racial Discrimination noted with regret in General Recommendation No. V that information on Article 7 of the *Racial Discrimination Convention*, if submitted, was often "general and perfunctory".[42] In recent resolutions, the United Nations General Assembly has urged the human rights monitoring bodies to place particular emphasis on the implementation by U.N. Member States of their international obligation to promote human rights education.[43] This state of affairs has prompted one leading commentator in this area to call for the creation of a mandate for a special rapporteur or working group on human rights education to systematically collect and scrutinise human rights teaching materials.[44] Mention should also be made of the informal monitoring role performed by non-governmental organisations. They maintain pressure on governments to honour their international commitments by monitoring governmental action or inaction, as the case may be. Indeed, it has been claimed that newsletters and bulletins published and circulated by N.G.O.s today constitute the best sources of information concerning human rights educational materials.[45]

Progress towards a fuller implementation of the human right to human rights education will continue to be hindered by a number of factors, including illiteracy, limited resources and vested political interests. One of the most pressing problems is the lack of adequate language translations of the major human rights instruments and teaching materials prepared by the United Nations and U.N.E.S.C.O. Secretariats. Language must be used which has been adapted to the needs of those being educated in order to transmit the message effectively and facilitate comprehension.[46] Translations in languages other than those officially adopted within the United Nations (Arabic, Chinese, English, French, Russian and Spanish) must be undertaken to ensure the more effective guarantee of the rights of individuals and groups.

Notes

1   M. Seck "A Plea for Human Rights Education in Africa" (1990) 11 *Human Rights Law Journal* 283, 295.
2   D. Ray and N. Tarrow "Human Rights and Education: An Overview" in N. Tarrow (ed.) *Human Rights and Education* (1987) 3,4.
3   M. Nowak "The Right to Education" in A. Eide (ed.) *Economic, Social and Cultural Rights* (1995) 189-190.
4   G. Alfredsson "The Right to Human Rights Education" in id. 213.
5   Id. 222.
6   Preamble to United Nations General Assembly Resolution 49/184, 49 U.N. GAOR Supp. (No. 49) at 202, U.N. Doc. A/49/49 (1994).
7   The Congress adopted a *World Plan of Action on Education for Human Rights and Democracy.* See U.N. Doc. A/CONF. 157/PC/42/Add.6.
8   See to the same effect Article 13(1) of the *International Covenant on Economic, Social and Cultural Rights.*
9   See also Principles II and VI.
10   See *Final Act of the International Conference on Human Rights* (United Nations publication, Sales No. E.68.XIV.2).
11   Proclaimed by the United Nations General Assembly in Resolution 3447 (XXX) of 9 December 1975.
12   U.N. Doc. A/47/38.
13   U.N. Doc. A/CONF.157/23, Part I, para. 33.
14   As contained in the report of the Secretary-General A/49/261-E/1994/110/Add.1, annex.

15   See Chapter 3.
16   *Constitution of the United Nations Educational, Scientific and Cultural Organisation* (signed at London on 16 November 1945) 4 U.N.T.S. 275.
17   U.N.E.S.C.O. has organised several multilateral consultations concerning the revision of history, geography and social sciences textbooks for primary, secondary and higher education.
18   United Nations *United Nations Action in the Field of Human Rights* (1988) p. 356, para. 151.
19   See also Paragraph 7 (each Member State to formulate and apply national policies aimed at strengthening respect for, and application of, human rights); Paragraph 18(c) (education should relate to action to ensure the exercise and observance of human rights); Paragraph 33(a) (Member States should instil within teachers a commitment to human rights).
20   United Nations *United Nations Action in the Field of Human Rights* (1988) p. 357, paras. 165-166. In addition, a Voluntary Fund for the development of human rights teaching was adopted by the Executive Board of U.N.E.S.C.O. to provide funds for financing the implementation of the Plan for the Development of the Teaching of Human Rights.
21   Id. p. 358, para. 172. Article 1 of the *Regulations of the U.N.E.S.C.O. Prize for Human Rights Education* reads:
                The U.N.E.S.C.O. Prize for Human Rights Education shall be awarded in recognition of activities aimed at developing human rights education. The Prize shall be open to educational and training institutions, organizations and individuals that have made a particularly deserving and effective contribution to the development of human rights education, in keeping with the spirit of the Charter of the United Nations and the Constitution of U.N.E.S.C.O. and in the light of the principles set forth in the Universal Declaration of Human Rights, and in the International Covenants on Human Rights and with due account taken of the provisions of the U.N.E.S.C.O. Recommendation on Education for International Understanding, Co-operation and Peace, and Education relating to Human Rights and Fundamental Freedoms. The Prize shall be awarded to encourage or stimulate new educational initiatives in human rights education.
22   See also Article 5(3) of the U.N.E.S.C.O. *Declaration on Race and Racial Prejudice* which, *inter alia*, urges the mass media to contribute to the eradication of racism.
23   Other provisions of the *Declaration on Race and Racial Prejudice* which concern human rights education include Articles 5(3), 6(2) and (3) and 8(2) and (3).
24   United Nations *United Nations Action in the Field of Human Rights* (1988) p. 358, para. 174.
25   The *Malta Recommendations* are contained in U.N.E.S.C.O. doc. SHS-87/CONF.401/15 of 16 May 1988.

26   See also Article 45 of the *African Charter* concerning the role of the African Commission on Human and Peoples' Rights in this regard.
27   M. Seck, op. cit., 291.
28   Id. 284.
29   Id. 290.
30   United Nations *United Nations Action in the Field of Human Rights* (1988) p. 358, para. 171.
31   15 January 1989, (1989) 28 *International Legal Materials* 527.
32   As contained in Appendix III to the *Vienna Declaration* adopted at the Council of Europe Summit, 9 October 1993.
33   Paragraph 4 of the *Plan of Action.*
34   http://www.uni-marburg.de/dir/GRUPPEN/PROJEKTE/EYC/finalreport.html.
35   Alfredsson, op. cit., 223.
36   Seck, op. cit., 298.
37   Id. 297.
38   http://www.unicef.org/crc/success/wca.html.
39   http://www.unicef.org/pon96/corights.html.
40   http://www.unicef.org/pon96/cogowar.html.
41   Alfredsson, op. cit., 226.
42   U.N. Doc. A/32/18 (reproduced in U.N. Doc. HRI/GEN/1, pp. 57-58).
43   See operative Paragraph 9 of U.N. General Assembly Resolution 48/127 of 1993 and operative Paragraph 13 of U.N. General Assembly Resolution 49/184 of 1994.
44   Alfredsson, op. cit., 226.
45   Id. 226-7.
46   Seck, op. cit., 297.

PART IV

SPECIALISED EDUCATION AND SPECIFIC GROUPS AND ISSUES

9 The Educational Rights of the Disabled

[T]he physical and mental handicaps which affect millions of children all over the world ought also to be given particular attention, for it is essential, both for moral . . . and for economic reasons, that such children, to whom fate has been unkind but who are perfectly capable of overcoming their handicaps, should not be excluded from the life of society; they have a right to an education adapted to their situation.[1]

Introduction

Some fifty years have now elapsed since the behavioural and physical abnormalities of persons with disabilities marked them for destruction in Nazi Germany. According to one commentator, "[p]rejudice, discrimination, aversion and habit are factors explaining the prior invisibility of the world's disabled population as a human rights concern".[2] Paragraph 1 of the *Declaration on the Rights of Disabled Persons* proclaimed by the United Nations General Assembly in Resolution 3447 (XXX) of 9 December 1975 defines the term "disabled person" as "any person unable to ensure by himself or herself, wholly or partly, the necessities of a normal individual and/or social life, as a result of deficiency, either congenital or not, in his or her physical or mental capabilities".[3] Disabilities commonly result from mental and physical impairments such as hearing, sight and speech problems.

Recognition Within the United Nations of the Educational Rights of the Disabled

Only one reference to disability appears in the *Universal Declaration of Human Rights* of 1948 in a general rather than an educational context. Article 25(1) provides in part that "[e]veryone has the right to . . . security in the event of unemployment, sickness, disability, widowhood, old age or other lack of livelihood in circumstances beyond his control". The *Declaration of the Rights of the Child* of 1959 affirms the disabled child's right to special education. Paragraph 5 thereof states that "[t]he child who is physically, mentally or socially handicapped shall be given the special treatment, education and care required by his particular condition". The United Nations and various non-governmental organisations were not content with such broadly stated principles. At its 1968 International Congress in Jerusalem, the International League of Societies for the Mentally Handicapped proclaimed a *Declaration of General and Special Rights of the Mentally Retarded*. A consensus emerged amongst non-governmental organisations that specific declarations should complement universal declarations and that specifically defined rights of disabled persons contained in the former were in addition to, and not in lieu of, general human rights contained in the latter.[4] This appears to have been the intent of the *Declaration on the Rights of Disabled Persons* and the *Declaration on the Rights of Mentally Retarded Persons* proclaimed by the United Nations General Assembly in Resolution 2856 (XXVI) of 20 December 1971.

Although the 1971 and 1975 *Declarations* were not legally binding as a matter of international or municipal law, they did have powers of moral and political suasion which were used effectively by lobby groups in the 1970s and 1980s to secure important national policy changes.[5] Both the 1971 and 1975 *Declarations* were underpinned by a desire to assist mentally retarded and disabled persons to develop their abilities in various fields and to promote their integration as far as possible in normal life. Both *Declarations* sought to elaborate upon earlier human rights standards in the form of a set of minimum guidelines to inform national policy-making, and to provide a firmer foundation for the international evolution of even more detailed (and eventually binding) standards. Paragraph 2 of the *Declaration on the Rights of Mentally Retarded Persons* of 1971 stated that "[t]he mentally retarded person has a right to . . . such education, training, rehabilitation and guidance as will enable him to develop his ability and maximum potential".[6] The *Declaration of the Rights of Disabled Persons* of 1975 builds upon the 1971 *Declaration* and prescribes in somewhat more detail the entitlements of disabled persons to measures that will "enable them to become as self-reliant as possible" (Principle 5). Paragraph 6 of the 1975 *Declaration* recognises the right of disabled persons to " . . . education, vocational training and rehabilitation, aid, counselling, placement services and other services which will enable them to develop their capabilities and skills to the maximum and will hasten the processes of social integration or reintegration".

The importance of the integration of the disabled person within the community was reaffirmed by the Conference on the Legal Protection of the Rights of the Child held in Warsaw in January, 1979. Principle 7 of the *Official Statement of Principles* adopted by the Conference articulated the view that "[a]lthough it is desirable to provide special educational facilities for children who are exceptional either in their talents or in their handicaps, it is important that their education should, so far as possible, be integrated with that of other children".

In 1976, the United Nations General Assembly designated 1981 as the "International Year of Disabled Persons" (IYDP). The authorising resolution[7] declared "full participation and equality" as the year's central theme and set down a number of objectives to be carried out during the IYDP including the promotion of "efforts to provide disabled people with proper assistance, training, care and guidance", the education of the public concerning the rights of disabled persons, and the implementation of the 1971 and 1975 *Declarations*. The Advisory Committee on the IYDP issued recommendations on measures that U.N. Member States might adopt and urged the review of existing legislation "to eliminate possible discriminatory practices regarding the education and employment of disabled persons".[8]

The most important outcome of the IYDP, however, was the adoption of the *World Programme of Action concerning Disabled Persons* by the United Nations General Assembly in its Resolution 37/52 of 3 December 1982. The purposes of the *Programme of Action* included the promotion of effective measures for rehabilitation, for the prevention of disability and for the realisation of the goals of full and equal participation of disabled persons in social life and development. General Assembly Resolution 37/53 of 3 December 1982 proclaimed the period 1983-1992 the "United Nations Decade of Disabled Persons" as a long-term plan of action to implement the *Programme of Action*.

The most comprehensive international norms pertaining to the rights of the disabled child appear in Article 23 of the *Convention on the Rights of the Child*. The first three sub-articles of Article 23 read:

(1) States Parties recognize that a mentally or physically disabled child should enjoy a full and decent life, in conditions which ensure dignity, promote self-reliance, and facilitate the child's active participation in the community.

(2) States Parties recognize the right of the disabled child to special care and shall encourage and ensure the extension, subject to available resources, to the eligible child and those responsible for his or her care, of

sistance for which application is made and which is appropriate to the child's condition and to the circumstances of the parents or others caring for the child.

(3) Recognizing the special needs of a disabled child, assistance extended in accordance with paragraph 2 shall be provided free of charge, whenever possible, taking into account the financial resources of the parents or others caring for the child, and shall be designed to ensure that the disabled child has effective access to and receives education, training, health care services, rehabilitation services, preparation for employment and recreation opportunities in a manner conducive to the child's achieving the fullest possible social integration and individual development, including his or her cultural and spiritual development.

Like the previous instruments, Article 23 emphasises social integration and individual development. It does succeed in enhancing the legal protection of the rights of disabled children as, prior to the adoption of the *Convention on the Rights of the Child*, there existed relatively few binding international standards in this area.[9] Nevertheless, several deficiencies can be identified. First, the combined effect of sub-articles (2) and (3) of Article 23 is such that the disabled child's right to education is subject to available State resources and shall be provided free of charge "whenever possible, taking into account the financial resources of the parents or others caring for the child". A revised Polish draft of what is now Article 23, supported by Canada and the U.S.S.R., had unsuccessfully proposed that the special educational needs of disabled children should be provided free of charge.[10] Secondly, as one leading commentator in the children's rights area has observed, it is unfortunate that the *Convention on* *the Rights of the Child* fails to impose upon States Parties a legal obligation either to promote or to deliver pre-school educational services.[11] Through a combined operation of Articles 2(1) and 28(1) of the *Convention*, a disabled child has an equal right of access to education only as from the primary school level.[12] As the same commentator has pointed out, pre-school education is important for children with disabilities as it can be used for the early identification of impairment and as a method for involving parents in the educational process.[13]

The World Conference on Human Rights held in Vienna in June, 1993 reaffirmed in Paragraph 63 of its *Programme of Action* that:

. . . . all human rights and fundamental freedoms are universal and thus unreservedly include persons with disabilities. Every person is born equal and has the same rights to . . . education and work . . . Any . . .

discriminatory treatment of a disabled person is therefore a violation of his or her rights. The World Conference on Human Rights calls on Governments . . . to adopt . . . legislation to assure access to these . . . rights for disabled persons.

In Paragraph 65 of its *Programme of Action*, the World Conference called on the United Nations General Assembly "to adopt the draft standard rules on the equalization of opportunities for persons with disabilities" which had emerged from the *World Programme of Action concerning Disabled Persons* which the General Assembly had endorsed in 1982.

The United Nations General Assembly did indeed heed the World Conference's call by adopting in its Resolution 48/96 of 1993 the *Standard Rules on the Equalization of Opportunities for Persons with Disabilities* and requested U.N. Member States to apply the *Rules* in developing national disability programmes. After an unsuccessful attempt by the General Assembly to agree on an international convention on the elimination of all forms of discrimination against persons with disabilities, it was agreed to formulate the non-binding *Standard Rules* on the basis of the experience gained during the United Nations Decade of Disabled Persons (1983-1992). The purpose of the *Rules* is to ensure that persons with disabilities may exercise the same rights as other persons. Although they are not legally binding, the *Rules* are founded on a strong moral and political commitment amongst U.N. Member States and provide a basis for mutual technical and economic co-operation. From the standpoint of persons with disabilities and their representative organisations, the *Rules* offer policy-making leverage and an advocacy platform.

Rule 6 of the *Standard Rules* comprises nine sub-rules which directly concern the educational entitlements of persons with disabilities. Since they are the most detailed norms yet to be developed, it is appropriate to set them out in full as follows:[14]

Rule 6. Education

States should recognize the principle of equal primary, secondary and tertiary educational opportunities for children, youth and adults with disabilities, in integrated settings. They should ensure that the education of persons with disabilities is an integral part of the educational system.

1. General educational authorities are responsible for the education of persons with disabilities in integrated settings. Education for persons with disabilities should form an integral part of national educational planning, curriculum development and school organization.

2.   Education in mainstream schools presupposes the provision of interpreter and other appropriate support services. Adequate accessibility and support services, designed to meet the needs of persons with different disabilities, should be provided.

3.   Parent groups and organizations of persons with disabilities should be involved in the education process at all levels.

4.   In States where education is compulsory it should be provided to girls and boys with all kinds and all levels of disabilities, including the most severe.

5.   Special attention should be given in the following areas:

(a)   Very young children with disabilities;

(b)   Pre-school children with disabilities;

(c)   Adults with disabilities, particularly women.

6.   To accommodate educational provisions for persons with disabilities in the mainstream, States should:

(a)   Have a clearly stated policy, understood and accepted at the school level and by the wider community;

(b)   Allow for curriculum flexibility, addition and adaptation;

(c)   Provide for quality materials, ongoing teacher training and support teachers.

7.   Integrated education and community-based programmes should be seen as complementary approaches in providing cost-effective education and training for persons with disabilities. National community-based programmes should encourage communities to use and develop their resources to provide local education to persons with disabilities.

Rule 6 is unremarkable to the extent that it reaffirms the principle of equality of educational opportunity for disabled children and the delivery of that education in most cases within an integrated mainstream setting. These entitlements were secured, as we have just seen, by Articles 2 and 23 of the *Convention on the Rights of the Child.* Several other features of Rule 6, however, are noteworthy. First, Rule 6 applies to all persons with disabilities. Secondly, Rule 6(3) innovatively recognises the involvement of parent groups and disabled persons themselves in the educational process. Thirdly, unlike the *Convention on the Rights of the Child*, Rule 6(5) singles out for special attention pre-school children with disabilities. Fourthly, Rule 6(7) introduces the notion that the education and training of persons with disabilities should be 'cost-effective'. This goes beyond the requirements stipulated by Article 23 of the *Convention on the Rights of the Child.* In its Resolution 49/153 of 1994, the United Nations General Assembly urged all governments to implement the *Standard Rules* and welcomed the appointment of a Special Rapporteur on Disability to monitor their implementation and to submit reports to the Commission for Social Development.

Various United Nations agencies and instrumentalities have made significant contributions to developing standards of treatment and protection for disabled persons. These include the World Health Organization, U.N.I.C.E.F., the United Nations Development Programme, the U.N. Commission for Social Development and the Disabled Persons Unit of the U.N. Secretariat. The most notable contributions in the educational sector have come from U.N.E.S.C.O. and the International Labour Organization. U.N.E.S.C.O.'s *Revised Recommendation concerning Technical and Vocational Education* of 1974 suggests that vocational and technical education should be available to disadvantaged and disabled persons in a manner which caters for their needs and facilitates an easier integration into society. As part of its drive towards the democratisation of education, U.N.E.S.C.O. adopted its *Second Medium-Term Plan (1984-1989) Education for All* which, *inter alia*, sought to promote the educational rights of particular groups, including the disabled. The learning needs of the disabled were also considered at the U.N.E.S.C.O.-sponsored 1990 World Conference on Education for All. Article 3(5) of the *World Declaration on Education for All* adopted by the Conference acknowledged that "[s]teps need to be taken to provide equal access to education to every category of disabled persons as an integral part of the education system". This call has been answered by Rule 6 of the *Standard Rules on the Equalization of Opportunities for Persons with Disabilities.* As for the International Labour Organization, Article 45(2) of the I.L.O. *Recommendation on Vocational Guidance and Vocational Training in the Development of Human Resources, 1975 (No. 150)* essentially reiterates U.N.E.S.C.O.'s *Revised Recommendation concerning Technical and Vocational Education.* Mention should also be made of the *Vocational Rehabilitation and Employment (Disabled Persons)*

Convention, 1983 (No. 159) adopted by the I.L.O. General Conference on 22 June 1983.

Regional Recognition of the Educational Rights of the Disabled

The African, American and European human rights systems have all recognised in treaty form the educational entitlements of persons with disabilities. Article 100(d) of the *Charter of the Organization of American States* of 1948 obliges the Inter-American Council for Education, Science, and Culture to "encourage the adoption of special educational programs directed toward integrating all sectors of the population into their respective national cultures". Special education programmes are also mentioned in the *Additional Protocol to the American Convention on Human Rights in the Area of Economic, Social and Cultural Rights* of 1988. States Parties to the *Additional Protocol* recognise in Article 13(3)(e) thereof that "[p]rograms of special education should be established for the handicapped, so as to provide special instruction and training to persons with physical disabilities or mental deficiencies".

The *African Charter on Human and Peoples' Rights* of 1981 is less explicit. Article 18(4) simply states that "[t]he aged and the disabled shall also have the right to special measures of protection in keeping with their physical or moral needs". As far as disabled children are concerned, Article 13 of the *African Charter on the Rights and Welfare of the Child* contains somewhat more detail. Pursuant to Article 13(2), States Parties "shall ensure that the disabled child has effective access to training, preparation for employment and recreation opportunities in a manner conducive to the child achieving the fullest possible social integration [and] . . . development". Recent Asian and Pacific initiatives include the launching of the "Asian and Pacific Decade of Disabled Persons, 1993-2002" and the adoption of the *Proclamation on the Full Participation and Equality of People with Disabilities in the Asian and Pacific Region* by the intergovernmental meeting to launch the Decade, convened by the Economic and Social Commission for Asia and the Pacific in December, 1992.

Within the Council of Europe, the rights of the disabled to vocational guidance and training are secured respectively by Articles 9 and 15 of the *European Social Charter* of 1961. Article 15(1) obliges the Contracting Parties to take adequate measures for the provision of training facilities and specialised institutions with a view to ensuring the effective exercise of the right of the physically or mentally disabled to vocational training and rehabilitation. The European Commission on Human Rights has dealt with several applications concerning placement of children with learning difficulties in special schools. In one case[15] the parents complained that this was contrary to their wishes and, as such, contravened Article 2 of *Protocol 1* to the *European Convention on the Protection of Human Rights and Fundamental Freedoms* which states:

> No person shall be denied the right to education. In the exercise of any functions which it assumes in relation to education and teaching, the State shall respect the right of parents to ensure such education and teaching in conformity with their own religious and philosophical convictions.

The Commission held that Article 2 required a balance to be struck between the expressed wishes of the parents and the disabled child's right to have as effective an education as possible. In the Commission's view, "there must be a wide measure of discretion left to the appropriate authorities as to how to make the best use possible of the resources available to them in the interests of disabled children generally".[16] The Commission's decision reflects in part the margin of appreciation it was willing to accord the State in the context of resource-intensive special education programmes competing with other social welfare claims in the context of a limited governmental budget.

Special Education

Special education is essentially education for persons suffering from physical or mental impairments. Such education can range from tuition in an integrated setting in a normal classroom within a mainstream school, through placement in a special unit within a mainstream school, to enrolment in a special school. Arguments supporting integration and 'mainstreaming' include egalitarianism and economic arguments concerning the untapped productive potential of disabled persons and the financial and opportunity costs of maintaining in specialised institutions those who could be self-sufficient and productive.[17] Advocates for specialised education point to its ability to deliver an education more tailored or better targetted to meet the special needs of disabled persons.

In a recent review, U.N.E.S.C.O. has concluded that the responsibility for special education should fall within the ambit of the national educational system, arguing against the establishment of two separate systems.[18] During the drafting of Article 23 of the *Convention on the Rights of the Child,* the debate touched upon but did not consider in any detail whether the best interests of disabled children would be served by the establishment of special schools for them, or by fully integrated schooling.[19]   At best the *Convention* leaves the matter open; at worst, its position is ambiguous.   On the one hand, Article 23(3) opens with the clause "[r]ecognizing the special needs of a disabled child".   On the other hand, Article 23(3) later states that the disabled child is to receive education and training "in a manner conducive to the child's achieving the fullest possible social integration and individual development".   Sub-rules (8) and (9) of Rule 6 of the *Standard Rules on the Equalization of Opportunities for Persons with Disabilities* constitute the latest United Nations pronouncement on this matter.   Sub-rules (8) and (9) respectively provide:

> (8) In situations where the general school system does not yet adequately meet the needs of all persons with disabilities, special education may be considered. It should be aimed at preparing students for education in the general school system. The quality of such education should reflect the same standards and ambitions as general education and should be closely linked to it. At a minimum, students with disabilities should be afforded the same portion of educational resources as students without disabilities. States should aim for the gradual integration of special education services into mainstream education.   It is acknowledged that in some circumstances special education may currently be considered to be the most appropriate form of education for some students with disabilities.

> (9) Owing to the particular communication needs of deaf and deaf/blind persons, their education may be more suitably provided in schools for such persons or special classes and units in mainstream schools. At the initial stage, in particular, special attention needs to be focused on culturally sensitive instruction that will result in effective communication skills and maximum independence for people who are deaf or deaf/blind.

Sub-rules (8) and (9) establish integration as the rule rather than the exception.   Special education is considered as a temporary expedient pending economic and material restructuring;   the trend is towards the gradual integration of special educational services into mainstream education.   There may be one exception, however.   Pending the development of new technologies and techniques, special education may continue to be the only viable option for deaf and deaf/blind persons.

In its 1988 *Review of the Present Situation of Special Education,* U.N.E.S.C.O. noted the absence of national special education planning and programmes addressing the needs and entitlements of children with disabilities. However, the experience of the United States of America in this area may well provide a model for other jurisdictions. Under the *Education for All Handicapped Children Act 1975*,[20] handicapped children are entitled to a "free appropriate education" in the "least restrictive environment".[21] Handicapped children are defined to include those who are mentally retarded, hard of hearing, deaf, speech or language impaired, visually handicapped, seriously emotionally disturbed, orthopaedically impaired, or other health impaired or who have a specific learning disability.[22] The legislative scheme is to provide financial assistance to Local Education Agencies (L.E.A.'s) for the cost of educating handicapped children over and above the costs of educating normal children. For those states deciding to adhere to it in order to qualify for such federal funding, the *Act* imposes several specific requirements on them. One such requirement is to ensure that the handicapped children receive a free, appropriate public education[23] and that "to the maximum extent practicable" this occurs in the normal classroom.[24] Another requirement is that the L.E.A. must have established procedures for drawing up an individualised education plan (I.E.P.) for each child in consultation with his or her parents.[25] The I.E.P. is a written agreement drawn up in a meeting between a representative of the L.E.A., the teacher, the child's parents, and, where appropriate, the child.[26] The I.E.P. must include a statement of the child's current educational standard, the child's annual goal, the services to be provided, the extent to which the child will be able to participate in the normal classroom, the starting date and duration of the services, and objective criteria by which it can be determined at least annually whether the child is meeting the educational objectives. In other words, the content of the educational services is narrowly targetted to meet the individual needs of each disabled child. The involvement of parents is a notable feature of the legislative scheme as it will be recalled that Rule 6(3) of the United Nations *Standard Rules on the Equalization of Opportunities for Persons with Disabilities* of 1993 recommends the involvement of parents of disabled children in the educational process at all levels. Thus, the educational rights of a child with disabilities are not left as vague entitlements in the legislation but are made the subject of negotiations in a contract-like procedure resulting in a written document which specifies in detail the educational services to be provided to the child.[27]

Contemporary problems experienced by countries in the delivery of special education programmes include an insufficient number of adequately trained special education teachers, lack of appropriate support staff, resource materials and facilities, inappropriate school placements, pessimistic views of the potential of disabled students, and a failure to allocate the resources necessary to give disabled children opportunity within the educational system equal to that provided for non-disabled children.[28]   Even when enlightened legislatures have legislated to proscribe discrimination on the ground of impairment, they have left in place exemptions when admission of a disabled child to an educational institution would require provision of additional services or facilities which, in the circumstances, cannot reasonably be provided.   Such exceptions to the operation of anti-discrimination legislation provide scope for the denial of funding for special education programmes on the basis of such considerations as cost-benefit analyses and allocation of public resources (which generally have fallen beyond the scope of judicial review in many common law jurisdictions).[29]   The drafters of the *Standard Rules on the Equalization of Opportunities for Persons with Disabilities* probably had such problems in mind when they drafted Rule 6(8) which requires that "[a]t a minimum, students with disabilities should be afforded the same portion of educational resources as students without disabilities".

Conclusion

Over the past quarter-century, the United Nations has pursued a trinity of aims in evolving international standards on behalf of persons with disabilities: promoting their independence, equalising opportunities available to them, and ensuring their full participation within the wider community.   Such is the reality, however, that the prosecution of these aims is highly resource-dependent.   Indeed, the United Nations General Assembly has identified in one of its recent resolutions[30] the "inadequate allocation of resources" as 'foremost' among the major obstacles to the pursuit of these aims.   This problem is compounded when one considers that the vast majority of persons who suffer from some form of serious impairment live in developing countries[31]   and that a disproportionate number of children in those countries are affected by various disabilities.[32]   It is perhaps not surprising that Article 23(4) of the *Convention on the Rights of the Child* states in part:

> States Parties shall promote in the spirit of international co-operation the . . . dissemination of and access to information concerning methods of rehabilitation education and vocational services, with the aim of enabling States Parties to improve their capabilities and skills and to widen their

experience in these areas. In this regard, account shall be taken of the needs of developing countries.

It is to be hoped that the States Parties, under the general co-ordination of U.N.E.S.C.O., will fulfil this obligation conscientiously and in good faith.

Notes

1   Amadou-Mahtar M'Bow   (former Director-General of U.N.E.S.C.O.) "Introduction" in G. Mialaret (ed.) *The Child's Right to Education* (1979) 9, 12-13.

2   S. Herr "Rights of Disabled Persons: International Principles and American Experiences" (1980) 12 *Columbia Human Rights Law Review* 2.

3   According to the World Health Organization, impairment is defined as "any loss or abnormality of psychological, physiological, or anatomical structure or function". Disability refers to any restriction or lack of ability, resulting from an impairment, to perform activities in the normal manner. Handicap refers to an essentially social disadvantage, resulting from an impairment or disability, that limits or prevents the fulfillment of a role that is normal for a given individual. See World Health Organization *International Classification of Impairments, Disabilities, and Handicaps* (1980) 27-29.

4   Herr, op. cit., 5.

5   A policy review conducted in the United States of America resulted in the *Education for All Handicapped Children Act 1975*, 20 U.S.C.A. ss. 1401-1461 (1976).   In England, the Committee of Enquiry into the Education of Handicapped Children and Young People (the "Warnock Committee") held a similar enquiry in the late 1970s.

6   The United Nations General Assembly has also adopted the *Principles for the Protection of Persons with Mental Illness and for the Improvement of Mental Health Care.*

7   Resolution 31/123.

8   United Nations Department of Public Information *First Session of Advisory Committee for 1981 Year for Disabled Persons, Recommends Draft International Programme for Year* Doc. No. SOC/4014 at 2 (press release issued, 26 March 1979).

9   The *International Covenant on Economic, Social and Cultural Rights* of 1966 did not directly address the rights of disabled persons.

10   Commission on Human Rights *Report of the Working Group on a Draft Convention on the Rights of the Child*   E/1982/12/Add.1 E/CN.4/1982/30/Add.1 p. 69, paras. 108 and 109.

11   G. Van Bueren *The International Law on the Rights of the Child* (1995) 359.

12   Article 2(1) of the *Convention on the Rights of the Child* explicitly refers to 'disability' as an anti-discrimination ground.   Article 28(1) refers to various types and levels of education but fails to mention pre-school education.

13   Van Bueren, op. cit., 359.

14   Sub-rules 8 and 9 of Rule 6 of the *Standard Rules* will be set out in full later in this chapter in a section dealing with the special educational requirements of disabled persons.

15   App. 13887/88, *Graeme v United Kingdom*, 5 February 1990, (1990) 64 DR 158.

16   Id. 166.

17   D. Neal   "The Right to Education: the Case of Special Education" (Winter, 1982) *The Australian Quarterly* 147, 150.

18   U.N.E.S.C.O.   *Review of the Present Situation of Special Education* (1988).

19   Van Bueren, op. cit., 359.

20   20 U.S.C.A. Ss. 1401-1461 (1976).

21   See nn. 23 and 24 below.

22   S. 1401(1).

23   S. 1414(a)(1)(C)(ii).

24   S. 1414(a)(1)(C)(iv).

25   S. 1414(a)(5).

26   S. 1401(19).

27   Neal, op. cit., 152-153.

28   R. Hayes and S. MacAlpine   "A Lawyers' View of Special Education: Past, Present and Future" (1986) 10 *Australian Journal of Special Education* 33, 35.

29   Id. 36.

30   Resolution 49/153 (1994).

31   Herr, op. cit., 2.

32   M. Black *The Children and the Nations* (1986) 369.

10 The Educational Rights of Women, Girls, Migrants and Refugees

The Educational Rights of Women and Girls

It has recently been reported that more than two-thirds of those children who never go to school or who drop out at an early stage are female. On a regional basis, a girl born in South Asia or in the Middle East has a less than one-in-three chance of completing primary education.[1] The fact that women and girls continue to be disproportionately represented in the statistics is a source of concern considering that the United Nations Organisation has been working virtually since its creation to eliminate discrimination against women in the educational field and to improve the status and role of women in education, science and culture.[2] In its Resolution 154 F (VII) of 23 August 1948, the United Nations Economic and Social Council (E.C.O.S.O.C.), on the recommendation of the Commission on the Status of Women (C.S.W.), requested Member States of the United Nations "to grant women equal educational rights with men and to ensure that they are afforded genuine educational opportunities, irrespective of nationality, race or religion". In the more detailed and demanding Resolution 547 K (XVIII) of 12 July 1954, E.C.O.S.O.C. recommended that U.N. Member States should:

> (a) Take the necessary steps to ensure that women have equal access with men to all types of education . . .
>
> (b) Enact the necessary laws and regulations to eliminate all forms of discrimination against women in education and to ensure access for women to all types of education, including vocational and technical education, and equal opportunities to obtain State scholarships for education in any field and in preparation for all careers;
>
> (c) . . . [T]ake full advantage of the facilities and resources of U.N.E.S.C.O. in developing additional educational opportunities for girls and women . . .

169

United Nations Educational, Scientific and Cultural Organization

Since the mid-1950s, U.N.E.S.C.O. has prepared and submitted at regular intervals reports on various aspects of the education of girls and women to the C.S.W. and E.C.O.S.O.C. These reports have formed the basis of recommendations made by E.C.O.S.O.C. to U.N. Member States on such subjects as the access of girls and women to primary, secondary and higher education, to technical and vocational education, and to the teaching profession. In 1966, the General Conference of U.N.E.S.C.O. adopted a long-term programme for the advancement of women through access to education, science and culture. Under this programme, the Director-General of U.N.E.S.C.O. was authorised by the General Conference to aid government projects within U.N.E.S.C.O.'s sphere of activity which are designed to advance the educational aspirations of women and girls in both urban and rural settings, and to give technical and financial support to the activities of international non-governmental organisations working within U.N.E.S.C.O.'s mandate.[3]

The General Conference of U.N.E.S.C.O. has also devoted a portion of its 1974 *Revised Recommendation concerning Technical and Vocational Education* to female education in the context of preparation for an occupational field. In pursuit of the goal of the democratisation of education, U.N.E.S.C.O. also adopted the *Second Medium-Term Plan (1984-1989) Education For All*. One of the programmes which was approved for this five-year period to realise this goal concerned equality of educational opportunity for girls and women. Specific themes of this programme included the identification of obstacles to educational equality, the increase of access to the sciences and to technical and vocational education, and a consideration of the educational role of women in society.

International Instruments

The question of discrimination against women in education was first specifically addressed by U.N.E.S.C.O. in its *Convention against Discrimination in Education* of 1960. Article 1(1) of the *Convention* defines the term 'discrimination' to include any distinction based on sex. This question has also been dealt with by international instruments concerning women's human rights issues. Article 9 of the non-binding *Declaration on the Elimination of Discrimination against Women*, which was proclaimed by the United Nations General Assembly in Resolution 2263 (XXII) of 7 November 1967, states:

All appropriate measures shall be taken to ensure to girls and women, married or unmarried, equal rights with men in education at all levels, and in particular:

(a) Equal conditions of access to, and study in, educational institutions of all types, including universities and vocational, technical and professional schools;

(b) The same choice of curricula, the same examinations, teaching staff with qualifications of the same standard, and school premises and equipment of the same quality, whether the institutions are co-educational or not;

(c) Equal opportunities to benefit from scholarships and other study grants;

(d)   Equal opportunities for access to programmes of continuing education, including adult literacy programmes;

(e) Access to educational information to help in ensuring the health and well-being of families.

Similarly, an entire provision of the *Convention on the Elimination of All Forms of Discrimination against Women* of 1979 is devoted to the right to education. Article 10 states:

States Parties shall take all appropriate measures to eliminate discrimination against women in order to ensure to them equal rights with men in the field of education and in particular to ensure, on a basis of equality of men and women:

(a) The same conditions for career and vocational guidance, for access to studies and for the achievement of diplomas in educational establishments of all categories in rural as well as in urban areas; this equality shall be ensured in pre-school, general, technical, professional and higher technical education, as well as in all types of vocational training;

(b) Access to the same curricula, the same examinations, teaching staff with qualifications of the same standard and school premises and equipment of the same quality;

(c) The elimination of any stereotyped concept of the roles of men and women at all levels and in all forms of education by encouraging coeducation and other types of education which will help to achieve this aim and, in particular, by the revision of textbooks and school programmes and the adaptation of teaching methods;

(d) The same opportunities to benefit from scholarships and other study grants;

(e) The same opportunities for access to programmes of continuing education, including adult and functional literacy programmes, particularly those aimed at reducing, at the earliest possible time, any gap in education existing between men and women;

(f) The reduction of female student drop-out rates and the organization of programmes for girls and women who have left school prematurely;

(g) The same opportunities to participate actively in sports and physical education;

(h) Access to specific educational information to help ensure the health and well-being of families, including information and advice on family planning.

Although there are some changes in the wording and new clauses, Article 10 essentially reaffirms the provisions of Article 9 of the *Declaration*. Article 10 does add three new sub-articles - (c), (f)and (g). Thus, what was only a programmatic statement of principle in Article 9 of the *Declaration* has been converted into a binding legal obligation by Article 10 of the *Convention*.

The international instruments also address the special needs of women and girls living in rural areas. A disproportionate number of women and girls living in such areas, particularly in developing countries, remain without access to education beyond the first few grades.[4] The World Conference on Agrarian Reform and Rural Development, convened by the United Nations Food and Agriculture Organization, met in Rome in July, 1979 to consider this and other problems. Several provisions of the "Programme of Action" annexed to the *Declaration of Principles* adopted by the Conference are relevant in this context. Section IV.D.(i) states that "[g]overnments should consider action to ensure educational opportunities of similar quality and content for both sexes and provide special incentives such as reduced fees for the increased enrollment of girls and women in schools and training programmes". Section IV.D.(iii) urges governments to consider action to "[e]stablish and strengthen non-formal educational opportunities for rural women, including leadership training, instruction in agricultural as well as non-farm activities, health care, upbringing of children, family planning and nutrition". Some of these recommendations soon became binding treaty obligations by virtue of their inclusion in Article 14 of the *Convention on the Elimination of All Forms of Discrimination against Women*. Article 14(2) obliges States Parties to take appropriate measures to eliminate discrimination against women in rural areas. According to Article 14(2)(d), States Parties shall ensure to rural women the right to obtain all types of formal and non-formal training and education including functional literacy programmes and extension services.

Recent Developments

In July, 1985 a world conference was held at Nairobi to review and appraise the achievements of the United Nations Decade for Women. The conference adopted *The Forward-looking Strategies for the Advancement of Women to the Year 2000* [5] which contained a number of measures for action in the educational sector. Education was identified in Paragraph 163 of *The Forward-looking Strategies* as the basis for the improvement of the status of women and for their role as full members of society. The most notable recommendations included the following:

- governments should strengthen the participation of women at all levels of national educational policy (Paragraph 163);

- special measures (including incentives) should be adopted by governments to increase access by girls and young women to scientific, technical, vocational and managerial subjects at all levels (Paragraphs 163 and 169);

- governments should identify and address the causes of high absenteeism and drop-out rates of girls in the educational system (Paragraph 165);

- special measures (including the setting of targets) should be taken by governments and U.N.E.S.C.O. to eliminate the higher rates of illiteracy amongst girls and women by the year 2000 (Paragraph 164);

- efforts should be made to promote functional literacy, with special emphasis on health, nutrition and viable economic skills (Paragraph 164).

The education of girls and women was also considered by the U.N.E.S.C.O.-sponsored World Conference on Education for All held in Jomtien, Thailand in March, 1990. Article 3(3) of the *World Declaration on Education for All* records the conviction of the Conference delegates that "[t]he most urgent priority is to ensure access to, and improve the quality of, education for girls and women, and to remove every obstacle that hampers their active participation". The Conference's *Framework for Action to Meet Basic Learning Needs* encourages the formulation and implementation of educational programmes which are designed to eliminate the social and cultural barriers which have inhibited women and girls from enjoying the full benefits of regular education.[6]

The Organization of African Unity has recently invoked special affirmative action measures to deal with gender discrimination in education. Two provisions of the *African Charter on the Rights and Welfare of the Child*, adopted by the O.A.U. in July, 1990, specifically target the female child. Article 11(3)(e) obliges States Parties to take special measures in respect of female children to ensure their equal access to education. Pursuant to Article 11(6) the States Parties assume a legal obligation to "take all appropriate measures to ensure that children who become pregnant before completing their education shall have an opportunity to continue with their education on the basis of their individual ability".

Gender-specific educational issues were also on the agenda of the Fourth United Nations World Conference on Women held in Beijing in September, 1995. One of the major aims of the Conference was to adopt a *Platform for Action* which would concentrate on the critical issues identified as representing fundamental obstacles to the advancement of women. Echoing the *World Declaration on Education for All*, the *Platform* earmarks education for women and girls as a priority issue. Like *The Forward-looking Strategies* the Beijing *Platform* is concerned with eliminating illiteracy. The *Platform* sets a target of 80 per cent primary school attendance by the year 2000 which curiously (or perhaps realistically) is 20 per cent below the target set by the 1990 World Conference on Education for All. The *Platform* provides additional arguments for programmes to focus on improving the access of women and girls not only to basic schooling but also to opportunities for life-long learning and skills training, and for the inclusion of science and technology subjects in these non-formal learning programmes.

Conclusion

It is clear from the foregoing that the United Nations has been concerned virtually from its inception with equalising educational opportunities for girls and women. It is equally clear that progress towards achieving actual, as well as formal legal, equality in this context has been grudgingly slow. As we have just seen, there are now sufficient treaty guarantees in place which recognise formal legal equality of educational opportunity for girls and women. Practical measures must now be resorted to in order to secure actual equality of opportunity. It is now up to treaty-monitoring bodies like the Committee on the Rights of the Child and the Committee on the Elimination of Discrimination against Women to question States Parties in a rigorous and searching manner on the extent to which they are fulfilling their relevant obligations conscientiously and in good faith. In terms of the provision of international financial, technical and material assistance, consideration might be given to attaching to the provision of such assistance conditions concerning the application of a portion thereof to specifically addressing gender-related educational issues.

The Educational Rights of Migrants and Refugees

Those persons who satisfy the definition of 'refugee' as contained in Article 1 of the *Convention relating to the Status of Refugees* of 1951 are entitled to the protection of Article 22 thereof. Article 22 deals with public education and its text states:

> 1. The Contracting States shall accord to refugees the same treatment as is accorded to nationals with respect to elementary education.

> 2. The Contracting States shall accord to refugees treatment as favourable as possible, and, in any event, not less favourable than that accorded to aliens generally in the same circumstances, with respect to education other than elementary education and, in particular, as regards access to studies, the recognition of foreign school certificates, diplomas and degrees, the remission of fees and charges and the award of scholarships.

The standard of protection for refugee children is regrettably lower in relation to secondary education. Nevertheless, the protection offered under the *Convention on the Rights of the Child* of 1989 may exceed that offered under the 1951 *Convention* by virtue of Article 22(1) of the former instrument which obliges States Parties to take appropriate measures to ensure that refugee children enjoy the rights set forth therein. Despite these treaty obligations, however, the fact remains that many developing States are not able to provide universal primary education even to their own children.[7] Article 29(1)(c) of the *Convention on the Rights of the*

Child is also relevant to child refugees. It states that the education of the child shall be directed to "the development of respect for the child's . . . cultural identity, language and values, for the national values of the country in which the child is living [and] the country from which he or she may originate . . .". The education of refugee children must therefore take into account not only the values of the country of asylum but of those of the country of origin as well. In terms of the appropriate language of instruction, U.N.E.S.C.O. has recommended that initially education should be in the refugee child's native tongue but that on attaining proficiency a second language ought to be introduced.[8]

The *Framework for Action to Meet Basic Learning Needs* adopted by the 1990 World Conference on Education for All recognises the importance of educational programmes for refugees. Paragraph 45.f. refers to the Conference's view that programmes run by such organisations as the United Nations High Commissioner for Refugees and the United Nations Relief and Works Agency for Palestine require more substantial and reliable long-term financial support. Paragraph 45.f. also urges the international community to share the burden countries of refuge experience in coping with the basic learning needs of refugees through increased international co-operation and financial and technical assistance. In 1994, the United Nations General Assembly in Resolution 49/172 called upon the United Nations High Commissioner for Refugees, the United Nations Children's Fund and other United Nations agencies to mobilise adequate assistance to unaccompanied refugee minors in the areas of relief, education, health and psychological rehabilitation. Unfortunately, this assistance was to be undertaken "within existing resources".

As far as the educational entitlements of migrants and their children are concerned, detailed reference has been made in Chapter 6 (*"Educational Rights of Minority Groups"*) to the *Council of the European Communities Directive on the Education of the Children of Migrant Workers 1977*. As part of its *Second Medium-Term Plan (1984-1989) Education for All*, U.N.E.S.C.O. has sought to promote the right to education of particular groups including, amongst others, migrant workers and refugees. The United Nations General Assembly has sought to guarantee educational access to aliens, albeit in non-binding form. In 1985, the General Assembly adopted the *Declaration on the Human Rights of Individuals Who Are Not Nationals of the Country in Which They Live*.[9] Article 8(c) of the *Declaration* provides in part that aliens lawfully residing in the territory of a State shall enjoy, in accordance with the national laws, the right to education "provided that they fulfill the requirements under the relevant regulations for participation and that undue strain is not placed on the resources of the state". It would appear by implication that undocumented or illegal aliens are beyond the scope of protection. It is interesting to note, however, that the United States Supreme Court held in *Plyler v Doe* [10] that the equal protection clause of the U.S. Constitution prohibits a state's discriminatory denial of public education to undocumented aliens. The Supreme Court's reasoning turned largely on its recognition of the critical importance of education to all individuals, regardless of their legal status or lack thereof.[11]

The United Nations General Assembly has recently adopted a treaty which seeks to secure the educational rights of the children of migrant workers. Article 30 of the *International Convention on the Protection of the Rights of All Migrant Workers and Members of Their Families* [12] states that "[e]ach child of a migrant worker shall have the basic right of access to education on the basis of equality of treatment with nationals of the State concerned". Unlike Article 22 of the *Refugees Convention*, Article 30 of the *Migrant Workers Convention* does not set a differential standard in relation to primary and secondary education.

Notes

1   U.N.I.C.E.F. *The World Summit for Children* (1990) 32.

2   United Nations *United Nations Action in the Field of Human Rights* (1988) 146.

3   Ibid.

4   S. Graham-Brown "The Role of the Curriculum" in *Education Rights and Minorities* (Minority Rights Group Report) (1994) 29.

5   *Report of the World Conference to Review and Appraise the Achievements of the United Nations Decade for Women: Equality, Development and Peace*, Nairobi, 15-26 July 1985 (United Nations publication, Sales. No. E.85.IV.10), chap. II, C.2.

6   See Paragraph 45.e. See also Principle 20 of the *Plan of Action for Implementing the World Declaration on the Survival, Protection and Development of the Child* adopted by the 1989 World Summit for Children (referring, *inter alia*, to the need to reduce female illiteracy and the current educational disparities between boys and girls).

7   G. Van Bueren *The International Law on the Rights of the Child* (1995) 369.

8   Ibid.

9   United Nations General Assembly Resolution 40/144 (1985).

10   457 U.S. 202 (1982).

11   Id. 221.

12   Adopted by the United Nations General Assembly in Resolution 45/158 of 18 December 1990. For the full text see (1991) 30 I.L.M. 1517.

11 Specialised Education

Adult Education

Although children are the main beneficiaries, the right to education has been recognised by various international and regional instruments as belonging to all persons. This acknowledges the life-long and continuous nature of the learning process as well as the ever-increasing demands for maintaining up-to-date information and skills.

The modern foundation for adult education is contained in Article 26(1) of the *Universal Declaration of Human Rights* of 1948 which states in part that "[e]veryone has the right to education".[1] The unqualified nature of this particular formulation of the right implies that it is to be enjoyed by adults and children alike and that 'education' should not be confined to only general education.

Adult education has been recognised by two major universal human rights treaties. Article 4(c) of the U.N.E.S.C.O. *Convention against Discrimination in Education* of 1960 imposes a legal obligation on States Parties to promote equality of opportunity in educational matters by encouraging and intensifying "by appropriate methods the education of persons who have not received any primary education or who have not completed the entire primary education course and the continuation of their education on the basis of individual capacity". Article 13(2)(d) of the *International Covenant on Economic, Social and Cultural Rights* of 1966 is in similar terms. In order to fully realise the right of everyone to education, States Parties recognise that "[f]undamental education shall be encouraged or intensified as far as possible for those persons who have not received or completed the whole period of their primary education". The term "fundamental education" generally refers to adult education and includes literacy, numeracy and basic orientation into society.[2] Unlike primary education which is made compulsory by the international instruments, adult or fundamental education is optional. Adults are permitted to choose whether or not they wish to avail themselves of adult education facilities provided to them by the State.

Adult education has also been identified as an important prerequisite to rural development. Section VII of the *Programme of Action* adopted by the World Conference on Agrarian Reform and Rural Development held in Rome in 1979 recognises the importance of the creation and expansion of

179

training and extension networks for both men and women residing in rural areas and their potential to develop and improve skills and to increase productivity and income-generating capabilities.

Regional human rights systems have also mentioned adult education in various instruments. The contribution of the Inter-American human rights system in this respect is the most outstanding. Article 48 of the *Charter of the Organization of American States* obliges the Member States to strengthen their adult education systems. Article 3 of the *Central American Convention on the Unification of the Fundamental Norms of Education* of 1962 goes so far as to require Central American educational systems to give priority to adult education. Article 13(3)(d) of the *Additional Protocol to the American Convention on Human Rights in the Area of Economic, Social and Cultural Rights* essentially repeats the text of Article 13(2)(d) of the *International Covenant on Economic, Social and Cultural Rights*. Within the Council of Europe, adult education has been recognised by Article 10 of the *European Social Charter* of 1961 in the context of the right to vocational training. Article 10(3) thereof obliges the Contracting Parties to provide and promote "adequate and readily available training facilities for adult workers".

U.N.E.S.C.O. has attempted to prescribe non-binding standards in the field of adult education. At its 19th session in 1976, the General Conference of U.N.E.S.C.O. adopted the *Recommendation on the Development of Adult Education* which reaffirmed Article 26 of the *Universal Declaration of Human Rights* and Article 13 of the *International Covenant on Economic, Social and Cultural Rights*. The aims of adult education were stated to be, *inter alia*, the development of aptitudes as well as the development of respect for the diversity of cultures and a deeper understanding of social problems. The *Adult Education Recommendation* urged each U.N.E.S.C.O. Member State to:

- recognise adult education as a necessary component of the educational system;

- promote the creation of programmes to meet the needs of all categories of adults without discrimination;

- eliminate the isolation of women from adult education;

- take measures to promote the participation of the underprivileged and illiterate segments of the population.[3]

The United Nations has also focussed on the development of adult education programmes for women and girls. Article 9(d) of the *Declaration on the Elimination of Discrimination against Women* of 1967 calls upon States to take appropriate measures to ensure to girls and women "[e]qual opportunities for access to programmes of continuing education, including adult literacy programmes". The *Convention on the Elimination of All Forms of Discrimination against Women* of 1979 elaborated upon the non-binding standard contained in Article 9(d). Sub-Articles (e) and (f) of Article 10 of the *Convention* state:

> States Parties shall take all appropriate measures to eliminate discrimination against women in order to ensure to them equal rights with men in the field of education and in particular to ensure . . .
>
> (e)   The same opportunities for access to programmes of continuing education, including adult and functional literacy programmes, particularly those aimed at reducing, at the earliest possible time, any gap in education existing between men and women;
>
> (f)   The reduction of female student drop-out rates and the organization of programmes for girls and women who have left school prematurely.

The development of adult education programmes tailored to the needs of women also formed part of the agenda of the World Conference to Review and Appraise the Achievements of the United Nations Decade for Women: Equality, Development and Peace held at Nairobi in 1985. Paragraph 165 of *The Forward-looking Strategies for the Advancement of Women to the Year 2000* adopted by the Conference urged governments to "encourage and finance adult education programmes for those women who have never completed their studies or were forced to interrupt their studies, owing to family responsibilities, lack of financial resources or early pregnancies".

Home Education

The issue of whether parents have a right to educate their children at home in lieu of formal institutional instruction is not addressed explicitly by international and regional human rights instruments. Whether or not such a right exists is therefore left to each State to decide as a matter of domestic law.

The State must strike a balance between two freedoms. On the one hand, parents can claim the right to freedom from State interference in how they raise their children on the basis of freedom of conscience, religion and respect for their family privacy.[4]   On the other hand, States which are party to the *Convention on the Rights of the Child* have an obligation under Article 29(1)(d) thereof to ensure that all children receive the kind of education that promotes understanding and tolerance apposite to harmonious and responsible life in a free society. It has been said that children who are educated at home, especially where it is for religious reasons, may have their freedom to explore a range of alternative viewpoints restricted.[5]   Where the State allows parents to educate their children at home as they see fit, it is therefore legitimate for public authorities to monitor the quality of education they receive. Such oversight would primarily involve ensuring that certain minimum standards of education and moral and social development are met and, in rare cases, protecting children from serious physical or emotional harm that may occur as a result of home instruction.

Some countries regard home education as sufficiently important to warrant constitutional recognition. For example, Article 76 of the Constitution of Denmark and Article 42 of the Irish Constitution respectively permit home education by parents or guardians provided that certain minimum requirements are satisfied.[6]   Article 45 of the former Constitution of the Union of Soviet Socialist Republics implicitly sanctioned home instruction in its reference to "the provision of facilities for self-education". In the absence of explicit constitutional protection, home education has been regulated by ordinary statute in a number of countries. In England, for example, the parental duty to educate may be discharged otherwise than by attendance at school. Section 36 of the *Education Act 1944* states that "[i]t shall be the duty of the parent of every child of compulsory school age to cause him to receive efficient full-time education, suitable to his age, ability and aptitude, either by regular attendance at school or otherwise". In the view of one commentator, however, it is unlikely that most attempts by parents to educate at home would be sufficiently structured as to comply with the requirements of Section 36.[7]   Indeed, the local education authorities in England have been known to question the suitability of the curriculum offered in the home environment.[8]   In the United States of America, an exception to compulsory school attendance is often allowed for 'adequate' home instruction. Most states of the Union simply require that home instruction be the equivalent of that offered in the public schools. The courts have generally required parents to discharge the burden of showing that their home instruction is equal to that obtainable in the public schools in terms of such matters as instruction in the required subjects, daily number of hours of instruction, number of days of instruction per year and adequacy of library materials.[9]

The question whether Article 2 of the *First Protocol* to the *European Convention on the Protection of Human Rights and Fundamental Freedoms* includes a right to educate, or be educated, at home has been considered by the European Commission of Human Rights. Article 2 states:

> No person shall be denied the right to education. In the exercise of any functions which it assumes in relation to education and to teaching, the State shall respect the right of parents to ensure such education and teaching in conformity with their own religious and philosophical convictions.

According to the European Commission, it is clear that Article 2 "implies a right for the State to establish compulsory schooling, be it in State schools or private tuition of a satisfactory standard, and that verification and enforcement of educational standards is an integral part of that right".[10] Thus, the State does not breach the requirement to respect parents' wishes by requiring them to co-operate in the assessment of their children's educational progress. Consistently with the position in other jurisdictions, home instruction is permitted subject to the requirement that the tuition is in accordance with prescribed national educational standards.

The topic of home and community education has been addressed recently at the international level by the 1990 U.N.E.S.C.O.-sponsored World Conference on Education for All. Article 5 of the Conference's *World Declaration on Education for All* acknowledges that "[s]upplementary alternative programmes can help meet the basic learning needs of children with limited or no access to formal schooling, provided that they share the same standards of learning applied to schools, and are adequately supported".

Technical and Vocational Education

Although the international and regional human rights instruments do not contain a definition of "vocational education", some assistance can be derived from two sources. First, the European Court of Justice has attempted to define the term in the context of interpreting Article 128 of the *Treaty of Rome.* Article 128 provides that "the Council [of Europe] shall . . . lay down general principles for implementing a vocational training policy".   In *Gravier v City of Liège* [11]   the Court defined "vocational training" as follows:

> Any form of education which prepares for a qualification for a particular profession, trade or employment or which provides the necessary training and skills for such a profession, trade or employment is vocational training, whatever the age and the level of training of the pupils or students and even if the training programme includes an element of general education.

U.N.E.S.C.O. has also attempted to define the concept of technical and vocational education in its *Revised Recommendation concerning Technical and Vocational Education, 1974.* Such education refers to "those aspects of the educational process involving, in addition to general education, the study of technologies and related sciences and the acquisition of practical skills, attitudes, understanding and knowledge relating to occupations in various sectors of economic and social life".

The right to technical and vocational education is mentioned in several international instruments.   Article 26(1) of the *Universal Declaration of Human Rights* requires technical education to be made generally available.   Article 6(2) of the *International Covenant on Economic, Social and Cultural Rights* requires each State Party to adopt and implement technical and vocational guidance and training programmes as one of the means to securing the full realisation of the right to work. Article 28(1) of the *Convention on the Rights of the Child* imposes two obligations on States Parties in this context.   Article 28(1)(b) requires States Parties to encourage the development of vocational education at the secondary level while Article 28(1)(d) requires them to "make . . . vocational information and guidance available and accessible to all children".

Vocational education also features prominently in regional human rights instruments.   Pursuant to Article 48 of the *Charter of the Organization of American States* the Member States pledge to strengthen vocational education systems. And, in terms reminiscent of Article 6(2) of the *ICESCR*, Article 6(2) of the *Additional Protocol to the American Convention on Human Rights in the Area of Economic, Social and Cultural Rights* obliges States Parties to adopt measures that will make the right to work fully effective including vocational guidance and the development of technical and vocational training projects. The most detailed provisions on the right to vocational education are to be found in the Council of Europe's

European Social Charter. Article 9 and the first two sub-articles of Article 10 of the *Charter* provide as follows:

Article 9

With a view to ensuring the effective exercise of the right to vocational guidance, the Contracting Parties undertake to provide or promote, as necessary, a service which will assist all persons, including the handicapped, to solve problems related to occupational choice and progress, with due regard to the individual's characteristics and their relation to occupational opportunity: this assistance should be available free of charge, both to young persons, including school children, and to adults.

Article 10

With a view to ensuring the effective exercise of the right to vocational training, the Contracting Parties undertake:

1. to provide or promote, as necessary, the technical and vocational training of all persons, including the handicapped, in consultation with employers' and workers' organisations, and to grant facilities for access to higher technical and university education, based solely on individual aptitude;

2. to provide or promote a system of apprenticeship . . . for training young boys and girls in their various employments;

Article 7(4) of the *Charter* obliges the Contracting Parties to limit the working hours of persons under 16 years of age in accordance with their need for vocational training. The Council of the European Communities has adopted the *Directive on the Implementation of the Principle of Equal Treatment for Men and Women as Regards Access to Employment, Vocational Training and Promotion, and Working Conditions* of 9 February 1976. Article 4(c) of the *Directive* provides that "Member States shall take all necessary measures to ensure that . . . vocational guidance [and] vocational training . . . shall be accessible on the basis of the same criteria and at the same levels without any discrimination on grounds of sex". The European Parliament has recently reaffirmed the right to vocational training. Article 16 of the *Declaration of the European Parliament of Fundamental Rights and Freedoms* of 12 April 1989 states in part that "[e]veryone shall have the right to education and vocational training appropriate to their abilities".

The two United Nations agencies which have been most active in formulating standards for technical and vocational education are the

International Labour Organisation and U.N.E.S.C.O. In 1962, the General Conference of the I.L.O. adopted the *Social Policy (Basic Aims and Standards) Convention.*[12] According to Article 14(1)(d) thereof, it shall be the aim of the national policy of each Member State to abolish all discrimination among workers in respect of opportunities for vocational training. Article 15(1) obliges States Parties to make adequate provision "to the maximum extent possible under local conditions, for the progressive development of broad systems of education, vocational training and apprenticeship, with a view to the effective preparation of children and young persons of both sexes for a useful occupation". Article 2 of the I.L.O. *Convention concerning Vocational Guidance and Vocational Training in the Development of Human Resources*[13] provides that Member States should gradually extend their vocational guidance to ensure that comprehensive information and the broadest possible vocational guidance are available to children. Apart from these two conventions, the General Conference of the I.L.O. has also adopted the following non-binding recommendations for the consideration of I.L.O. Member States:

> *Vocational Guidance Recommendation, 1949 (No. 87)*

> *Vocational Training (Agriculture) Recommendation, 1956 (No. 101)*

> *Vocational Training Recommendation, 1962 (No. 117)*

> *Vocational Guidance and Vocational Training in the Development of Human Resources Recommendation, 1975 (No. 150)*

The major contribution of U.N.E.S.C.O. in this field has been the adoption by its General Conference of the *Revised Recommendation concerning Technical and Vocational Education, 1974.* This instrument is notable in a number of respects. It seeks to contribute to greater democratisation by striving for equality of access to such education for men and women and by making special provision for women, migrants, out-of-school youth, and the physically and mentally disadvantaged. The *Revised Recommendation* also recites that the acquisition of an understanding of the technological aspects of contemporary civilisation and an introduction to the working world must be an essential component of general education above primary level as well as of continuing education.

Health Education

As the 1990 World Conference on Education for All recognised, learning does not take place in isolation. The success of teaching initiatives will depend in large part on the extent to which communities ensure that students receive the nutrition, health care and support they require in order to participate in, and benefit from, their education.[14]   It has also been observed that education is strongly associated with better health and nutrition, higher child survival rates, and lower fertility.[15]   Education is therefore a cause as well as a consequence of better health.

Several major human rights instruments recognise the child's right to basic health education. Article 24(2)(e) and (f) of the *Convention on the Rights of the Child* respectively oblige States Parties to take appropriate measures to ensure that parents and children receive basic knowledge of child health and nutrition, and to develop preventive health care and family planning education and services. The importance of health education has also been acknowledged recently by the Organization of African Unity. Article 11(2)(h) of the *African Charter on the Rights and Welfare of the Child* of 1990 states that the education of the African child shall be directed to the promotion of the child's understanding of primary health care.

Although health care is important for children of both sexes, it is especially so for girls and young women. Paragraph 164 of the *Forward-looking Strategies for the Advancement of Women to the Year 2000* [16] identified the close link between raising the level of health education among women and child survival and spacing. The World Health Organisation and U.N.I.C.E.F. have been the most active amongst the United Nations agencies in promoting basic health education. Both agencies have emphasised the importance of female literacy in the context of the child's right to survival.[17]

Notes

1   See also Article 27 of the *Universal Declaration of Human Rights.*
2   P. Arajärvi "Article 26" in A. Eide (ed.) *The Universal Declaration of Human Rights: A Commentary* (1992) 405, 409.
3   See also U.N.E.S.C.O.'s *Second Medium-Term Plan (1984-1989) Education for All* which aims, *inter alia*, to intensify literacy training for adults.

4   Articles 17 and 18 of the *International Covenant on Civil and Political Rights.*

5   P. Hobson and R. Cresswell "Parental Rights, Education and Liberal Tolerance" (1993) 14 *Discourse* 44, 50.

6   Arajärvi, op. cit., 424; B. Walsh "Existence and Meaning of Fundamental Rights in the Field of Education in Ireland" (1981) 2 *Human Rights Law Journal* 319.

7   A. Bainham *Children, Parents and the State* (1988) 160.

8   D. Milman *Educational Conflict and the Law* (1986) 41.

9   S. Davis and M. Schwartz *Children's Rights and the Law* (1987) 134-135.

10   *Family H v United Kingdom* (1984) 37 D & R 105.

11   Case 293/83, [1985] E.C.R. 593.

12   No. 117.

13   No. 142 (1975).

14   Article 6 of the *World Declaration on Education for All.*

15   U.N.I.C.E.F. *The World Summit for Children* (1990) 32. See also Principle 21 of the *Plan of Action for Implementing the World Declaration on the Survival, Protection and Development of the Child* (" . . . progress in education and literacy can contribute significantly to improvement in maternal and child health . . . ").

16   Adopted by the World Conference to Review and Appraise the Achievements of the United Nations Decade for Women: Equality, Development and Peace (Nairobi, 1985).

17   D. Hodgson "The Child's Right to Life, Survival and Development" (1994) 2 *The International Journal of Children's Rights* 369, 383-384.

12 Parental Educational Rights

Introduction

In his *Second Treatise of Government*, John Locke referred to the obligation of parents to educate their children until they become able to make full and proper use of their freedom.[1]   Thomas Jefferson considered this obligation so important and unique that he was reluctant to support the compulsory education of children over "the will of the parent".[2]   In contemporary society, the education of children is now shared between their parents or guardians and the formal education system.   In today's terms, the conception of parental obligations in the educational field has been superseded to a significant extent by that of parental rights or liberties.   Although the trend today is towards a diminution of parental rights in this field, their impact is still considerable.

A number of justifications have been put forward for acknowledging a legitimate decision-making role for parents in the matter of their children's education. The conventional wisdom is that the natural ties of love and affection between parent and child make it likely that the parents are best placed to perceive what will be in the best interests of their children. It is argued, therefore, that parents should have the right to make decisions on behalf of their children about whether to send them to school, what type of school to send them to, and what they should learn there.[3] Other rationales include the societal interest in diversity and pluralism, protection against State-sponsored indoctrination, and the desire not to unduly interfere with family life so as to permit parents to induct their children into the beliefs and practices of the particular way of life to which the parents are committed.[4]

Recognition by International Instruments of the Right of Parents to Choose the Kind of Education for Their Children

The right of parents to choose their children's education according to their own religious or philosophical convictions is regulated by international human rights instruments either as a component of freedom of religion or belief or within the framework of the right to education. Article 26(3) of the *Universal Declaration of Human Rights* is an example of the latter

189

whereby parents are acknowledged to have "a prior right to choose the kind of education that shall be given to their children". The United Nations *Declaration of the Rights of the Child* of 1959 is less explicit. Principle 7 thereof merely states that "[t]he best interests of the child shall be the guiding principle of those responsible for his education". During the drafting of the *Children's Declaration*, the International Catholic Child Bureau wanted explicit mention of the parental right to choose the religious education of their children while the representatives of Guatemala and Israel proposed that the child have the right to be raised in the faith of his or her parents. These proposals were rejected, however,[5] but have been largely incorporated into the United Nations *Declaration on the Elimination of All Forms of Intolerance and of Discrimination Based on Religion or Belief.* [6]   Article 5(2) thereof states:

> Every child shall enjoy the right to have access to education in the matter of religion or belief in accordance with the wishes of his parents or, as the case may be, legal guardians, and shall not be compelled to receive teaching on religion or belief against the wishes of his parents or legal guardians, the best interests of the child being the guiding principle.

Several international human rights conventions place the parental right on a much firmer footing.[7]   Article 5(1)(b) of the U.N.E.S.C.O. *Convention against Discrimination in Education* records the agreement of the States Parties that it is essential to respect the liberty of parents to choose for their children private educational institutions which conform to State-prescribed minimum standards, and their liberty to ensure the religious and moral education of their children in conformity with their own convictions.[8]   Article 13(3) of the *International Covenant on Economic, Social and Cultural Rights* is in virtually identical terms. Article 18(4) of the *International Covenant on Civil and Political Rights* also obliges States Parties "to have respect for the liberty of parents and, when applicable, legal guardians to ensure the religious and moral education of their children in conformity with their own convictions". Unlike the equivalent provisions in the U.N.E.S.C.O. *Convention* and the *Covenant*, however, the parental liberty is set within the framework of a provision guaranteeing freedom of thought, conscience and religion. So fundamental and important is this freedom that Article 18 as a whole is one of the few provisions of the *ICCPR* that cannot be derogated from by a State Party.[9]   The *travaux préparatoires* of the *ICCPR* reveal the purposes underlying Article 18(4) - the protection of the beliefs of parents and their provision with a means to protect their children from the risk of indoctrination by the State in public schools. During the drafting debates, numerous State representatives recalled the abuses of the German educational system perpetrated by the Nazis.[10]

The parental right to choose the type of education to be undertaken by their children is stated in somewhat weaker terms in the *Convention on the Rights of the Child*. Article 14(2) thereof states that "States Parties shall respect the rights and duties of the parents . . . to provide direction to the child in the exercise of his or her right [to freedom of thought, conscience and religion] in a manner consistent with the evolving capacities of the child". The primary right-holder is the child rather than the parent who merely exercises a right to provide guidance until the child is sufficiently mature to make his or her own informed judgment. Unlike other international conventions, the *Children's Convention* does not contain a provision respecting the parental right to have children educated in conformity with parental convictions, presumably because it would be inappropriate for an instrument on children's rights to incorporate such a provision. Nevertheless, during the second reading of the *Convention*, concern over the absence of such a provision was expressed by the Netherlands, Italy, the Holy See, Ireland, Canada and the United States of America.[11]

Recognition by Regional Instruments of the Right of Parents to Choose the Kind of Education for Their Children

All three regional human rights systems recognise in treaty form the right of parents to choose the kind of education for their children. As we shall see shortly, however, the European system has led the way in defining its parameters.

The *American Convention on Human Rights* provides for the relevant right in the context of a provision concerning freedom of conscience and religion. Article 12(4) thereof states that "[p]arents or guardians, as the case may be, have the right to provide for the religious and moral education of their children, or wards, that is in accord with their own convictions". By contrast, the *Additional Protocol to the American Convention on Human Rights in the Area of Economic, Social and Cultural Rights* recognises the parental right within the framework of a provision devoted to the right to education. In language reminiscent of Article 26(3) of the *Universal Declaration of Human Rights*, Article 13(4) of the *Additional Protocol* recognises the parental right to select the type of education to be given to their children. In terms of the Organisation of

African Unity, Article 11(4) of the *African Charter on the Rights and Welfare of the Child* provides that States Parties shall respect the rights and duties of parents to ensure the religious and moral education of their children.[12]

Within the Council of Europe, the relevant parental right appears in Article 2 of *Protocol 1* to the *European Convention on Human Rights and Fundamental Freedoms* which states:

> No person shall be denied the right to education. In the exercise of any functions which it assumes in relation to education and to teaching, the State shall respect the right of parents to ensure such education and teaching in conformity with their own religious and philosophical convictions.[13]

The second sentence of Article 2 is the result of a compromise and it has provoked more reservations than any other provision in the *Convention.* [14] The second sentence is principally a protection against indoctrination by the State.[15] As the main provider of educational services, the State has a duty not to use its powerful and influential position to promote one set of opinions or values to the exclusion of all others.[16]

The scope and meaning of the phrase "religious and philosophical convictions" have been tested a number of times before the European Court of Human Rights. In 1976, the Court was called on in the case of *Kjeldsen, Busk Madsen and Pedersen*[17] to consider whether compulsory sex education within schools breached the second sentence of Article 2. Sex education had been an optional subject in Danish public schools for many years. In 1970, the Danish Parliament decided to follow Sweden and passed legislation amending the *State Schools Act 1966* in order to introduce compulsory sex education into public primary schools. Under the legislative amendment, sex education would not be presented as a separate subject but would be integrated instead with the teaching of other subjects. Consequently, Danish parents would lose their existing right to exempt their children from sex education classes. The parents of a number of children objected that the amendment infringed their right to ensure their children's education in conformity with their own Christian religious convictions and, as such, constituted a breach of Article 2. While acknowledging the parents' right to require the State to respect their religious and philosophical convictions, the Court held that the setting and planning of the curriculum was within the competence of the State authorities. The extent of the requirement imposed on the authorities by the second sentence of Article 2 was stated by the Court as follows:

... the State, in fulfilling the functions assumed by it in regard to education and teaching, must take care that information or knowledge included in the curriculum is conveyed in an objective, critical and pluralistic manner. The State is forbidden to pursue an aim of indoctrination that might be considered as not respecting parents' religious and philosophical convictions.[18]

It was thus not open to State authorities to pursue a policy of indoctrination. The Court concluded, however, that there had been no breach of Article 2 since, in its view, the Danish legislation did not amount to an attempt at indoctrination aimed at advocating a specific kind of sexual behaviour. Rather, the legislation sought to present information to children in a more objective and precise manner than they would otherwise acquire it from other sources.[19]

In the case of *Campbell and Cosans v U.K.* [20] the European Court of Human Rights faced the daunting task of trying to set limits upon what constitutes a philosophical conviction for the purposes of the second sentence of Article 2 of *Protocol 1*. Both applicants had sought and been refused assurances from the local education authority that their sons would not be subjected to measures of corporal punishment at school. The applicants alleged that this refusal infringed their right under Article 2 to ensure their son's education in conformity with their own philosophical convictions. The United Kingdom Government argued that the views of the applicants concerning corporal punishment did not constitute "philosophical convictions" for the purposes of Article 2. The Court considered that the expression "philosophical convictions" denotes "such convictions as are worthy of respect in a 'democratic society' . . . and are not incompatible with human dignity; in addition, they must not conflict with the fundamental right of the child to education, the whole of Article 2 being dominated by its first sentence".[21] The Court held that the parental objections to corporal punishment were based on philosophical convictions for the purposes of Article 2 because they attained "a certain level of cogency, seriousness, cohesion and importance".[22]

If the parents' objection is sufficiently well founded on a religious or philosophical conviction, the duty of the State Party to the *European Convention* is to 'respect' their right. The obligation to 'respect' such convictions only just escaped being the weaker obligation to "have regard to" those convictions.[23] Generally speaking, the State will respect the parental right if the authorities permit their children to be excused from the offending lessons. As the European Court of Human Rights observed in *Campbell and Cosans v U.K.*, however, the child retains his or her right to education. Thus, if the State cannot arrange public education in a manner which is sensitive to the convictions of the parents, it must permit them to establish private schools.[24]

Recognition of the Right of Parents to Choose the Kind of Education for Their Children Under Domestic Law

The right of parents to choose the kind of education for their children is considered sufficiently important to receive constitutional protection under the laws of some States. For example, Article 20(1) of the *Constitution of Cyprus (1960)* recognises the right of parents to secure for their children such education as is in conformity with their religious convictions. Pursuant to Article 42 of the Constitution of Ireland, the State guarantees to respect the inalienable right and duty of parents to provide, according to their means, for the religious and moral, intellectual, physical and social education of their children. The State cannot oblige parents to send their children to public schools in violation of their conscience and lawful preference.[25]

Respect for parental convictions in the educational field in the United States of America is protected by the "Free Exercise" and "Establisment" clauses of the First Amendment concerning freedom of religion[26] and the Equal Protection Clause of the Fourteenth Amendment to the U.S. Constitution. Early decisions of the United States Supreme Court have been interpreted as supporting the principle that the State is not entitled to interfere with the religious convictions of parents without an exceptional reason for doing so. For example, as early as 1925 the Supreme Court in the case of *Pierce v. Society of Sisters* [27] declared unconstitutional a state law which permitted only public school attendance to satisfy compulsory education laws. That case involved a direct clash between state authority over education and the right of parents to select for their children a private school. The Oregon *Compulsory Education Act 1922*, which required parents of children between the ages of eight and sixteen years to send them to public schools only, was declared an unreasonable interference with the right of parents to direct the upbringing of their children. The choice between a public education and a private education (religious or otherwise) for their children was described as a "fundamental liberty" of parents under the Constitution's Fourteenth Amendment. The Supreme Court stated that there is no "general power of the State to standardize its children by forcing them to accept instruction from public teachers only".[28]

In 1972 the U.S. Supreme Court was called upon in *Wisconsin v. Yoder* [29] to adjudicate a conflict between freedom of religious belief and the State of Wisconsin's compulsory school attendance law. The Amish parents claimed that enforcement of the compulsory formal education requirement after the eighth grade would seriously undermine the free exercise of their religious beliefs. The Court held that the combined effect of the First and Fourteenth Amendments prevent a state from compelling Amish parents to cause their children who have graduated from eighth grade to attend formal public or private high school to age sixteen. The Court thus further limited the state's control over education, stating that:

> A state's interest in universal education . . . is not totally free from a balancing process when it impinges on fundamental rights and interests, such as those specifically protected by the Free Exercise Clause of the First Amendment, and the traditional interest of parents with respect to the religious upbringing of their children.[30]

The Right of Children to Participate in Decisions Affecting Their Education

An important contemporary issue is whether children have, or should have, a right to participate in decisions concerning the type of education they receive, so that their education is in conformity with their own religious and philosophical convictions. Although the wishes of parent and child often coincide in this area, this is not always the case. The child may have an independent interest in such matters as sex education, language tuition and certain activities considered by parents as contrary to family beliefs or values.

The international instruments have traditionally considered the role of parents in determining their children's education as a right of the parents rather than a parent's exercise of the child's right on the latter's behalf.[31] Until recently, children had no recognised legal right to determine their own education, with it being assumed that the interests of the child and parent would coincide. However, there has been a growing call by both educationalists[32] and jurists[33] that international human rights law provide stronger protection of the right of young persons to have a greater say in choosing their own educational paths. It has been argued that the incapacity of childhood is not absolute and that a child gradually develops the ability, and therefore the right, to make responsible decisions.[34] Children should therefore be allowed to participate in making educational decisions affecting them to an extent commensurate with their age and understanding.[35]   Indeed, one educationalist has argued that during the years of primary schooling, parents should have the determining voice as children are not yet in a position to make reflective decisions for themselves. However, as students progress through secondary schooling, the case for making their own educational choices becomes stronger.[36]

Judicial decisions from several jurisdictions during the 1970s and 1980s began to embrace this new "functional capacity" approach. In its 1972 decision in *Wisconsin v Yoder* the majority of the Supreme Court of the United States failed to deal with a potential conflict of interest between Amish parents and their children concerning the latter's kind of education. Douglas J. considered, however, the independent interests of the Amish children which were at stake. His Honour considered the possibility that students might wish to opt out of the Amish tradition and that they should be given an opportunity, therefore, to present their views to the court before parents withdrew them from formal education.   Douglas J. considered by way of an *obiter dictum* that if an Amish child wished to attend high school and was sufficiently mature to make a responsible and informed decision, the State would be able to override the religious objections of parents.[37] The same issue was considered within the Council of Europe by Mr Kellberg in *Kjeldsen, Busk Madsen and Pedersen v Denmark*. In a separate concurring opinion, Mr Kellberg stated that insufficient stress had been put on the rights of the child. He recognised that as students grow older, they will develop the capacity to hold and assert their own independent views concerning religious and philosophical convictions and what they consider to be in their own educational best interests.[38]   In 1986, the House of Lords considered the issue of a clash between the convictions of parents and the independent interests of their child in the case of *Gillick v West Norfolk and Wisbech Area Health Authority*.[39] In that case, Lord Scarman identified the underlying principle of the English common law in this area - the "parental right yields to the child's right to make his own decisions when he reaches a sufficient understanding and intelligence to be capable of making up his own mind on the matter requiring decision . . .".[40]

The evolving capacity of children has also been recognised by international conferences, parliamentary resolutions and international human rights instruments. In January, 1979, participants from 19 countries of Western and Eastern Europe attended a Conference on the Legal Protection of the Rights of the Child held in Warsaw. The Conference adopted an *Official Statement of Principles*,   Principle 5 of which acknowledged the important role of children in deciding on the content and form of educational programmes. Principle 7 of the European Parliament Resolution of 14 March 1984 concerning freedom of education in the European Community states in part that "[i]t is the parents' right to choose a school for their children until the latter can do so for themselves". Article 11(4) of the 1990 *African Charter on the Rights and Welfare of the Child* provides in part that the States Parties shall respect the rights and duties of parents "to ensure the religious and moral education of the child in a manner consistent with the evolving capacities of the child".

The most comprehensive and far-reaching recognition of the evolving capacity of children, however, is to be found in various provisions of the *Convention on the Rights of the Child.* Article 5 obliges States Parties to respect the rights of those legally responsible for the child "to provide, in a manner consistent with the evolving capacities of the child, appropriate direction and guidance in the exercise by the child of the rights recognized in the . . . Convention". Article 14(2) casts the same obligation on States Parties specifically in relation to the child's right to freedom of thought, conscience and religion.[41] Article 12(1) obliges States Parties to "assure to the child who is capable of forming his or her own views the right to express those views freely in all matters affecting the child, the views of the child being given due weight in accordance with the age and maturity of the child". The combined effect of these provisions as well as Article 28(1) (dealing with the child's right to education) is such that older and more mature children are provided under the *Convention* with the right to participate in decisions to help ensure that their education is more in conformity with their own religious and philosophical convictions.[42] In the context of the child who wishes to participate in school activities which the parents consider to be contrary to their convictions, if the child is sufficiently mature and responsible enough to make an informed decision on his or her own, that decision should be allowed to stand in most circumstances.[43]

The Liberty of Individuals and Entities to Establish and Direct Private Schools

International human rights law permits the existence of non-State schools but does not oblige States to take positive measures to assist them.[44] Several international and regional treaties speak not of a 'right' to establish and direct private educational institutions but rather of a 'liberty' or 'freedom' to do so.

The U.N.E.S.C.O. *Convention against Discrimination in Education* of 1960 identifies two types of educational institutions whose establishment and operation shall not be deemed to constitute discrimination.   First, Article 2(b) refers to the establishment or maintenance, for religious or linguistic reasons, of separate educational institutions if attendance is optional and the education provided conforms to minimum standards prescribed by State authorities.   Secondly, Article 2(c) refers to the establishment or maintenance of private secular educational institutions if their object is not to secure the exclusion of any group but to provide educational facilities in addition to those provided by the public authorities and the education provided conforms to minimum State standards.   Article 13(4) of the *International Covenant on Economic, Social and Cultural Rights* recognises "the liberty of individuals and bodies to establish and direct [private] educational institutions" provided they observe the aims of education specified by Article 13(1) and conform to State-prescribed minimum standards.   Article 29(2) of the *Convention on the Rights of the Child* is virtually in identical terms. It is important to note that the drafters chose the word 'liberty' rather than the word 'right' to avoid any implication that the State might be obliged to provide material assistance for the education of children outside State schools.[45]   According to the *travaux préparatoires*, the reference to State minimum educational standards was adopted partly to allay fears that the exercise of excessive individual liberty might result in teaching contrary to the aims of education referred to in Article 13(1), and partly to avoid the possibility that "foreign bodies" might spread subversive propaganda under the guise of education.[46]

Regional human rights systems have also recognised the liberty or freedom of individuals and entities to establish and direct private schools. Article 13(5) of the *Additional Protocol to the American Convention on Human Rights in the Area of Economic, Social and Cultural Rights* recognises "the freedom of individuals and entities to establish and direct educational institutions in accordance with the domestic legislation of the States Parties". Within the Council of Europe, the text of Article 2 of *Protocol 1* to the *European Convention for the Protection of Human Rights and Fundamental Freedoms* does not make it clear whether there is a right to establish schools outside the State system.   As some commentators have persuasively argued, the requirements of the second sentence of Article 2 - namely, that the State respect the religious and philosophical convictions of parents - arguably creates a practical imperative to permit the operation of some private schools.[47]   In *Jordebo v Sweden* [48] the European Commission of Human Rights took the view that

Article 2 guarantees the right to start and run a private school which is subject to State regulation in order to ensure the quality of education. The State may not use its regulatory power, however, to make it impossible to establish private schools.[49]

Generally, States do not have any objections to the establishment of private schools. The most controversial issue in this area is whether States have, or should have, an obligation to provide financial and material assistance to private schools equal to that provided to public schools. As minority groups are often economically disadvantaged, they argue that the State has an obligation to do more than permit private schools; it must fund them as well.[50] Representatives of organisations which maintain private schools maintain that freedom of education can only be achieved on an equal basis if private schools are free of charge, which is only possible through public financing.[51]

The minorities treaties under the League of Nations system did provide for an equitable provision of public funds to minority schools. For example, Article 9 of the *Treaty Between The Principal Allied and Associated Powers and Poland*[52] provided in part as follows:

> In towns and districts where there is a considerable proportion of Polish nationals belonging to racial, religious or linguistic minorities, these minorities shall be assured an equitable share in the enjoyment and application of the sums which may be provided out of public funds . . . for educational, religious or charitable purposes.

Contemporary international law, however, does not impose upon States any obligation to subsidise private education or to create conditions, such as tax advantages, in which private schools can more easily operate.[53] States Parties to the *International Covenant on Civil and Political Rights* are only obliged by Article 18(4) thereof to permit parents to choose from among different types of education, if such schools exist.[54] The *travaux préparatoires* of the *I.C.C.P.R.* make it clear that there is no legal duty thereunder to subsidise education according to parental preference.[55] The United Nations Human Rights Committee has ruled that the failure by a State to fund private schools does not constitute discrimination under Article 26 of the *I.C.C.P.R.* In the cases of *Blom, Lindgren et al.* and *Hjord et al. v Sweden* the Human Rights Committee held that Sweden had not breached Article 26 in refusing subsidies for school meals and textbooks. It had been alleged that the Swedish Government had discriminated against private schools by giving preferential treatment to public sector schooling in the form of such educational benefits as free bus transport and free textbooks and school meals. The Committee rejected the applicants' arguments, however, reasoning that "a State Party cannot be deemed to discriminate against parents who freely choose not to avail themselves of benefits which are generally open to all".[56]   It would appear to be beyond doubt, therefore, that States Parties are not obliged under the *I.C.C.P.R.* to subsidise private schools either directly or indirectly.

The same question has arisen for consideration under the *European Convention for the Protection of Human Rights and Fundamental Freedoms.* The *travaux préparatoires* disclose that the second sentence of Article 2 of *Protocol 1* was introduced primarily to protect the rights of parents against State use of public schools for the indoctrination of the pupils, rather than for the establishment or continued operation of private schools.[57]   The decisions of the European Court of Human Rights and the European Commission of Human Rights have confirmed that States Parties to the *European Convention* are not obliged thereunder to subsidise, or create favourable conditions for the establishment or continuance of, private schools. In the *Belgian Linguistic* case, the European Court of Human Rights considered that the States Parties did not accept, and so the *Convention* did not require, an understanding of the right to education that " . . . would require them to establish at their own expense, or to subsidise, education of any particular type or at any particular level".[58]   The European Commission of Human Rights has rejected a number of applications submitted by private educational institutions from various countries under Article 2 of *Protocol 1.* The Commission held in *W and KL v Sweden* [59] that a State Party has no obligation under the *European Convention* to fund or subsidise private systems of education which it has permitted. Consequently, refusal of a subsidy to pupils at a private school for such items as textbooks and other educational aids will not breach Article 2. Thus, in the Commission's view, merely permitting private schools to be established is sufficient compliance with Article 2.

The U.N.E.S.C.O. *Convention against Discrimination in Education*, the most comprehensive international instrument concerning the right to education, is silent on the issue of the funding of private educational systems. In the face of such silence, the issue will be ultimately resolved as it is with many other social and economic rights, as one of State resources.[60]   The funding issue is important since, as one commentator has observed, States which seek to abolish private education directly would clearly breach international law but the same goal may be achieved with impunity through indirect methods such as the fiscal system.[61]   An indication of the direction of the future development of the law on this issue might be gleaned from Principle 7 of the European Parliament

Resolution of 14 March 1984 concerning Freedom of Education in the E.C. which provides in part that "it is the duty of the State to provide the necessary facilities for state or private schools".

Religious Education

There are basically two approaches to religious education. The first has been described as the 'dogmatic' approach whereby children receive instruction in the tenets of one particular faith in a doctrinaire fashion. The second might be described as the 'ecumenical' approach whereby the aim of religious education is perceived as the promotion of knowledge and understanding of the significance of religious experience without any attempt being made to inculcate a specific set of beliefs.[62] The latter approach attempts to develop an attitude of objective enquiry to the major religious belief systems as well as non-religious convictions. The main difference between the two approaches lies in the intention of the former to convert while the latter seeks to inform.

Some contend that it is no longer appropriate for a modern State to teach religion as contemporary society grows increasingly secularised. As concerns the 'dogmatic' approach to religious education, it has been argued that the teaching of religion is best achieved outside the formal educational system in the hands of those with a real conviction and qualification. It should therefore be the function of the home and the parents' own religious community to instruct the child in the beliefs of a particular faith. The role of the school is merely to inform students about the nature of religion and provide them with a platform from which to enter into the religious realm. As one commentator has stated, religious education of the 'ecumenical' type would seem to be unexceptionable on liberal democratic grounds.[63] In his view, a reasonable compromise would be classes which give broadly equal treatment to the whole range of major world religions and belief systems.[64] In England, there appears to be widespread parental support, even among those who hold no firm religious beliefs, for the idea that children should receive some religious education at school.[65] Some parents hope and expect that their children will thereby acquire a religious faith or conviction or some basic moral values.

International and regional human rights instruments generally do not recognise the right to religious education *per se*. A right to religious instruction had been recognised in treaty form within the League of Nations system. Article 106 of the *Treaty of Paris, Poland-Danzig*[66] provided in part that "[r]eligious instruction shall be part of the regular school curiculum". However, Article 106 was stated in terms to be without prejudice to the State's right of supervision. Despite intense lobbying and a plea by the International Catholic Child Bureau for explicit mention of the right to religious education, the final text of Principle 7 of the United Nations *Declaration of the Rights of the Child* did not contain any such reference.[67] What the international instruments do contain, however, is a parental right to withdraw children from any religious instruction which may be permitted by the individual State. Such a right is based on the offence which attendance at religious education classes would otherwise cause to the basic values and beliefs of the parents. Indeed, this right was explicitly recognised by Article 106 of the *Poland-Danzig Treaty* which provided that "the right to withdraw a child from religious instruction . . . shall be granted in accordance with the expressed wishes of the person who is responsible for the religious upbringing of the child". Later instruments have recognised the right of withdrawal in more indirect terms in a manner which suggests that the right may be exercised by the child himself or herself. For example, Article 5(1)(b) of the *Convention against Discrimination in Education* states in part that "no person or group of persons should be compelled to receive religious instruction inconsistent with his or their conviction". Of similar effect is Article 18(2) of the *International Covenant on Civil and Political Rights* which provides that "[n]o one shall be subject to coercion which would impair his freedom to have or adopt a religion or belief of his choice". To ensure compliance with these provisions, it may be necessary for the State Party to permit exemptions from the offending classes or practices and the holding of separate classes.[68]

The obligation to respect personal beliefs contained in both Sub-Articles (2) and (4) of Article 18 of the *I.C.C.P.R.* extends to all forms of belief, including non-religious beliefs. In the case of *Hartikainen v Finland* [69] the Applicant complained that free thinkers' rights were violated by the fact that children who were exempted from compulsory religion classes in school were obliged to take a course in the history of religion and ethics, even though they received no religious instruction outside school. He alleged that the substitute course was in fact biased toward the teaching of the Christian religion and morality. Although the Finnish Government denied these allegations, it did concede that difficulties existed with the teaching of the course which was undergoing a review. The United Nations Human Rights Committee, echoing the approach taken by the European Court of Human Rights in *Kjeldsen*, ruled:

The Committee does not consider that the requirement of the relevant Finnish legislation that instruction in the study of the history of religions and ethics should be given instead of religious instruction is in itself incompatible with Article 18(4), if such alternative course of instruction is given in a neutral and objective way and respects the convictions of parents and guardians who do not believe in any religion . . . the Committee believes that appropriate action is being taken to resolve the difficulties . . .[70]

With regard to the Council of Europe, it would appear that the second sentence of Article 2 of *Protocol 1* concerning respect for the right of parents to ensure the education of their children in conformity with their own convictions implicitly allows parents to make alternative arrangements if they so wish in cases where compulsory education is provided in State schools.[71] The European Commission of Human Rights was presented with this issue in *Karnell and Hardt v Sweden* [72] The applicants, members of the Evangelical-Lutheran Church of Sweden, complained that they were prevented from giving their children appropriate religious instruction. Their children attended State schools where they were obliged to take compulsory religious instruction, and their Church had been refused permission to provide alternative religious instruction. The Commission approved a friendly settlement of the case when the Swedish authorities agreed to satisfy their complaint in full. By the terms of the decision, children belonging to the Church would be exempted from compulsory religious instruction if their parents so requested.

In some countries, the parental right to withdraw children from religious education classes is regulated by statute. Pursuant to Section 25(4) of the English *Education Act 1944*, parents may withdraw their children from religious instruction classes which are otherwise required by the *Act.* [73] Furthermore, if parents desire that their children receive a form of religious instruction which is not available at the school, they can demand that the education authority make suitable arrangements for the children to receive it at another school or, if this is not possible, elsewhere during school hours.[74] By contrast, in the United States of America, religious education classes in state schools are broadly prohibited by the First Amendment to the U.S. Constitution which prohibits Congress from making any law "respecting an establishment of religion". In the leading case of *Illinois ex rel. McCollum v Board of Education*,[75] the U.S. Supreme Court held that a release-time programme whereby students were released to attend religious instruction in public school classrooms violated the First Amendment. With the permission of the local board of education, religious teachers were employed (under the supervision of the superintendent of public schools) by a private religious group, including representatives of Catholic, Protestant and Jewish faiths, to give religious instruction in public school buildings once each week. On their parents' request, students were released from class for this instruction but other students were not released from their public school duties. The Supreme Court held as follows:

> Pupils compelled by law to go to school for secular education are released in part from their legal duty upon the condition that they attend the religious classes. This is beyond all question a utilization of the tax-established and tax-supported public school system to aid religious groups to spread their faith. And it falls squarely under the ban of the First Amendment . . . [76]

Notes

1   As quoted in F. Volio "The Child's Right to Education: A Survey" in G. Mialaret (ed.) *The Child's Right to Education* (1979) 19, 20.

2   Letter dated 9 September 1817 from Thomas Jefferson to Joseph Caball in 17 *Writings of Thomas Jefferson* 417.

3   K. Forster   "Parents' Rights and Educational Policy"   (1989) 21 *Educational Philosophy and Theory* 47.

4   The 'family' is recognised and protected by Article 10 of the *International Covenant on Economic, Social and Cultural Rights* and Articles 17 and 23 of the *International Covenant on Civil and Political Rights.*

5   P. Veerman   *The Rights of the Child and the Changing Image of Childhood* (1992) 173.

6   Proclaimed by the General Assembly in Resolution 36/55 of 25 November 1981.

7   The religious and moral convictions of parents are also recognised in the context of their children's education by international humanitarian law. See Article 78(2) of *Protocol Additional to the Geneva Conventions of 12 August 1949, and relating to the Protection of Victims of International Armed Conflicts (Protocol I)* and Article 4(3)(a) of *Protocol Additional to the Geneva Conventions of 12 August 1949, and relating to the Protection of Victims of Non-International Armed Conflicts (Protocol II).*

8   See also Article 2(b) which provides that the establishment of separate educational institutions for religious reasons which offer an education in keeping with the wishes of the pupils' parents shall not be deemed to constitute discrimination.

9   By virtue of Article 4(2) of the *ICCPR.*

10   U.N. Doc. E/CN.4/SR227. See also G. Van Bueren "Education: Whose Right is it Anyway?" in L. Heffernan (ed.) *Human Rights: A European Perspective* (1994) 339, 342.

11   Commission on Human Rights *Report of the Working Group on a Draft Convention on the Rights of the Child* E/CN.4/1989/48 (2 March 1989) pp. 86-87, para. 491.
12   See also Article 7(b) of *The Cairo Declaration on Human Rights in Islam.*
13   See also Article 16 of the *Declaration of the European Parliament of Fundamental Rights and Freedoms* ("Parents shall have the right to make provision for [education and vocational training] in accordance with their religious and philosophical convictions."), and Principle 7 of the European Parliament's Resolution of 14 March 1984 Concerning Freedom of Education in the E.C. ("It is the parents' right to choose a school for their children . . .").
14   F. Jacobs and R. White *The European Convention on Human Rights* (2nd ed., 1996) 264.
15   *Kjeldsen, Busk Madsen and Pedersen v Denmark* A 23 para. 53 (1976).
16   D. Harris, M. O'Boyle and C. Warbrick *Law of the European Convention on Human Rights* (1995) 540.
17   Judgment of 7 December 1976, Series A, No. 23; (1979-80) 1 E.H.R.R. 711.
18   Series A, No. 23, p. 26, para. 53.
19   In an earlier case, the European Court of Human Rights had held that the inclusion of the phrase "philosophical convictions" within the second sentence of Article 2 was not intended to guarantee respect for parental preferences or opinions in linguistic or cultural matters. See the *Belgian Linguistic Case* Judgment of 23 July 1968, Series A, No. 6, p. 32, para. 6; (1979-80) 1 E.H.R.R. 252.
20   Series A, No. 48 (1982).
21   Id. para. 36.
22   Ibid.
23   A. Robertson "The European Convention on Human Rights: Recent Developments" (1951) 28 *British Yearbook of International Law* 359, 363-4.
24   *X v U.K. No. 7782/77*, 14 DR 179 (1978).
25   B. Walsh "Existence and Meaning of Fundamental Rights in the Field of Education in Ireland" (1981) 2 *Human Rights Law Journal* 319-320.
26   The First Amendment provides in part: "Congress shall make no law respecting an establishment of religion, or prohibiting the free exercise thereof . . .".
27   268 U.S. 510 (1925).
28   Id. 535.
29   406 U.S. 205 (1972).
30   Id. 214.
31   See Article 26(3) of the *UDHR*; Article 18(4) *ICCPR*; Article 5(1)(b) of the U.N.E.S.C.O. *Convention against Discrimination in Education*; Article 2 of *Protocol 1* to the *European Convention on Human Rights and Fundamental Freedoms.*

32   J. Holt *Escape from Childhood* (1974) Dutton, New York, 240-1.
33   M. Nowak "The Right to Education" in A. Eide (ed.) *Economic, Social and Cultural Rights* (1995) 189, 205.
34   H. Cullen "Education Rights or Minority Rights?" (1993) 7 *International Journal of Law and the Family* 143, 161.
35   A. Bainham *Children, Parents and the State* (1988) 168-169.
36   B. Crittenden "The Rights of Children" (1989) 5 *Melbourne Report* 4, 6.
37   *Wisconsin v Yoder* 406 U.S. 205, 242 (1972).
38   Series B, No. 21 (1975), at p. 50.
39   [1986] A.C. 112.
40   Id. 186.
41   Article 14(2) provides: "States Parties shall respect the rights and duties of the parents and, when applicable, legal guardians, to provide direction to the child in the exercise of his or her right in a manner consistent with the evolving capacities of the child".
42   G. Van Bueren "Education: Whose Right is it Anyway?" in L. Heffernan (ed.) *Human Rights: A European Perspective* (1994) 339, 346.
43   Cullen, op. cit., 162.
44   Van Bueren, op. cit., 347.
45   Report of the Third Committee, 12 U.N. GAOR Annexes (Agenda Item 33) 1, at 4 (1957).
46   Ibid.
47   Harris, O'Boyle and Warbrick, op. cit., 544.
48   App. 11533/85, 6 March 1987, (1987) 51 DR 125.
49   Id. 128.
50   Cullen, op. cit., 169.
51   Nowak, op. cit., p. 207 and n. 54.
52   112 Great Britain T.S. 232 (signed 28 June 1919).
53   Van Bueren, op. cit., 348.
54   Id. 343.
55   U.N. Doc. A/C3/SR 1023; U.N. Doc. A/C3/SR 1024.
56   Communication No. 191/1985, paragraphs 10.2 - 10.3; Communications Nos 298 and 299/1988, paragraphs 10.2 - 10.4.
57   Official Report of the 35th Sitting of the Consultative Assembly, 8 December 1951. *Collected Editions*, V at pp. 1229-30.
58   Series A, No. 6, p. 31 (1968).
59   Application No. 10476/83, (11 December 1985), 45 DR 143 at 148-149 (1986).
60   Cullen, op. cit., 169.
61   Van Bueren, op. cit., 348.
62   S. Poulter *English Law and Ethnic Minority Customs* (1986) 165.
63   Ibid.
64   Ibid.
65   Regan *Local Government and Education* (2nd ed., 1979) 67.
66   6 L.N.T.S. 190 (signed 9 November 1920).

67   P. Veerman *The Rights of the Child and the Changing Image of Childhood* (1992) 177.

68   Cullen, op. cit., 169.

69   Communication No. 40/1978 (United Nations Human Rights Committee).

70   Id. para. 10.4.

71   Jacobs and White, op. cit., 264.

72   Application No. 4733/71, 13 December 1971, (1971) 14 *Yearbook* 676.

73   Section 25(4) provides in part: "If the parent of any pupil . . . requests that he be . . . excused from attendance at religious worship in the school, or from attendance at religious instruction in the school, . . . then, until the request is withdrawn, the pupil shall be excused from such attendance accordingly".

74   Section 25(5) of the *Education Act 1944*.

75   333 U.S. 203 (1948).

76   Id. at 209-210.

PART V

CONCLUSION

13 International Co-operation and Development

International Co-operation

Since its inception in 1945, the United Nations has recognised the necessity of "international co-operation in solving international problems of an economic, social, cultural, or humanitarian character".[1]   The whole of Chapter IX of the *United Nations Charter* is devoted to "International Economic and Social Co-operation" with Article 55 thereof providing, *inter alia*, that the United Nations shall promote "international cultural and educational co-operation".   U.N.E.S.C.O. has been at the forefront in the effort to realise Article 55.   Article I.2.(c) of its Constitution refers to U.N.E.S.C.O.'s role in diffusing knowledge "by encouraging co-operation among the nations in all branches of intellectual activity, including the international exchange of persons active in the fields of education, science and culture and the exchange of publications, objects of artistic and scientific interest and other materials".   Article I.2.(b) of its Constitution also obliges U.N.E.S.C.O. to collaborate with States in order to develop educational activities and to advance the ideal of equality of educational opportunity.   International co-operation in the educational field has also been undertaken at the regional level.   The purpose of the Inter-American Council for Education, Science, and Culture, as stated by Article 99 of the *Charter of the Organization of American States*, is "to promote friendly relations and mutual understanding between the peoples of the Americas through educational, scientific, and cultural co-operation and exchange between Member States . . . ".   The Council's duty in this regard is more clearly spelled out by Article 100.   Pursuant to Article 100(f), the Council shall foster the exchange of professors, research workers, technicians, students and study materials, and encourage the conclusion of multilateral agreements on the progressive co-ordination of the curricula and on the validity and equivalence of degrees and certificates.[2]

In furtherance of the aims stated in the U.N.E.S.C.O. Constitution, several international agreements have been concluded to facilitate the free flow of books, publications and educational, scientific and cultural materials between the Contracting States.   The *Agreement for Facilitating the International Circulation of Visual and Auditory Materials of an Educational, Scientific and Cultural Character* of 15 July 1949 and the *Agreement on the Importation of Educational, Scientific and Cultural Materials* of 22 November 1950 essentially exempt the imported educational materials from customs duties, import restrictions and import licences.   The United Nations General Assembly and the General Conference of U.N.E.S.C.O. have also been active in promoting the exchange of human and material resources between States.   Principle 4 of the *Declaration on the Promotion Among Youth of the Ideals of Peace, Mutual Respect and Understanding Between Peoples*[3] states that "[e]xchanges, travel, tourism, meetings, the study of foreign languages, [and] the twinning of towns and universities . . . should be encouraged and facilitated among young people of all countries . . . ".   The General Conference of U.N.E.S.C.O. has devoted Part X of its *Recommendation Concerning Education for International Understanding, Co-operation and Peace and Education Relating to Human Rights and Fundamental Freedoms 1974* to the subject of "International Co-operation".   Principle 43 thereof calls on Member States to, *inter alia*, strengthen their programmes for the reception of foreign students, research workers, teachers and educators and to promote reciprocal visits by schoolchildren and student, teacher and textbook exchanges.   Strengthening international solidarity in the educational field was a prominent item of the agenda of the World Conference on Education for All held in Jomtien, Thailand in March, 1990.   Article 10(1) of the Conference's *World Declaration on Education for All* proclaims that meeting basic learning needs requires international solidarity and acknowledges that all nations have valuable knowledge and experiences to share for designing effective educational policies and programmes.

The State duty to co-operate with other States in the educational field was placed on a quasi-legal footing by Article 15(4) of the *International Covenant on Economic, Social and Cultural Rights.* Article 15(4) records the recognition by the States Parties of "the benefits to be derived from the encouragement and development of international contacts and co-operation in the scientific and cultural fields". The most recent and comprehensive formulation of the duty to co-operate internationally appears in Article 28(3) of the *Convention on the Rights of the Child* which states:

> States Parties shall promote and encourage international co-operation in matters relating to education, in particular with a view to contributing to the elimination of ignorance and illiteracy throughout the world and facilitating

access to scientific and technical knowledge and modern teaching methods. In this regard, particular account shall be taken of the needs of developing countries.

Article 28(3) essentially transforms into a binding legal obligation Article 10(a) of the U.N.E.S.C.O. *Recommendation concerning the Status of Teachers 1966* regarding co-operative projects, the exchange of research findings, teacher preparation and in-service training. Article 4 of the *Convention* also mentions that in regard to economic, social and cultural rights, States Parties shall undertake all appropriate measures to implement the rights recognised in the *Convention* "to the maximum of their available resources and, where needed, within the framework of international co-operation".[4] Article 4 of the *Convention* is similar to Article 2(1) of the *International Covenant on Economic, Social and Cultural Rights* which obliges States Parties to take steps, individually and through international co-operation, to the maximum of their available resources with a view to achieving progressively the full realisation of the rights recognised in the *Covenant*. According to Principle 26 of *The Limburg Principles on the Implementation of the International Covenant on Economic, Social and Cultural Rights*,[5] the phrase "its available resources" which appears in Article 2(1) of the *I.C.E.S.C.R.* refers to both the resources within a State and those available from the international community through international co-operation and assistance. This phrase has also been interpreted by the Committee on Economic, Social and Cultural Rights as referring to the amount of resources available to the international community as a whole and that can be distributed through international co-operation and assistance.[6] This suggests that the responsibility to provide basic education extends beyond that of individual States and that their economic and resource limitations may be overcome by joint efforts and a pooling of joint resources at the international level.[7]

Development

International co-operation, through the transfer of information, knowledge and technology, is essential to the effective realisation of the right to education for children in the less developed countries. It has been repeatedly observed, moreover, that the right to education is an economic necessity upon which the development of these countries depends.[8] The gap between educational facilities in industrialised countries and those in developing countries demands an active policy of academic co-operation which would assist in contributing to the implementation of the right to development.[9]

The provision of education should be considered by all States as a long-term, high-priority investment because it develops individual human resources as an asset in the process of national development.[10]   As U.N.I.C.E.F. has recognised, a society's failure to invest in education will disable all other developmental efforts, whether it be the effort to increase agricultural production or the effort to reach people with new knowledge about child care.[11]   Educational expenditure ought to be regarded as an investment in human capital because, according to the World Bank, development will not occur without education.[12]   World Bank studies consistently show that economic returns from education are higher than from most other kinds of investment.[13]   Education is therefore a cause as well as a consequence of economic development. The General Conference of U.N.E.S.C.O. has also acknowledged that education is an essential factor in a country's economic growth and has called on States to include educational planning as an integral part of any comprehensive social programme undertaken to improve living conditions.[14]

Latin American States were among the first to stress the importance of the link between education and the development of their peoples.[15] Article 100(e) of the *Charter of the Organization of American States* obliges the Inter-American Council for Education, Science, and Culture to "[s]timulate and support scientific and technological education and research, especially when these relate to national development plans". Article 8 of the *Central American Convention on the Unification of the Fundamental Norms of Education* of 1962 states:

> The signatory States recognize that funds allocated to education must be considered a capital investment. Therefore, in their general budgets they shall give priority to education, in order to accelerate the economic and social development of their peoples.

This theme was picked up at the International Conference on Human Rights held at Teheran in 1968. In its Resolution XII, the Conference invited U.N.E.S.C.O. to stimulate efforts for enhancing the contribution which literacy could make to economic and social development. On 11 December 1969, the United Nations General Assembly proclaimed the *Declaration on Social Progress and Development* [16] which listed the eradication of illiteracy in Article 10(e) as one of the goals to be attained in the raising of the standards of living of all members of society. The United Nations General Assembly has more recently proclaimed in Article 8(1) of its *Declaration on the Right to Development* [17] of 4 December 1986 that the realisation of the right to development entails, *inter alia*, "equality of opportunity for all in their access to . . . education". Although Article 28(3) of the *Convention on the Rights of the Child* does not place development on a legal footing in the educational context, it does have positive implications for developing countries in so far as it succeeds in facilitating access to scientific and technical knowledge and modern teaching methods. The *World Declaration on Education for All* adopted by the 1990 World Conference on Education for All has reaffirmed that basic education is fundamental to the capacity of countries to achieve self-reliant development. The *Declaration* describes basic education as the foundation for human development[18] and "the most profound investment in people and in the future of a country which can be made".[19]

Over the past two decades, international attention has focussed on the crucial role of basic education in the human, economic and social development of the rural sector. A child's ability to read and write and understand basic arithmetic will have a significant bearing on his or her future. If, for example, a boy drops out of school at an early age and becomes an illiterate adult farmer, he will be unable to read directions, weigh fertilisers, calculate his earnings and prepare a budget, and protect himself from unscrupulous creditors. With a view to tackling these and other problems, the World Conference on Agrarian Reform and Rural Development met in Rome in July, 1979 under the auspices of the United Nations Food and Agriculture Organization. The Conference adopted a *Declaration of Principles* as well as a *Programme of Action.* Section VII of the *Programme of Action* states in part as follows:

> Education, including preschool and primary education, and training and extension services are fundamental needs for human development in rural areas and also for expansion and modernization of rural economies. Basic literacy and numeracy and free education for all children, including those in rural areas, deserve the highest priority. No less essential is [sic] the creation and expansion of training and extension networks for both men and women to develop and improve skills and to increase productivity and income-generating capabilities.

Section VII.A.(iii) urged governments to consider action to strengthen programmes of non-formal education which emphasise such matters as functional literacy, health, home economics, nutrition and family planning. U.N.E.S.C.O. has also been active in this area. As part of its *Second Medium-Term Plan (1984-1989) Education for All,* U.N.E.S.C.O. approved a programme to extend and improve education in rural areas. The three subprogrammes related to the extension of educational services, the improvement of educational standards and the contribution of education to development.

Since the 1960s, many developing States have embarked upon reforming traditional educational systems to overcome their colonial past and to make them more attuned to the needs of their citizens. In numerous instances, these States have been assisted in this task by U.N.E.S.C.O., U.N.I.C.E.F., bilateral donors and private aid agencies. For instance, President Julius Nyerere of Tanzania introduced his "Education for Self-Reliance" throughout the primary school system in 1967. Pursuant to this initiative, textbooks were rewritten to emphasise the needs of rural areas and farming methods became part of the regular curriculum.[20] Some developing States have also begun to move over the past two decades towards out-of-school or non-formal education for children who have never been in school or who dropped out at an early age. In 1971, U.N.I.C.E.F. commissioned the International Council for Educational Development to conduct research into what might be done, outside the formal school system, to help prevent the social and economic waste represented by millions of children who had either dropped out of school or had never begun school. The Council recommended that States formulate, on the basis of their particular educational needs, a "minimum package" so that every child would acquire the following:

- functional literacy and basic arithmetic for use in simple agriculture;

- proper nutrition in the family diet;

- a basic understanding of nature and environmental protection;

- knowledge of the social environment to allow constructive participation in community affairs;

- information concerning child care, family planning and sanitation.[21]

Several developing States took up this call. Kenya, for example, opened "village polytechnics"; Thailand offered school drop-outs another opportunity in mobile training schools; Upper Volta introduced a network of rural education centres. The aim of these initiatives was to impart a basic education consisting of knowledge and skills which would empower those living in rural areas to make a modest, but better, living.[22]

The United Nations *Convention on the Elimination of All Forms of Discrimination Against Women* of 1979 addresses in considerable detail the plight of women and girls living in rural areas. It obliges States Parties to take all appropriate measures to eliminate discrimination against them in order to ensure that they participate in, and benefit from, rural development on an equal basis with men. Article 14(2) of the *Convention* requires States Parties, *inter alia*, to ensure that women living in rural areas have the right to participate in the elaboration and implementation of development planning as well as the right to obtain all types of formal and non-formal training and education in order to increase their technical proficiency.[23]

Notes

1   Article 1(3) *United Nations Charter.*

2   Other relevant provisions of the O.A.S. *Charter* are Sub-Articles (c) and (i) of Article 100 which relate respectively to supporting the collective efforts of the Member States to improve and extend education at all levels, and fostering co-operation and technical assistance for preserving the cultural heritage of the American States.

3   Proclaimed by the General Assembly in Resolution 2037 (XX) of 7 December 1965.

4   See also the last preambular paragraph of the *Convention* (concerning the importance of international co-operation for improving the living conditions particularly in developing countries) and Article 23(4) (relating to the obligation of States Parties to promote in the spirit of international co-operation the exchange of appropriate information concerning methods of rehabilitation education and vocational services for disabled children).

5   U.N. Doc. E/CN.4/1987/17, Annex.

6   Committee on Economic, Social and Cultural Rights, *General Comment No. 3*, 1990.

7   C. Beyani "The Prerequisites of Education" in *Education Rights and Minorities* (1994) (A Minority Rights Group Report) 14, 15.

8   M. El Fasi "The Right to Education and Culture" (1968) 9 *Journal of the International Commission of Jurists* 33, 37-38; A. M'Bow "Introduction" in G. Mialaret (ed.) *The Child's Right to Education* (1979) 9, 15.

9   M. Nowak "The Right to Education" in A. Eide (ed.) *Economic, Social and Cultural Rights* (1995) 189, 198.

10   Beyani, op. cit., 15.

11   U.N.I.C.E.F. *The World Summit for Children* 32.

12   World Bank *Education in Sub-Saharan Africa* (1988).

13   For example, four years of primary education is associated with an average increase in farm productivity of at least 10 per cent: U.N.I.C.E.F., op. cit., 32.

14   See U.N.E.S.C.O.'s *Recommendation concerning the Status of Teachers 1966.*

15   The Conference on Education and Economic and Social Development in the Latin American Countries was held at Santiago, Chile in March 1962.

16   Resolution 2542 (XXIV).

17   Resolution 41/128.

18   Article 1(4).

19   Article 9(1).

20   M. Black   *The Children and the Nations: The Story of Unicef* (1986) 318.

21   Id. 320-321.

22   Id. 318.

23   See particularly Article 14(2)(a) and (d).

14 Conclusion

> [T]he effective application of the child's right to education is primarily a question of will. Only the political will of governments and of the international community will be able to promote this essential right to a point at which it will contribute to the fulfilment of every individual and to the progress of every society.[1]

The Minimum Core Content of the Right to Education

It is readily apparent from the foregoing survey that over the past fifty years the international community has embraced education as a basic human right. Even a minimalist approach to the interpretation of those provisions concerning the right to education which appear in the major international and regional human rights instruments discloses a number of important State obligations.

The standard formulation of "a right to education" as opposed to "a right of access to education" implies that governments are obliged to provide education even if schools do not yet exist.[2] Under international human rights law, States are required at the minimum to provide for the existence and maintenance of adequate educational facilities. States may be assisted in fulfilling this requirement by the private sector in so far as the latter invokes its well-established right under international conventional law to establish and direct private educational institutions for religious, linguistic of other recognised reasons. States are also obliged to ensure that all conditions prescribed by international law such as free and compulsory primary education are satisfied.

The relevant provisions of the major international and regional human rights instruments generally recognise the following State obligations:

a) primary education shall be compulsory and available free to all;[3]

b) secondary education shall be made generally available and accessible to all; free secondary education and financial assistance in case of need shall be introduced on a progressive basis;[4]

219

c) higher education shall be made equally accessible to all on the basis of capacity; free tertiary education shall be introduced on a progressive basis;

d) special education programmes shall be established for persons with disabilities and those persons who have not completed the whole period of their primary education;

e) access to, and treatment in, educational programmes at all levels shall be on the basis of non-discrimination and equality of educational opportunity;[5]

f) subject to certain conditions, States must respect the liberty of individuals and bodies and minority groups to establish and direct educational institutions.

Old Problems: New Directions

As one commentator has aptly observed, it is not enough to proclaim lofty principles if they are to remain a dead letter because the methods used to implement them are absent or defective.[6]

It must, of course, be appreciated that the right to education belongs primarily to the "second generation" class of human rights comprising economic, social and cultural rights. Unlike most political and civil rights, these rights often require huge amounts of capital expenditure progressively over time for their effective implementation. Indeed, in the experience of many countries, health, education and defence constitute the leading governmental expenditure items. This is recognised by Article 2(1) of the *International Covenant on Economic, Social and Cultural Rights* which requires States Parties to take steps " . . . to the maximum of [their] available resources, with a view to achieving progressively the full realization of the rights recognized in the present Covenant . . . ". The *Convention on the Rights of the Child* also concedes a margin of appreciation to each State Party. The *chapeau* of Article 28(1) thereof also recognises that the child's right to education will be achieved on a progressive basis. During the drafting deliberations, the representative of China, supported by other delegates, pointed out the different levels of economic development of States and their impact on the provision of free education.[7]

Writing some 30 years ago, Mohammed El Fasi said that although the world has recognised the right to education and has attempted to make it a reality, far greater resources must still be devoted to it.[8]   Sadly, these sentiments ring truer today. The *Human Development Report* prepared by the United Nations Development Programme discloses that the current level of educational expenditure by States is inadequate for meeting contemporary educational needs in the world.[9] In the words of Article 10(2) of the 1990 *World Declaration on Education for All* "[s]ubstantial and long-term increases in resources for basic education will be needed". As governments of developed States are expected to do more for their citizens particularly in the social welfare field, budget allocations for education tend to be the casualty. The Preamble of the *World Declaration on Education for All* alludes to cutbacks in governmental expenditure over the 1980s in certain industrialised countries which have led to the deterioration of their educational systems.

The main obstacle frustrating the child's exercise of the right to education in developing countries is poverty. The problem is not so much that children do not have schools to go to. Over 90% of the developing world's children do begin primary schooling. The problem is the very high wastage rates in terms of students dropping out of school or repeating their year. U.N.I.C.E.F. has estimated that of the 100 million six-year-olds who will begin school in 1990, over 40 million will drop out before completing their primary education.[10] An ever-increasing imbalance exists in the provision of education between developed and developing States, due mainly to the lack of economic resources within the latter. A matter of concern is the trend of continuing decline in financial support for education particularly in developing States.[11] On average, the number of years of free full-time compulsory education in the industrialised countries in 1989 was nine;[12] by contrast, the average number of years spent in such education in developing countries was seven in 1988.[13] Lack of funds prevents the authorities from building new schools and maintaining existing ones, operating teacher training colleges, recruiting competent teaching and administrative staff, ensuring teaching materials and other supplies, and providing adequate transportation systems for students. All of these are directly dependent upon the economic resources at the State's disposal. Poverty makes it difficult for families either to pay school fees and the cost of books and school materials or, when schooling is free, to send a child to school when his or her work contributes to the meagre family budget.[14] A study conducted by the Save the Children Fund revealed that as a result of their debt burden, African States have been forced in some cases to impose or increase school fees, increasing the cost of education to families.[15] In the result, millions of children either never attend school or fail to complete their basic education.

A lack of economic resources and poverty can also prevent children from participating in and benefiting from their educational opportunities.

Poverty produces hunger and malnutrition which can irreversibly damage the child's developing brain.[16]   A lack of resources prevents States from locating schools within a reasonable distance of the residences of pupils or providing an adequate transportation system in lieu thereof. Nevertheless, as Article 6 of the 1990 *World Declaration on Education for All* recognises, learning does not take place in isolation and States must therefore ensure that all learners receive the nutrition, health care and general support they require in order to participate actively in, and benefit from, their education. As one commentator has suggested, for a State Party to implement its duty to provide compulsory education effectively, a legislative framework which transcends a bald statement requiring compulsory education to a certain minimum age is needed.   Such a framework ought also to include adequate provision for such matters as transportation and nutritional provision at school.[17]

Article 9 of the *World Declaration on Education for All* stresses that special protection for basic education will be required in countries undergoing structural adjustment and facing severe debt burdens.   The capacity of developing countries to provide basic education has been particularly adversely affected by the policy of structural adjustment.[18] Pursuant to this policy, the terms of international financial assistance to countries in Africa, Asia, Eastern Europe and Russia require them to adjust the structure of their public-monopoly-based economies to private enterprises.[19]   Apart from the substitution of free enterprise and market forces for price and foreign exchange controls, the policy of structural adjustment entails a decrease in state involvement in economic management and the provision of social services, including education. The provision of education in developing States has been adversely affected by the removal of state subsidies and the introduction of, or increase in, school fees which exceed the means of many lower income families.[20]   The burden of costs is being transferred increasingly to families, not only by the imposition of fees, but also by increased demands for payments for books and school materials which may discourage poor families from keeping their children at school.   One commentator has pointed out the dangers posed by structural adjustment:

> Structural adjustment, in essence, seems to detract from the obligations of states to provide economic, social and cultural rights.   It questions the assumption that the provision of social services is the responsibility of government and sets a trend towards greater involvement of private organizations in providing social services. Non-governmental organizations

are increasingly becoming involved, even at primary level, and the price of their involvement is that education is no longer free.[21]

The greatest danger of structural adjustment policies particularly for developing States lies in the neglect of the development of human resources. Considering the implications for national development, States should therefore reflect carefully before making any decisions to divest themselves of responsibility in the educational sector.

For developing States, there is also a direct link between the management of foreign debt and whether or not children go to school. Article 10(2) of the *World Declaration on Education for All* accordingly calls on creditor and debtor nations to seek innovative and equitable measures to relieve heavy debt burdens in order to increase the capacity of many developing countries to respond effectively to basic educational needs. One commentator has urged developing States to make more effective use of their treaty obligations in renegotiating their international loan agreements. These States can and should invoke these obligations as leverage in negotiations with international financial institutions such as the World Bank against accepting any conditions in their rescheduled interest payments which would obstruct them in progressively implementing the right to basic education.[22] The argument has also been made that school enrolment and literacy could be improved, even within existing budgets, by restructuring national expenditure so that more resources are allocated to primary schools for the many rather than to higher education for the few.[23] The 1990 World Conference on Education for All called for a transfer to educational expenditure of a portion of the massive amounts governments allocate each year from their budgets to military expenditure in order to meet the urgent task of meeting basic learning needs.[24]

The lack of economic resources available to States and general poverty are not the only obstacles to the realisation of the right to education. International and internal armed conflicts and civil strife can disrupt normal patterns of life. Regular schooling for students may be impossible when schools are located near the regions of conflict. Despite being protected under international humanitarian law,[25] schools are often objects of attack.[26] Over the past two or three decades, children of school age have been increasingly conscripted into rebel armed factions as child soldiers. The preoccupation of nations with the arms race diminishes national budget allocations which would otherwise be targetted for the educational sector. Successes of international humanitarian and disarmament law in mitigating these problems will have positive flow-on effects for the effective implementation of the right to basic education.

The right to education also suffers from a political perception which undervalues it.[27]   The 1990 World Conference on Education for All proclaimed that the effective provision of basic education for all depends on political commitment and political will backed by appropriate and supportive fiscal, economic, trade, labour, employment and health policies.[28]   International aid donors must also accord basic education a higher priority.   A scant one per cent of the industrialised world's educational aid supports primary education.[29]

Entrenched intergroup rivalry, prejudice and mistrust can also frustrate implementation of the right to education. Members of the more affluent and influential social classes may fear that their privileged position may be eroded if members of the lower social strata are provided with more favourable educational opportunities. Similarly, members of the dominant religious or ethnic group may be unwilling to accord equal rights to those outside their group.[30]   This in turn may lead to discrimination against various groups. The Committee on Economic, Social and Cultural Rights, which is entrusted with the monitoring of the implementation of the *International Covenant on Economic, Social and Cultural Rights*, has requested States Parties to provide information on educational discrimination against various groups of children particularly at the primary level.   These groups include girls, children with disabilities, indigenous and minority children, children living in rural communities, children from low income families, and children of immigrants and migrant workers.[31]   The World Conference on Education for All has called for an active commitment to remove educational disparities so that these "underserved groups" may no longer suffer any discrimination in access to educational opportunities.[32]

Although international human rights law recognises the right to education, there is little practical guidance on what constitutes a meaningful and relevant education or which skills children should acquire by the end of their primary education.   The Preamble of the *World Declaration on Education for All* has called for basic education to be made more relevant.   For example, the educational curricula of those newly independent States which were ruled until recently by colonial powers must be revised so as to become more attuned to the developmental needs and aspirations of their peoples.   The recognition of the vital role of teachers is particularly important. As the World Conference on Education for All has recognised, their terms and conditions of service and their status, an important determining factor in the implementation of the right to education, must be improved as a matter of urgency in all countries in line with the joint I.L.O./U.N.E.S.C.O. *Recommendation concerning the Status of Teachers 1966.*[33]

Lack of effective monitoring of the implementation of the right to education is yet another obstacle preventing its fuller realisation. While international human rights instruments have generally excelled over the past fifty years at articulating rights in a comprehensive and detailed manner, they have been less successful in creating effective machinery to oversee their implementation. States are, of course, reluctant to open themselves up to external scrutiny and the educational field appears to be no exception. Pursuant to Article 7 of the *Convention against Discrimination in Education* States Parties are required to submit periodic reports to the General Conference of U.N.E.S.C.O. providing information on the legislative and administrative measures which they have adopted to implement the *Convention.* Regrettably, however, this reporting process has not elicited the information and guidance from States Parties which is required to ensure effective implementation of the objects of the *Convention.* [34] The reporting process has been characterised particularly by low response rates from Member States and the poor quality and incomplete nature of the reports submitted.[35] The lack of complaints initiated under the *Protocol Instituting a Conciliation and Good Offices Comission to be responsible for Seeking a Settlement of any Disputes which may arise between States Parties to the Convention against Discrimination in Education 1962* is yet another example of the futility of pursuing interstate complaints as an implementation mechanism as opposed to an individual complaints procedure.

The fuller realisation of the right to education can be achieved by improvements in the reporting and monitoring processes and a greater resolve on the part of States Parties to fulfil their reporting requirements and obligations under the international instruments conscientiously and in good faith. Armed with the *Limburg Principles on the Implementation of the International Covenant on Economic, Social and Cultural Rights* [36] and with the assistance and co-operation of international and national non-governmental organisations, it is now up to the United Nations Committee on Economic, Social and Cultural Rights and the Committee on the Rights of the Child to aggressively question States Parties on their reports. As with other economic, social and cultural rights, the monitoring of the implementation of the right to education on a progressive basis will benefit from the adoption and use of reliable indicators.[37] An important objective of such indicators is to distinguish an unwillingness to satisfy treaty obligations from an incapacity to do so.[38] Therefore, the documentation and analysis of trends will produce a more accurate picture than the more conventional use of cross-national comparisons and country rankings.[39] Consequently, it has been suggested that the performance of each country should be assessed over a period of several years on a cross-temporal basis. In the educational sector, reliable cross-temporal indicators might include literacy rates, enrolment ratios, completion and drop-out rates, pupil-teacher ratios, and public expenditure on education as a percentage of total public expenditure or in comparison with other sectors such as the military.[40] These indicators must be assessed, however, in the context of the overall political and economic situation obtaining in each State Party, taking into account such factors as the health of the economy, the balance of payments situation and the existence of armed conflict or internal strife.[41]

Considering the interdependence of the right to education with other human rights such as the right to health, the right to an adequate standard of living and the right not to be arbitrarily discriminated against, it may be expected that improvements to the latter will produce salutary results for the former. The transfer of information and technology from developed to developing States within the framework of international co-operation, and through the United Nations and its agencies such as U.N.E.S.C.O., U.N.I.C.E.F., the I.L.O. and the F.A.O., must continue and increase to prevent a widening of the gap between these States in terms of the incidence and quality of educational opportunities available for their citizens.

Notes

1　Amadou-Mahtar M'Bow (former U.N.E.S.C.O. Director-General) "Introduction" to G. Mialaret (ed.) *The Child's Right to Education* (1979) 9, 16.

2　U. N. Doc. E/CN.4/SR 285.

3　Although the right to education belongs to adults and children alike, compulsory education only applies to children. The principle of compulsory primary education was introduced in many Western nations long before education was recognised as a human right, and implies that it is in the best interests of children that they undertake a basic minimum of education. This principle is related to the principle of free education in the sense that by imposing an obligation on States Parties to provide free primary education, attendance can more easily be made compulsory.

4　Unlike primary education, secondary education has not been made compulsory, partly due to recognition that many families particularly in developing countries require the income generated by children of secondary school age in order to survive. The provision of free secondary education would, however, make a significant contribution to secondary education being accessible to all.

5   One method of achieving equality of educational opportunity is to make education free and compulsory until a specified minimum age.

6   M. El Fasi "The Right to Education and Culture" (1968) 9 *Journal of the International Commission of Jurists* 33, 34-35.

7   Commission on Human Rights *Report of the Working Group on a Draft Convention on the Rights of the Child* E/CN.4/1985/64 (3 April 1985) p. 11, para. 58.

8   El Fasi, op. cit., 39.

9   United Nations *Human Development Report* (1991) 2.

10   U.N.I.C.E.F. *The World Summit for Children* (1990) 32.

11   United Nations *Human Development Report* (1993).

12   United Nations *Human Development Report* (1991) 181 (Table 33).

13   Id. at 146-147 (Table 14).

14   M'Bow, op. cit., 13.

15   Save the Children Fund *Prospects for Africa's Children* 113.

16   M'Bow, op. cit., 12.

17   G. Van Bueren *The International Law on the Rights of the Child* (1995) 238-239.

18   C. Beyani "The Prerequisites of Education" in *Education Rights and Minorities* (A Minority Rights Group Report) (1994) 14.

19   United Nations *Report of the Special Rapporteur on the Realization of Economic, Social and Cultural Rights* E/CN.4/Sub.2/1992/16 pp. 11-31.

20   Beyani, op. cit., 14.

21   Beyani, op. cit., 15.

22   Van Bueren, op. cit., 237.

23   U.N.I.C.E.F., op. cit., 14.

24   Article 9(2) of the *World Declaration on Education for All.*

25   See Article 52 of the *Protocol Additional to the Geneva Conventions of 12 August 1949, and relating to the Protection of Victims of International Armed Conflicts (Protocol I).*

26   Beyani, op. cit., 16.

27   Van Bueren, op. cit., 256.

28   Article 8 of the *World Declaration on Education for All.*

29   U.N.I.C.E.F., op. cit., 14.

30   N. Tarrow *Human Rights and Education* (1987) 11.

31   U. N. Doc. E/1988/5.

32   Article 3(4) of the *World Declaration on Education for All.*

33   Article 7 of the *World Declaration on Education for All.*

34   States Parties are obliged to submit periodic national reports to the Committee on Conventions which writes its own report based on these submissions. Unlike the Human Rights Committee established under the *International Covenant on Civil and Political Rights,* the Committee on

Conventions does not engage in dialogue with States Parties concerning their reports.

35   U.N.E.S.C.O. Document 23 C/72; U.N.E.S.C.O. Document 26 C/31: 3-4, 22.

36   U.N. Doc. E/CN.4/1987/17, Annex.

37   See the report of the United Nations Seminar on Appropriate Indicators to Measure Achievements in the Progressive Realization of Economic, Social and Cultural Rights, held in Geneva in January, 1993:   U.N. Doc. A/CONF.157/PC/73.

38   M. Nowak "The Right to Education" in A. Eide (ed.) *Economic, Social and Cultural Rights* (1995) 189, 200.

39   Ibid.

40   Ibid.

41   Ibid.

Bibliography

Alfredsson, G. (1995), 'The Right to Human Rights Education', in A. Eide, C. Krause and A. Rosas (eds), *Economic, Social and Cultural Rights: A Textbook*, Martinus Nijhoff, Dordrecht, pp. 213-227.

Arajärvi, P. (1992), 'Article 26', in A. Eide, G. Alfredsson, G. Melander, L. Adam Rehof and A. Rosas (eds), *The Universal Declaration of Human Rights: A Commentary*, Scandinavian University Press, Oslo, pp. 405-428.

Bainham, A. (1988), *Children, Parents and the State*, Sweet and Maxwell, London.

Beyani, C. (1994), 'The Prerequisites of Education', in *Education Rights and Minorities*, The Minority Rights Group, London, pp. 14-17.

Black, M. (1986), *The Children and the Nations: The Story of Unicef*, P.I.C. Pty Ltd, Sydney.

Brownlie, I. (ed.) (3rd ed., 1992), *Basic Documents on Human Rights*, Clarendon Press, Oxford.

Capotorti, F. (1979), *Study on the Rights of Persons Belonging to Ethnic, Religious and Linguistic Minorities*, E/CN.4/Sub.2/384/Rev.I, United Nations, New York.

Christopher, C. (1984), '*Plyler v. Doe* and the Right of Undocumented Alien Children to a Free Public Education', *Boston University International Law Journal*, vol. 2, pp. 513-536.

Cresswell, R. and Hobson, P. (1993), 'Parental Rights, Education and Liberal Tolerance', *Discourse*, vol. 14, pp. 44-51.

Crittenden, B. (1989), 'The Rights of Children', *Melbourne Report*, vol. 5, pp. 4-6.

Cullen, H. (1993), 'Education Rights or Minority Rights?', *International Journal of Law and the Family*, vol. 7, pp. 143-177.

Davis, S. and Schwartz, M. (1987), *Children's Rights and the Law*, D. C. Heath and Company, Lexington, Massachusetts.

De la Vega, C. (1994), 'The Right to Equal Education: Merely a Guiding Principle or Customary International Legal Right?', *Harvard Black Letter Law Journal*, vol. 11, pp. 37-60.

Detrick, S. (ed.) (1992), *The United Nations Convention on the Rights of the Child: A Guide to the "Travaux Préparatoires"*, Martinus Nijhoff Publishers, Dordrecht.

El Fasi, M. (1968), 'The Right to Education and Culture', *Journal of the International Commission of Jurists*, vol. 9, pp. 33-40.

Forster, K. (1989), 'Parents' Rights and Educational Policy', *Educational Philosophy and Theory*, vol. 21, pp. 47-52.

Foster, W. and Pinheiro, G. (1987-88), 'Constitutional Protection of the Right to an Education', *Dalhousie Law Journal*, vol. 11, pp. 755-832.

Gould, M. (1990), 'Children's Education and the European Court of Justice', in D. Freestone (ed.), *Children and The Law: Essays in Honour of Professor H. K. Bevan*, Hull University Press, Hull, pp. 172-200.

Graham-Brown, S. (1994), 'The Role of the Curriculum', in *Education Rights and Minorities*, The Minority Rights Group, London, pp. 27-32.

Hannum, H. (ed.) (1993), *Documents on Autonomy and Minority Rights*, Martinus Nijhoff Publishers, Dordrecht.

Harris, D., O'Boyle, M. and Warbrick, C. (1995), *Law of the European Convention on Human Rights*, Butterworths, London.

Hayes, R. and MacAlpine, S. (1986), 'A Lawyers' View of Special Education: Past, Present and Future', *Australian Journal of Special Education*, vol. 10, pp. 33-39.

Herr, S. (1981), 'Rights of Disabled Persons: International Principles and American Experiences', *Columbia Human Rights Law Review*, vol. 12, pp. 1-55.

Hodgson, D. (1992), The Historical Development and "Internationalisation" of the Children's Rights Movement', *Australian Journal of Family Law*, vol. 6, pp. 252-279.

Jacobs, F. and White, R. (2nd ed.,1996), *The European Convention on Human Rights*, Clarendon Press, Oxford.

Jones, C. and Warner, R. (1994), 'Language and Education', in *Education Rights and Minorities*, The Minority Rights Group, London, pp. 18-23.

Knight, S. (1995), 'Proposition 187 and International Human Rights Law: Illegal Discrimination in the Right to Education', *Hastings International and Comparative Law Review*, vol. 19, pp. 183-220.

Martínez Cobo, J. (1986), *Study of the Problem of Discrimination Against Indigenous Populations*, E/CN.4/Sub.2/1986/7/Add.4, United Nations, New York.

Mialaret, G. (ed.) (1979), *The Child's Right to Education*, U.N.E.S.C.O., Paris.

Neal, D. (1982), 'The Right to Education: The Case of Special Education', *Australian Quarterly*, vol. 54, pp. 147-160.

Nowak, M. (1995), 'The Right to Education', in A. Eide, C. Krause and A. Rosas (eds), *Economic, Social and Cultural Rights: A Textbook*, Martinus Nijhoff Publishers, Dordrecht, pp. 189-211.

Opekokew, D. and Pratt, A. (1992), 'The Treaty Right to Education in Saskatchewan', *The Windsor Yearbook of Access to Justice*, vol. 12, pp. 3-51.

Pogany, I. (1982), 'Education: The Rights of Children and Parents Under the European Convention on Human Rights', *New Law Journal*, vol. 132, pp. 344-346.

Poulter, S. (1986), *English Law and Ethnic Minority Customs*, Butterworths, London.

Seck, M. (1990), 'A Plea for Human Rights Education in Africa', *Human Rights Law Journal*, vol. 11, pp. 283-299.

Skutnabb-Kangas, T. (1990), *Language, Literacy and Minorities*, The Minority Rights Group, London.

Snook, I. (1979), *Education and Rights*, Melbourne University Press, Melbourne.

Tarrow, N. (ed.) (1987), *Human Rights and Education*, Pergamon Press, New York.

Thornberry, P. (1991), *Minorities and Human Rights Law*, The Minority Rights Group, London.

Thornberry, P. (1994), 'International Standards', in *Education Rights and Minorities*, The Minority Rights Group, London, pp. 10-13.

Turner, J. (1992), 'The Rights of the Child Under the U. N. Convention', *Law Institute Journal*, vol. 65, pp. 38-45.

U.N.E.S.C.O. (1990), *World Declaration on Education for All and Framework for Action to Meet Basic Learning Needs*, Inter-Agency Commission, New York.

U.N.I.C.E.F. (1990), *The World Summit for Children*, P. & L.A., Oxfordshire.

United Nations (1980), *United Nations Action in the Field of Human Rights*, United Nations, New York.

United Nations (1988), *United Nations Action in the Field of Human Rights*, United Nations, New York.

Van Bueren, G. (ed.) (1993), *International Documents on Children*, Martinus Nijhoff Publishers, Dordrecht.

Van Bueren, G. (1994), 'Education: Whose Right is it Anyway?', in L. Heffernan (ed.), *Human Rights: A European Perspective*, The Round Hall Press, Dublin, pp. 339-349.

Van Bueren, G. (1995), *The International Law on the Rights of the Child*, Martinus Nijhoff Publishers, Dordrecht.

Van Der Wolf, W.J.F.M. (ed.) (1994), *Human Rights Selected Documents*, Global Law Association, Boxtel, The Netherlands.

Veerman, P. (1992), *The Rights of the Child and the Changing Image of Childhood*, Martinus Nijhoff Publishers, Dordrecht.

Walsh, B. (1981), 'Existence and Meaning of Fundamental Rights in the Field of Education in Ireland', *Human Rights Law Journal*, vol. 2, pp. 319-327.

Weisberg, D. (1978), 'Evolution of the Concept of the Rights of the Child in the Western World', *The Review* (International Commission of Jurists), vol. 21, pp. 43-51.

Wringe, C. (1981), *Children's Rights: A Philosophical Study*, Routledge and Kegan Paul, London.

Wringe, C. (1992), 'The Ideology of Liberal Individualism, Welfare Rights and the Right to Education', in M. Freeman and P. Veerman (eds), *The Ideologies of Children's Rights*, Martinus Nijhoff Publishers, Dordrecht.

Yudof, M. (1993), 'Articles 13 and 14 - Right to Education', in H. Hannum and D. Fischer (eds), *U. S. Ratification of the International Covenants on Human Rights*, Transnational Publishers, Inc., New York, pp. 235-245.